D1523149

METAPHORS OF FAMILY SYSTEMS THEORY

PERSPECTIVES ON MARRIAGE AND THE FAMILY
Bert N. Adams and David M. Klein, Editors

WIFE BATTERING: A SYSTEMS THEORY APPROACH
Jean Giles-Sim

COMMUTER MARRIAGE: A STUDY OF WORK AND FAMILY
Naomi Gerstel and Harriet Gross

HELPING THE ELDERLY: THE COMPLEMENTARY ROLES OF
INFORMAL NETWORKS AND FORMAL SYSTEMS
Eugene Litwak

REMARRIAGE AND STEPPARENTING:
CURRENT RESEARCH AND THEORY
Kay Palsey and Marilyn Ihinger-Tallman (Eds.)

FEMINISM, CHILDREN, AND THE NEW FAMILIES
Sanford M. Dornbusch and Myra F. Strober (Eds.)

DYNAMICS OF FAMILY DEVELOPMENT:
A THEORETICAL PERSPECTIVE
James M. White

PORTRAIT OF DIVORCE:
ADJUSTMENT TO MARITAL BREAKDOWN
Gay C. Kitson with William M. Holmes

WOMEN AND FAMILIES: FEMINIST RECONSTRUCTIONS
Kristine M. Baber and Katherine R. Allen

CHILDREN'S STRESS AND COPING: A FAMILY PERSPECTIVE
Elaine Shaw Sorensen

WHEN LOVE DIES: THE PROCESS OF MARITAL DISAFFECTION
Karen Kayser

FAMILES BEFORE AND AFTER PERESTROIKA:
RUSSIAN AND U.S. PERSPECTIVES
*James W. Maddock, M. Janice Hogan,
Anatolyi I. Antonov, and Mikhail S. Matskovsky (Eds.)*

METAPHORS OF FAMILY SYSTEMS THEORY:
TOWARD NEW CONSTRUCTIONS
Paul C. Rosenblatt

Metaphors of Family Systems Theory

Toward New Constructions

PAUL C. ROSENBLATT

THE GUILFORD PRESS
New York   London

© 1994 The Guilford Press
A Division of Guilford Publications, Inc.
72 Spring Street, New York, NY 10012

Printed in the United States of America

This book is printed on acid-free paper.

Last digit is print number: 9 8 7 6 5 4 3 2 1

Library of Congress Cataloging-in-Publication Data

Rosenblatt, Paul C.
    Metaphors of family systems theory ; toward new constructions /
  Paul C. Rosenblatt.
        p.   cm. — (Perspectives on marriage and the family)
        ISBN 0-89862-321-9
        1. Family.   2. System theory.   3. Family psychotherapy.
    I. Title.   II. Series.
HQ734.R7572   1994
306.85—dc20
                                                      93-19476
                                                         CIP

Acknowledgments

David M. Klein and Bert Adams were enormously helpful and encouraging in moving this project to completion and in stimulating me to take on a number of issues dealt with in this book. Useful suggestions about ways to think and to organize my work, stimulating comments, helpful references, new ways of thinking, moral support, and/or helpful reading of chapter fragments, whole chapters, or even the entire manuscript were provided by Herbert Barry III, Pauline Boss, Anna Hagemeister, Terri Karis, James W. Maddock, Cynthia J. Meyer, David Olson, Naomi Quinn, Barbara Settles, Jetse Sprey, Patricia J. Thompson, Stephen G. Wieting, Sara E. Wright, and approximately two dozen students who took my seminars on metaphor and the family. Two students whose continued interest and conversations helped to sustain the work were Terri Karis and Janice Nadeau. Terri Karis also provided crucial bibliographical assistance at the beginning of the project.

My start on learning about metaphor and the family was funded by the University of Minnesota Summer Session, an organization that wanted to develop a new course. The Summer Session funded the bibliographic digging that began my education about metaphor and family systems and supported my teaching a course that enabled me to fuel this project with the intellectual and motivational benefits of teaching. Work on this project was advanced by a University of Minnesota sabbatical with supplementary funding from the University's Bush Sabbatical Fellowship program. I am grateful to my faculty colleagues in the Department of Family Social Science at the University of Minnesota, who have maintained an environment in which theory is valued, and to my two department heads during this project, Jan Hogan and Hal Grotevant, who fostered an environment in which progress on this project was possible and valued.

Contents

Introduction

This book, which is intended to stimulate new theoretical thinking about family systems, investigates how the standard metaphors of family systems theory structure family phenomena, highlighting some aspects of families and obscuring others. Throughout the investigation, the uses and limitations of the standard metaphors of family systems theory are outlined and alternative theoretical metaphors are generated.

Since the book focuses on metaphor, a definition of the term is in order. A metaphor is a figure of speech in which words or actions that literally denote one kind of object or idea are used in place of another, suggesting a resemblance or analogy.

Beginning with pioneering work by Erickson (1967), Haley (1973), Kopp (1972), and Bandler and Grinder (1975) and including a plethora of more recent writings (e.g., Barker, 1985; Lankton & Lankton, 1989; Mills & Crowley, 1986; Papp, 1982), the family literature has been rich in sensitivity to client metaphors and rich in the therapeutic use of metaphor to facilitate family change. The theoretical literature that informs family therapy is rich in metaphors for family systems, yet those theoretical metaphors have not received the intensive examination and the searching exploration of alternatives that have been devoted to client metaphors and to metaphors used to facilitate client family change. With so much attention to the metaphors used by clients and to therapeutic metaphors, it is an appropriate next step to explore the foundational metaphors, the theoretical metaphors that are the basis for thinking about family systems.

Some of the reasons why attention to metaphor has been so useful in therapy suggest why probing the standard theoretical metaphors and exploring alternative metaphors may be worthwhile. An understanding of client metaphor has often revealed client perceptions, biases, misunderstandings, and resistance to therapeutic intervention; it has helped to uncover why clients are stuck in family difficulties and why they have serious problems with issues that other families seem to handle effortlessly. Therapeutic metaphors have been helpful because they speak to client realities, because they are rich in meaning, and because they speak to clients at many levels. The literature provides many striking accounts of how therapeutic metaphors have moved families into healthier, energizing, problem-solving, freeing, and satisfying new places. Why not the same payoffs from analyzing theoretical metaphors?

Studying theoretical metaphors can bring new insights and much else. The capacity to recognize metaphor enables one to identify biases, hidden implications, reifications, and what has been over-looked. It helps to organize and to remember information. It helps one see the multilayered nature of "reality" and to take alternative perspectives. Perhaps most important of all, it can help one discover phenomena, ways of organizing experience and understandings, relationships among phenomena, and areas of life that one has overlooked.

This book is written for professionals who specialize in studying or helping families. It is written from a social constructionist perspective. According to that perspective, there is no true reality but only what is socially constructed and maintained. Such a perspective has strong advocates among those who are outside of family systems therapy as well as among therapists who work with families (Anderson & Goolishian, 1988; Hoffman, 1990). No doubt there are therapists who reify the family systems view, but many see their theories as temporary lenses (Anderson & Goolishian, 1988; Hoffman, 1990). This is a book about the standard lenses and about the value of trying out other lenses.

Chapter 1 defines metaphor as a transfer of meanings and

entailments from one domain to another. The chapter develops the Lakoff and Johnson (1980) perspective on metaphor, namely, that it saturates thought and is necessary for organizing and focusing thought but that it also obscures what is not within the reality defined by the metaphor currently being entertained. The chapter discusses the value of family systems theory and the value of exploring how the standard metaphors of the theory highlight and structure some things while obscuring other things. Although family systems theory has been a key source of therapeutic and research insight and energy, it has also been increasingly criticized and rejected. It is argued in Chapter 1 that part of the dissatisfaction with the theory may be that the standard metaphors of the theory are limiting. With the analysis of the standard metaphors that this book provides, it may be possible to continue working within a systemic perspective while developing metaphors that not only highlight what the standard metaphors obscure but also provide fresh insights and perspectives on family phenomena.

Chapter 2 explores a foundational metaphor in family systems theory: the metaphor of the family as an entity. It shows how the metaphor highlights aspects of the family as an entity (e.g., proximity and similarity) and explores much that the entity metaphor obscures, such as the extent to which each person in a given family is considered by self and others to be in other families in which no other member of the given family is counted and the fact that family members and others may differ on who and what can be counted in the family. Much that is obscured by a generic entity metaphor can become clear when specific entity metaphors are applied to the family. The chapter offers examples of insights that arise from the application of two specific entity metaphors—the family as a river and the family as a house.

Chapter 3 continues the analysis of the metaphors of family systems theory by exploring the metaphor of a system, as well as the major systemic metaphors—system circularity, system linkage, system goals, system dynamics, subsystem, larger system, system input, and system output, and the metaphor of family types. What these system metaphors highlight is crucial in making family systems theory as useful and powerful as it is. However, these metaphors have important limitations. There are useful nonsystem views. There are also compelling alternative ways to understand families and family systems that are loyal to systems thought but not to the standard metaphors. One thing obscured is the extent to which systems analysis involves observer subjectivity (e.g., in punctuating social relationships in order to say what is and what is not a family system), a subjectivity that may overlook important aspects of the uniqueness of events and impose pattern where it might be more useful to keep track of ambiguity, uniqueness, and difference. The system metaphors may make it harder to detect the randomness of family events, the importance in families of precedents and of one-of-a-kind events, the ways in which the individual functions in isolation from the family, the unboundedness of families, the likelihood that each member of a given family is also in one or more other families which contain no other members of the given family, and the variability and fluidity of families and of what goes on in them. The chapter concludes with a discussion of the ubiquity of systems and of the possibility that the language and concepts used in analyzing any system other than a family can provide useful metaphors for understanding family systems.

Chapter 4 extends the analysis of the metaphors of family systems theory to the metaphor of family boundary and to the closely related metaphors of family subsystem, family boundary permeability, family boundary ambiguity, and the metaphor of gender differences in boundaries. The chapter shows how these are metaphors and explores what each metaphor highlights and obscures. The boundary metaphor, which has been helpful in conceptualizing families and in intervention, highlights heterogeneity in the social world, patterns of connection, family barriers to all sorts of things that might enter or leave the family, ways of organizing and controlling interactions, limits on autonomy, bounding processes, what goes on at the margins and edges of families, the ways families are confining, and the regulation and enforcement of family barriers. The metaphor obscures the artificiality of the boundary concept and of any apparent boundary. It obscures the ambiguous location of family boundaries, the two-sidedness of any boundary, the perspectival nature of boundaries, the ways public versus private is a false dichotomy, the fluidity and processual nature of boundaries, and the complex nature of what might be called boundaries. The chapter offers suggestions about alternative metaphors for the interface of families with other socially constructed entities. The chapter discusses what each of the metaphors related to boundaries highlights and obscures, and it concludes with a discussion of the metaphor of the family as a container. By developing a particular container metaphor, the family as an aquarium, the chapter examines some implications of the notion of family boundaries—the importance of the sustaining medium that contains the family, the possible lack of perspective for those confined within the family boundaries—and the potential for missing the larger context of a family, which comes with focusing on the container and the contained.

Chapter 5 explores metaphors of family structure. All structural metaphors highlight systematic family arrangements, family stability, and the extent to which families can be known. All obscure the indistinct, ever-changing, situation-bound nature of family relationships, the difficulty of observing most of what is called family structure, the perspectival nature of assertions about family structure, and the ways in which family structures are never complete. The structural metaphor of family role highlights the inherently interactional nature of family roles, how family members play to audiences, how what is out of role is hidden or suppressed, how roles and situations trap family members, how members may unquestioningly play their parts, and how feelings, commitments, and actions may be consequences of the parts played. The family role metaphor obscures the unpredictability of what family members do, think, and feel; how roles are in process; the consequences of playing roles where time is never condensed (as in dramatic productions); how people play their parts to their perceptions of the roles of other family members; and how role analyses make it more difficult to know or to value how family members understand what is going on. The metaphors of family differentiation and cohesion highlight the ways that separation and distance are normal and inevitable in families and important in enabling family members to stay together. The metaphors obscure the place of the larger society in family differentiation and cohesion, the implicit valuing in systems theories of differentiation, how families may prefer and gain from functioning at so-called pathological extremes of differentiation and cohesion, the internal diversity of family differentiation and cohesion, the ways that a family may be simultaneously differentiated in some regards and cohesive in others, and the importance of looking at membership in groups besides the family in order to understand the place of differentiation and cohesion in an individual's life. The Circumplex Model, a particular approach to family assessment that includes consideration of family cohesion and differentiation, is discussed as a metaphor. Also discussed are the metaphors of generational structure (a metaphor that obscures how the metaphoric transfer of the concept of generation into family systems theory transforms the concept of generation into a matter of morality and pathology) and the metaphor of gender structure in family systems theory (which can be criticized from feminist perspectives). The chapter also offers an analysis of the metaphors of triangulation and of family coalitions and explores how alternative structural metaphors (e.g., the family is a tapestry) may highlight what the standard structural metaphors obscure.

Chapter 6 explores the metaphor of systems control and the related metaphors of family rules and of negative and positive feedback. Control metaphors highlight regularity and regulation in family interaction. The rules metaphor highlights the possibility of unverbalized but effective family understandings, the status of the therapist/researcher as someone who can understand what family members cannot, the possibility of patterned family constraints, and the possible origins of family understandings about what should and should not be done. The metaphor obscures the possibility that there is no need for family rules and the possibility that so-called rules are after-the-fact inventions. The metaphor of feedback highlights the need for family stability and change and the possibility of multiple levels of system guidance, so that change on one level maintains stability on another. The feedback metaphor obscures how family stability and change are matters of observer interpretation, the inherent ambiguity of family realities, and the complexity of interpreting negative and positive feedback when both may be going on. The feedback metaphor also obscures the possibility that what appears to be morphostasis may be something else—for example, a lack of system guidance about how to change. All family control metaphors obscure that there may be no regularities and that it is unlikely that family monitoring and regulating of family process is continual. All family control metaphors also obscure the existence and importance of areas of autonomy in family life, the extent to which what appear to be family controls may more properly be understood as societal or cultural controls, and the dialogic relationships between control and power. In this chapter aspects of the metaphor "the family is a government," are outlined in order to provide alternative perspectives for thinking about family control systems. The government metaphor leads to the idea that family control mechanisms function to control externalities and to the idea that there are limits to the development of controls (due, for example, to lack of consensus about what or how to control). The government metaphor highlights the ways in which processes other than social construction may shape control systems in families (e.g., the exercise of vetoes or passive opposition) and the extent to which conflict and disharmony may be normal in family life, with family controls seen as a way of channeling, not eliminating, conflict and disharmony.

Chapter 7 explores the metaphors of communication, open and closed communication, metacommunication, paradox, and communication pathology. The concept of "communication" used in family systems theory is metaphoric in that it imports concepts that go far beyond the everyday meaning of the term. The metaphor of communication highlights the potential of communication to accomplish more than communicators may realize, the extent to which family systems are communication systems, and the ways the aspects of communication incorporated in the metaphoric meaning of the term (e.g., boundary maintenance, feedback) are as basic to family system functioning as are the aspects of communication that are part of its everyday conception. The metaphor of communication obscures the degree to which all communication is challenging to capture and interpret, how much systems analysis of communication privileges the observer's view, how much people get by with imperfect communication, the many situations in which communication content is irrelevant, and the place of reflexivity in family communication. The metaphor of open and closed communication highlights the idea that there are real things to communicate and the way families seem to differ on how much is disclosed. The metaphor obscures how a family that is closed to one version of a communication may be open to another and how topics and situations, as opposed to families, may be crucial in understanding openness–closedness. The metaphor of openness–closedness obscures the place of individual dispositions in family communication and how closedness may have more to do with avoiding certain kinds of processing than with avoiding sending certain messages. The metaphor of metacommunication highlights the distinction between communications that are about communication and those that are not and the potential of metacommunication to facilitate communication or to create problems. It may obscure the extent to which people function with no metacommunicative reality and the extent to which realities may be so fluid that metacommunication is of little value. The metaphor of metacommunication, resting on distinctions among types of communications, obscures the extent to which all content comments on all other content and on the relationship between the communicators. The metaphor of paradox in family communication highlights the ways in which family members may communicate to one another things that cannot simultaneously be true and the problems that can occur in relationships as a result of such communication. The metaphor of paradoxical communication obscures the extent to which what is a paradox to one person is not to another and the extent to which communication in families is not necessarily subject to the logic of the family system observer. The metaphor of pathology in family communication, borrowed from concepts of physical disease, highlights how communication patterns can be harmful in families and the possibilities for diagnosis, prevention, and cure. The pathology metaphor obscures the ways in which a disease concept of communication may not be appropriate (e.g., what one person considers a pathology may not be a pathology for another or what is harmful communication in one family may not be harmful in another).

Chapter 8 explores three key metaphors in family systems therapy, the metaphors of therapeutic goals, of the therapist in the system, and of family response to intervention. Because of the focus on intervention, many of the metaphors of family systems therapy are metaphors that accommodate intervention. With goals other than intervention different metaphors could be used. The focus on intervention may also obscure transformative processes in families and in their environments. The active nature of intervention is masked by the metaphor of the presenting problem, which downplays the role of the therapist in defining therapeutic goals and belies the complexity and fluidity of what may be labeled therapeutic goals. The metaphors applied to families in therapy often characterize families as freestanding and objectively real, yet the therapist is very much in the system in making it "real." Among the metaphors used in manufacturing the reality of a family are those of family health, stuckness, coping, reconnecting, and insight. In addition to these metaphors, this chapter discusses the metaphoric nature of family test scores and those aspects of the feminist critique of family therapy that are relevant to the metaphors applied to family therapy. The chapter also explores how the metaphors of family therapy obscure the "shadow realities" of family therapy, including ways therapy might be in the therapist's interests, and practical and customary constraints on therapist action that limit therapeutic metaphors and alternative approaches to healing. The chapter explores the use of one of the many conceivable alternative metaphors for what therapists do: listening. The chapter concludes with a framing of the metaphoric approach toward family therapy within the ecosystemic framework, indicating that the metaphoric approach is one way of bridging differing levels of systemic therapy.

Chapter 9 begins by making a case for continuing to focus on family systems, working toward new insights with a variety of experience-based metaphors. It explores cultural barriers to thinking systemically and ways of developing new theoretical metaphors for family systems. One approach to developing new theoretical metaphors is to turn to what seems to be the core, metaphors for family systems—the family is a thing, the family is a living entity, the family is a primary relationship, the family is a container, and the family is a machine. The core metaphors can guide the search for more specific and lively metaphors. However, a challenge in the search for new theoretical metaphors is to hold on to what seems basic in the phenomena we are trying to understand, to hold on to a kernel of "reality" that is captured by the metaphors we want to leave behind. In the end the question to be asked is, what do new metaphors give us that standard metaphors do not? While rejecting any notion of ultimate truth, the chapter offers a number of approaches to evaluating new theoretical metaphors. In addition, because multiple and seemingly mutually inconsistent metaphors are appropriate in analyzing families, we need metaphoric frames for combining metaphors that seem on face not to fit together. The chapter suggests two such frames: the crossroads and the city. The chapter concludes with an outline of some of what all family systems theory metaphors obscure and with the hope that this book will lead to renewed enthusiasm and creative growth in systems thought.

Metaphors and Theory

T he metaphors of family systems theory
form the conceptual foundation of a great deal of theory, therapy,
research, education, and policy making in the family field. Metaphor
is essential and inescapable in thinking about anything, and anyone
who thinks about families or a specific family uses metaphor. Although
they are necessary in theorizing about families, the metaphors of family
theories, like all metaphors, focus thinking in ways that make it
difficult, if not impossible, to think in terms of alternative metaphors.
It is a step toward more powerful, creative, and flexible theorizing to be
able to recognize the metaphors we use for what they are, to explore
what they highlight and obscure, and to acquire fluency in developing
and applying alternative theoretical metaphors.

Because family systems theory has been and continues to be
central in the family field, it is appropriate to explore how the
metaphors of the theory organize thinking and to examine what they
highlight and what they obscure. This book offers extensive analysis of
the major metaphors of family systems theory and explores what is
gained by using these metaphors, as well as what these metaphors
obscure. The discussion includes illustrative development of alternative theoretical metaphors to explore some of what the standard
metaphors obscure. The book is not intended to replace family systems
theory but to increase awareness of what is gained and lost while
working with standard versions of the theory and to encourage the

generation of alternative systemic metaphors that can highlight what is obscured by the standard versions.

A metaphor is a figure of speech in which a word or phrase that ordinarily applies to one kind of object or idea is applied to another, thus suggesting a likeness or analogy between them. The word "metaphor" originates in Latin and Greek roots that refer to a transfer. Saying "My love is a red, red rose" transfers the meanings of a red rose (beauty, freshness, striking color, delicacy, life, impermanence) to the loved one, thus communicating a richer sense of why the person is loved. To say "My family is a military unit" transfers the meanings associated with military units (rigid hierarchy, strict rules, disciplined activity, inattention to feelings, acting in accordance with roles and statuses rather than individual preferences and desires, arming against enemies) to a family, thus communicating a richer sense of how the speaker's family is experienced.

The word "metaphor" should be distinguished from three words with which it is sometimes confused: "metonymy," "simile," and "concept." Metonymy occurs when the name of one thing is used in place of the name of another with which it is associated, for example, the sign for the thing signified, the container for the thing contained, the cause for the effect. In the case of a family, one might use the alcoholism of a single family member to characterize the entire family ("the alcoholic family"). Or one might say, "I'll be visiting the Ortega house tonight," when what is meant is that the Ortega family will be visited. Metonymy, like metaphor, facilitates thinking and communication. However, it can lead to problems if one confuses the symbolic marker with the thing symbolized, for example, the sign (what one family member says, a score on a diagnostic test, a problem of one member of the family) with the thing signified (the entire family). (See Gubrium & Holstein, 1990, pp. 72–73, for further discussion of metonymy and the family.) Although issues of perspective, facilitation of thinking, the displacement of signs from one meaning location to another, and potential conceptual confusion are present when dealing with both metonymy and theoretical metaphor, there are major differences. With metonymy, the movement of a sign is to something already associated with it, and the sign is often a specific descriptive name, like "alcoholic" or "house." With metaphor, the movement of a sign is to something not obviously associated with it—at least not before the metaphor becomes known—and the sign is often much more elaborate than a specific descriptive name, quite often, in fact, an elaborate conceptual structure.

A simile is a figure of speech by which one thing, action, or relation is likened or explicitly compared to something different, usually with the word "as" or "like" used to make the comparison explicit. For example, "My family is like a cast of actors who can never stop playing their parts or acknowledge that they are playing parts." Or, "That family is as immoral and as focused on victimizing those who can't protect themselves as a pirate crew." Simile and metaphor are similar, and in some writings (even at places in this book) they are treated as interchangeable. The basic difference is that with a simile the comparison is drawn explicitly ("It is as though families have boundaries"), whereas with a metaphor the fact that a comparison or transfer of meaning is being made is often implicit ("family boundaries"). Simile makes reification more difficult because the comparison is explicit (Merkel & Searight, 1992). On the other hand, metaphor may make it easier to transfer the full range and impact of conceptual structure to the new domain because the transfer of meaning is not marked or limited by such words as "like" or "as." Similes are not used in family systems theory—and perhaps are not used in any other social science theory. Simile does not seem to be accepted as an appropriate form for theoretical language. Perhaps this is because a simile is inherently ambiguous about what it asserts to be true.

A concept is an idea or a mental notion of something based on generalization from particulars. A concept may or may not be metaphorical. The concept of philosophy in the sentence "Logic and ethics are areas of philosophy" seems not to be a metaphor, seems not to be drawn from other areas of experience. Without metaphoric connections, a concept imports none of the associated meanings, implications, and conceptual structure of a metaphor. Concepts underlie metaphors. Metaphors that are new to us may or may not lead us to new concepts, but they have the potential to qualify, change, or add to the concepts they are applied to.

All social science and psychological theories and conceptual frameworks draw heavily on metaphors (Brown, 1977, chap. 4; Gergen

& Gergen, 1986). Social psychological theories, for example, build on metaphors from drama (role theory, dramaturgical theory), causal analysis in law and scientific research (attribution theory), and economics (exchange theory). Theories of cognitive process build on metaphors from computer science and electronics. Family systems theory, which has been the key conceptual framework for family therapy and for research and teaching about families, also builds on metaphors (Allman, 1982).

Thinking about metaphor is not new in the family field. Gubrium and Holstein (1990) have carried out a rich and insightful analysis of how some Americans think about family. The family therapy literature is rich in discussions of the value of understanding client metaphors and the value of using metaphors in therapeutic intervention (e.g., Andolfi, Angelo, Menghi, & Nicolo-Corigliano, 1983, chap. 6; Atwood & Levine, 1991; Dolan, 1986; Griffith, Griffith, & Slovik, 1990; Jordan, 1985; Laird, 1989; Lankton & Lankton, 1989; Palazzoli, Boscolo, Cecchin, & Prata, 1977; Papp, 1982; Watzlawick, 1978). Family therapists are keenly aware that understanding client metaphors is a key to understanding how client realities are constructed. Client metaphors provide the context of a client family's problems, reflect and create client realities, and limit the ways in which the family comes to terms with its problems. Family therapists are also keenly aware of how the therapeutic use of metaphor can alter client realities and influence what clients do and experience (see, e.g., Dell, 1980; Seltzer & Seltzer, 1983).

Family therapists are no different from their clients in that metaphors guide and limit their thinking. The theoretical metaphors used by family therapists contextualize, reflect, and create their therapeutic realities and limit the ways in which they understand client words and actions and come to terms with client problems. Any way of thinking about anything can be useful, but it is always limiting. A family therapist's way of thinking, whatever it is, is limiting.

Practitioners, researchers, theoreticians, and policymakers, like families, can be stuck with problems that seem intractable and theories that seem to lead nowhere but to ideas and insights that seem stale, unhelpful, and trite. Moving to alternative realities by working with alternative metaphors may, as with clients, enable family professionals to come unstuck, to deal with problems that have resisted solution, and to achieve new and valuable discoveries. Entering these alternative realities may allow new developments in family theory and theory-based family research, in providing help to families, and in family policy making.

In light of the potential value of exploring the theoretical metaphors used by professionals who work with, study, and think about families, it seems appropriate to extend the family field interest in metaphors to consider the theoretical metaphors commonly used in analyzing family systems. Interest in theoretical metaphors for family systems is not new. Kantor and Lehr (1975, pp. 6–8) were clear about the importance of theoretical metaphors for family systems and deliberately developed their framework of ideas about family systems around a spatial/territorial metaphor. Jackson (1965b) was clear that his concept of family rules was a metaphor to facilitate thinking systemically instead of in terms of individuals. In this book the standard family system metaphors are explored in a search for how they organize knowledge and what they obscure. In analyzing the standard metaphors and revealing what they obscure, the book shows how alternative metaphors are useful, even necessary, and provides a variety of alternatives to the standard metaphors.

In exploring the metaphors of family systems theory, it is important to keep track of the distinction between the study of the family as a system and the study of family therapy as a system (de Shazer, 1982). This is a book about the study of the family as a system.

It is also important to keep track of the distinctions among (1) phenomena, (2) conceptual frameworks, and (3) theories. The phenomena are what many social scientists consider the focus of social science. From this perspective, phenomena are to be accounted for. Phenomena come into prominence as a result of the ways we perceive and understand things, and those ways are dependent on the conceptual filters of our culture, language, occupation, social class, and other experience bases. A conceptual framework is an overview of a domain that includes a general focus on the domain; a sensitization to certain issues, concepts (often, if not always, expressed metaphorically); concept definitions (often, if not always, expanding on the metaphoric expression of a concept and often connecting the initial expression of the concept to other concepts, also often expressed metaphorically); and general ideas about relations among concepts (with the relations quite possibly expressed metaphorically). Conceptual frameworks lack integrated, tightly constructed, phenomena-comprehensive propositions about relations among concepts. A theory, on the other hand, rests on metaphor as much as a conceptual framework does but ideally provides those integrated, tightly constructed, phenomena-comprehensive propositions. This is a book about the metaphoric base of a particular theory—or, to be more accurate, a particular conceptual framework (since family systems theories are typically not theories in the sense of offering tightly constructed, integrated, comprehensive propositions). To keep things simple, I will continue to call family systems theory a theory even if it is not a theory by standard definitions of theory and will use the terms "conceptual framework" and "theory" interchangeably when writing about generic conceptual schemes.

From the perspective taken in this book, phenomena do not exist independently of our frameworks for thinking about them, for considering them to be phenomena, and for knowing them. That is part of why it is so important to understand that our frameworks are frameworks and to learn how to step outside of the familiar frameworks and into new ones.

THE STUDY OF METAPHOR

In the fields of philosophy, anthropology, linguistics, cognitive psychology, and literary criticism there are rich discussions of metaphor. Metaphors may be nonlinguistic (e.g., musical, ritual, pictorial, or gestural), but linguistic metaphors receive most of the attention in the literature on metaphors. This is so largely because linguistic metaphors saturate language, and language is key to human relationships and to most thought, including the thought represented in social theories. In fact, many of the early family systems theorists were linguistically sensitive and saw family systems theory as a language for facilitating thought about relationships (e.g., Jackson, 1965b). Consistent with notions that language is crucial in understanding relationships and that linguistic metaphors saturate language, this book is about the linguistic metaphors of family systems theory.

A linguistic metaphor is not drawn randomly from all of language and experience but rests on conceptual connections between the metaphor and the object to which it is applied. Things associated by metaphor have a "family resemblance" (Turner, 1987, p. 12). The family resemblance of a metaphor and its object arise because they, like two family members, are similar in certain ways. They have similar elements, patterning, implications, or associations. Consider the central metaphor of this paragraph, Turner's "family resemblance" metaphor. It is useful because the idea of a family resemblance draws on a widely shared experience of seeing family members who look similar and who have similar personalities, preferences, and behavioral patterns. Thus, when applying a metaphor to an object, we can use the conceptual lens of family resemblance to search for and organize what seem to be similarities. A useful metaphor, moreover, can be developed and extended beyond a brief statement of applicability or relevance. For example, Turner (1987, chap. 2) shows how the family concepts of distant relative and close relative provide insight into metaphor. Compare the two metaphors in the following statements: "Theorizing about families is the drawing of family portraits" and "Theorizing about families is gossip." The concepts of the former metaphor and its object have a close kinship; theorizing about families is associated with such actions of family portraiture as depicting the family as a group, providing a representation of family members that has some sort of validity, and composing the group in an aesthetically appropriate arrangement. The concepts of the gossip metaphor, by contrast, have a more distant kinship. The theorizing may involve evaluating families and communicating about them in a way that could seem gossipy, so there is some appropriateness to the metaphor. But the metaphor of gossip emphasizes moral judgment and the enthusiastic disclosure of secrets rather than the stuff of social science theorizing—understanding and generalizing.

The literature on metaphor goes back to Aristotle's *Rhetoric* and *Poetics*. Key sources of the renaissance in 20th-century writings on metaphor are works by I. A. Richards (1936) and Max Black (1962). Some philosophers, linguists, and social scientists distinguish metaphor from literal language and consider metaphor a decorative addition, conveying perhaps no more than literal language would, and perhaps conveying less. At best, from this perspective, metaphor simply shows a similarity or provides novel words when the standard words seem trite. Many others, certainly since the work of Richards and Black, see metaphor as essential to language, not mere decoration, and capable of accomplishing much that could scarcely (if at all) be accomplished with literal language. Among these uses for metaphor are identifying something that otherwise has no name, generating hypotheses, clarifying perspectives when alternative metaphors are uninspiring or too hard to understand, and providing insights, truths, knowledge, and conceptual frames that otherwise would have been missed. Scholars who see these gains from metaphor would argue that comparatively little language actually is literal and that the meanings of words are not freestanding but are conveyed by the context of their usage and their nuanced connections.

In the debates around these issues one would find scholars differing enormously about something like the metaphor of family rules. Some might say the metaphor is absurd, unless families literally have rules. Some might say the metaphor tells us no more than the more literal words for which the metaphor of family rules substitutes, for example, that there is enough regularity in some family interactions that it seems as though rules are operating. Some would say that the metaphor of family rules actually proposes a new meaning for "rules," a meaning that can be understood only when we translate "family rules" into more basic terms, and that the more basic terms are really what the metaphor is about. Some, myself included, would say that the metaphor of family rules takes us to interesting conceptual places that other metaphors for apparent patterning and control in families would not. This is so because of the other ideas that come along with the idea of rules. From this last perspective, there may not be concepts independent of our metaphors. We might not, for example, be able to conceive of family rules without having a metaphor like that of family rules.

Some social scientists working in traditions stemming from logical positivism may consider what they study and theorize about to be concrete realities. Those social scientists may consider metaphor to be irrelevant, not the stuff of social science, or they may consider metaphor to be a conduit for thoughts already available, not as a source of new thought (see Brown, 1977, p. 31; Kittay, 1987, pp. 1–11). Yet the rejection of metaphor seems like a choice to overlook the meta-phoric nature of the concepts, theories, variables, measurement proce-dures, and epistemological standards and procedures that are central in the social sciences (Brown, 1977, chap. 4). The metaphors are inevita-bly present: Many concept labels are rooted in other areas of discourse; the theories have connections to other areas of experience; the names of variables often have metaphoric connections. The measurement procedures may involve verbal material to which the people studied must respond, and these verbal materials often have metaphoric qualities and are conceptualized metaphorically by the researcher. The epistemology used will have metaphoric connections to other ways of knowing. Even when social scientists working in the logical positivist tradition attempt to minimize the metaphoric carryover of meaning, to limit what they talk about to something very concrete, they are unlikely to escape using metaphor. As Brown (1977) argued in *A Poetic for Sociology*, what people know, they know through frames of vision; all knowledge is perspectival. To achieve perspective requires a view from something else, which entails metaphor (Brown, 1977, chap. 4). Indeed, to work to limit the use of metaphor is to work at limiting knowledge and experience.

Although logical positivism is foundational for a great many researchers in the family field, it has been left behind by analytic philosophers and by scholars in a number of family-related disciplines and subdisciplines. Having rejected logical positivism, analytic philos-ophers have turned to, among other things, metaphor (Kittay, 1987, pp. 6–7). Metaphor is seen not as a frill or a source of surplus meaning that obscures "facts" but as a key to the conceptual processes involved in framing them, in knowing them, in evaluating them, in deciding what a fact is, and in deciding that there are facts to be known. From such a perspective there is no dichotomy between metaphor and scientific thought.

THE LAKOFF AND JOHNSON
VIEW OF METAPHOR

Lakoff and Johnson (1980), in an insightful and influential analysis of metaphor, argued that metaphor is pervasive in everyday language, thought, and action. They further argued that thought processes rely heavily on metaphors and that these metaphors arise in and reflect a cultural, historical, and linguistic context. Thus, people from different cultures or historical periods and people speaking different languages may come to different metaphors and hence to different realities. Different cultures give rise to different metaphors in part because they are associated with different experiences, in part because they may give different meanings to experiences that from a distance might seem to be the same, and in part because they provide different linguistic tools for characterizing things.

Although this book uses the Lakoff and Johnson approach in order to analyze a scholarly theory, it is clear that Lakoff and Johnson were writing about ordinary language. Although not all of ordinary language is metaphoric, and although some scholars think that Lakoff and Johnson exaggerate how much ordinary language is metaphoric and create problems by the way they draw distinctions between literal and metaphoric speech (Way, 1991, pp. 17–18, 22, 25), ordinary language is saturated with metaphor. That we may not be aware of the metaphoric richness of ordinary language does not make that language any less metaphoric. As Richards (1936) wrote many years ago, "Our skill with metaphor, with thought, is one thing—prodigious and inexplicable; our reflective awareness of that skill is quite another thing—very incomplete, distorted, fallacious, over-simplifying" (p. 116).

The importance of cultural context (and life experience) in shaping the metaphors by which people live and with which they think and communicate means that across cultures there will be major differences in metaphors about family experience and perhaps major differences in the family systems theory metaphors that make sense. Consider the importance to most Balinese of the *dadia*, which Geertz and Geertz (1975) describe as "an agnatic, preferentially endogamous, highly corporate group of people who are convinced, with whatever reason, that they are all descendants of one common ancestor" (p. 5). Consider further the crucial importance to most Balinese of the *banjar*, a defined neighborhood that plays a central role in religion, cooperative work, identity, politics, decision making, and celebration

(Geertz & Geertz, 1975, pp. 16–19). Even without getting into other aspects of Balinese culture, we can comprehend that a lifetime of experience in dadia and banjar provides the Balinese with a very different basis for thinking about phenomena that are counted as familial in family systems theories. For example, a Balinese family systems theory might make heavy use of metaphors dealing with the processes of defining and maintaining dadias and with the blurring of family and banjar.

Even among cultures within the United States there are major differences in family experience. Consider such terms, from a black community studied by Stack (1974), as "old man," "old lady," "going for sisters," "going for cousins," and "play daddy." The terms cataloged by Stack are foreign to family systems theory and to most textbooks in the family field, yet they are meaningful and powerful metaphors in a substantial segment of the U.S. population. Such terms might well be sources of systems theory metaphors that would provide perspectives missed by the standard metaphors. Those alternative metaphors might also be central to a systems theory that would make the most sense in trying to understand and help families in those communities.

That metaphors have a cultural context also means that "the most fundamental values in a culture will be coherent with the metaphorical structure of the most fundamental concepts of the culture" (Lakoff & Johnson, 1980, p. 22). Thus, something is known about a people's values by knowing their frequently expressed metaphors, and something is known about their frequently expressed metaphors by knowing their values. For example, knowing that many Americans use such financial metaphors as "bottom line" and "investment," one might expect them to value money and activities that will generate money. Similarly, knowing that Americans value health, one might expect them to frequently use health-related concepts metaphorically in talking about family relationships, for example, "a sick family," "an epidemic of child abuse," or "a prescription for a more rewarding family life." More to the point of a book on family systems theory, the way American culture deals metaphorically with families may be incorporated into family systems theory in ways that make the metaphors of the theory imperfect tools for seeing and understanding American families. For example, many Americans may both value families and value an obscuring of the differentiation of family experience (Thorne, 1982). Some may not want to attend to gender differences within their own family (or in families in general) in terms of privilege, responsibility, capacity to threaten or carry out physical violence, or social sensitivity. There is a danger that family systems theory may incorporate this cultural value of obscuring so that it too misses the differentiation of family experience.

More generally, American values influence how Americans theorize about people (Kirschner, 1990). Even as I attempt to expand the ways we might think about family systems theory, I am still a captive of American culture. For example, I am still concerned with solving problems, verbalizing issues, and the importance of families.

There may be, as Lakoff and Johnson (1980, chap. 6) suggested, metaphoric processes that are panhuman, for example, the use of metaphors of entity and substance to categorize and delimit. English speakers, for example, make feelings into things that have labels and that they can quantify. Thus, the statement "I am carrying around a lot of sadness" labels how one is feeling, makes the feeling into a thing, and quantifies it. The metaphors of entity and substance are also used to categorize and delimit families and, as a consequence, to differentiate them from one another and from things that are not called families. Thus, saying "The Rosenblatts are located in Minnesota" makes a certain group of people into an entity and separates that group from similar groups that have a different name or locality.

Two other metaphoric processes that Lakoff and Johnson (1980, chap. 12) suggested may be panhuman are the conceptualization of the nonphysical in terms of the physical and the conceptualization of the less clearly delineated in terms of the more clearly delineated (see also Johnson, 1987; Lakoff, 1987). The physical and more clearly delineated metaphors quite often rely on our most primary physical experiences, including our location in space (up–down, front–back, close–distant, in–out), and on distinctions based on the nature of our bodies and on our body functioning (female–male, warm–cold, light–dark, quiet–loud). Take the term "family." A family is not a clearly bounded physical entity but one defined by culture and custom (Gubrium & Holstein, 1990; Schneider, 1980). (Do we define family as the people who care about us? Are in-laws counted as in or out of a typical American's family? Is a spouse a relative? What about the cousins one has never met or the cousins one does not know exist?) Families are made concrete with physical terms—recall, for example, the biblical reference to the "house of Abraham"—and with locational terms, like "close relative" (cf. Constantine, 1986, pp. 147). In American English and American culture the family is metaphorically given a status as a physical object through the metaphoric application of concepts that are typically applied to physical objects. Thus, people talk about *close* kin, people *in* the family, a family *bouncing* back from a setback, and a family being *moved* to a new location.

The physical world has many regularities. It is harder to move things uphill than down, large things are generally heavier and harder to move than small ones, things broken into pieces are not easy to put together. Such physical regularities shape and limit how language is used (Lakoff, 1987, p. xv). Thus, in talking about families, Americans might refer metaphorically to family problems that involve an uphill struggle, that are big, or that lead to a broken family.

Metaphoric Entailments

From the Lakoff and Johnson perspective, once people think in terms of a metaphor, its entailments stimulate and direct their thinking in a coherent and systematic way. Entailments are the necessary and automatic associations of a concept; for example, in the preceding paragraph, "harder to move" is an entailment of big. Using a metaphor makes entailed associations, connections, and creative leaps likely, if not certain, and makes nonentailed associations, connections, and creative leaps difficult or impossible to consider at the same time. Thus, the computer metaphor in cognitive theory highlights the guiding systems that are used in processing information and the importance of understanding how information is stored and retrieved, but it obscures intuitive processes, the ways in which input is multiple, chaotic, fluid, or out of control, and the instability and multiple transformations of what is stored in human thought. The computer metaphor in cognitive theory indicates linkages, causal relationships, hierarchy, differences in degree of importance of various cognitive mechanisms, and the mechanisms themselves. It gives us notions of discrete operations in thought, hierarchical organization in processing and information storage, operational sequences like those engaged in by computers, and a sense of what sequences there are to processes and what can go wrong. With a different metaphor (e.g., that of a lending library or a town meeting) we would come to different views of the structures and systems of cognitive processes.

Just as entailments in the metaphoric application of the concept of computer to human thinking shape how we think about thinking, the metaphors applied to families shape how we think about families. For example, the biblical metaphor for family as the "house" of somebody brings with it entailments that stimulate us to think about the solidity of the house and the way it contains a group of people and separates them from those outside. We may also think about the house as having a roof, needing repairs, and having internal divisions. These entailments cohere and are systematic in that they all relate to the single idea of a house. While working within that metaphor, we are less likely to have associations that are unrelated to it, for example, associations related to the family as a growing organic thing or the family as a bureaucratic organization.

One critic of the Lakoff and Johnson approach (Fogelin, 1988, pp. 83–86) has argued that Lakoff and Johnson used the term "metaphor" to refer to comparisons that many people would not call metaphors. Although that is an issue to keep in mind in considering potential problems in working within a Lakoff and Johnson framework, I think the basic conceptual issues apply—the experiential foundation of metaphors, potential reification, importance of entailments—whether one considers family systems theory to be laden with metaphors or laden with implicit and explicit comparisons.

RECOGNIZING METAPHORS

Metaphors may often seem to be grounded, real, and literally accurate rather than expressions that are drawn from one area of discourse and applied to another. People are easily captured by metaphors. For example, it is hard at first to realize that when we speak of close relatives we are using a distance metaphor. But relatives differing in genealogical distance or emotional relationship to us are not literally close or far. Similarly, stepparents are not literally a step away, but the culture counts them as in some sense a step further away than a person who has been a parent from one's birth. (Actually, the concept of step relationship is taken from an early English word dealing with bereavement; the term originally applied to orphans.) Half siblings are not literally cut in half, not related through only half of their feelings, and not committed to dealing with each other with literally 50% of the commitment for full siblings. Half siblings are only half in that they are biologically linked to half the number of parents to whom full siblings are linked. But it is still a metaphor to call them half siblings, with the concept of half taken from other areas of experience.

Metaphors are also hard to identify because they may be hidden by layers or chains of derivation. The recognition of a metaphoric base for a concept may stop us from seeing that there are other bases for that concept. For example, recognizing that the concept of family power has roots in thoughts about governmental and organizational control may stop us from thinking in terms of physical strength or electrical energy. Recognizing a metaphoric base for a concept may also stop us from seeing how the concept is being used as a metaphor for other things. For example, when we speak about relationship losses, we are using a metaphor that might have its roots in the destruction or disappearance of something valued. But loss may also be a metaphor for other things, for example, our attachment that existed prior to the loss or our continuing sense of attachment to a person who was lost (Vaillant, 1985). Thus, expressions of loss may reflect true feelings of grief but also may be metaphoric expressions of how attached one was or still is to the person lost.

How can we recognize that a linguistic expression is a metaphor? Sometimes a metaphor can be recognized as metaphor simply by asking where else those words are used. Where else are words like "close," "step," or "half" used? Where else do we use such family systems theory terms as "structure," "feedback," and "boundary?" Sometimes a metaphor can be recognized because a literal reading seems to be bizarre, false, nonsensical, a violation of the rules of speech, incongruent with the surrounding text, or in some other way anomalous (see Tourangeau, 1982, for a discussion of the complexities in recognizing metaphors). One way to recognize a concept as metaphoric is to extend the implications of the concept (Turbayne, 1970, pp. 57–59). If, say, the concept of family boundaries seems real and not metaphoric, one can develop implications of the concept by asking the following questions: Who surveyed the boundaries? Are there boundary disputes? Can a rustler come in the night, cross the boundary, and steal some of what's behind it? Can a boundary be broken? If it is broken, can it be repaired? Sometimes, however, it is more difficult to recognize that a linguistic expression is a metaphor, such as when a metaphoric usage becomes the dominant one. When, for example, family professionals use the word "scapegoat" only in talking about families, they may lose track of the biblical reference that is the metaphoric base for the family systems theory usage.

Although it is often hard at first to recognize that a metaphor is not literally true, a metaphor succeeds only because it is imperfect (Romanyshyn, 1981). A metaphor helps us to understand things because we can think in terms of it and still think in some other terms. As an example of the necessary imperfection of a metaphor, Romanyshyn discussed the metaphor of the heart as a pump. We can believe that the heart is truly a pump because it has many of the characteristics of a pump. Yet we must also realize that the heart is not only a pump. We may for the moment become captured by the reality that the pump metaphor creates, but for the pump metaphor to be perceived as a metaphor and for it to enlighten us we must escape the reality of thinking of the heart as a pump and only that. Thus, we must see how at least one other usage applies—for example, the heart as a biological organ, as a symbol (of courage, strength, love, life), or a switching point for blood. Similarly, a family systems metaphor of family rules succeeds because we can think about family patterning in terms other than rules.

People may often be temporary prisoners of their metaphors (Lakoff & Johnson, 1980, p. x; Turbayne, 1970). It is hard to step back from a compelling metaphor in order to see alternative realities. When a metaphor becomes a reality for us—when, for example, we think of the metaphor of the family system as a reality rather than as one of many different ways of talking about a group of people called a family—we are functioning as people normally do. But in doing so, we lose the imagination and creativity that come with the complexity and ambiguity of multiple meanings and multiple realities (Hillman, 1975, chap. 3). Being captured by a metaphor is like being captured by the view from a telescope. If we only see the world through the telescope, never removing our eye from it to look at the world through other lenses or through the naked eye, we will see quite a bit but miss so much more.

Recognizing metaphors requires practice. Hearing and seeing them become easier the more practice one has. One can also learn to recognize metaphors by creating them. With greater practice at creating them, one can recognize them more easily in the language of others. However, it is possible to be captured by one's own metaphors so that one loses track of how they are metaphors; they become one's reality (Turbayne, 1970).

THE VALUE OF EXAMINING THEORETICAL METAPHORS

If we allow ourselves to be captured by the reality provided by Lakoff and Johnson, it becomes obvious that any theory structures the domain with which it deals and highlights some phenomena while obscuring others. It often seems that the most difficult task of working with a theory is to be fully loyal to its concepts and meanings, but it is also difficult to step outside of a theory that organizes one's thinking in order to see what it has been obscuring. Metaphoric analysis can lead to the recognition of structures of experience and thought, of phenomena and relationships among phenomena, and of perspectives that have been out of awareness and thought. An analysis of theoretical metaphors that leads to alternatives to the theoretical metaphors that have captured our thinking can enable us to see what we have been missing and can lead us to fascinating and important new lines of thought. An example from outside of the family field is Morgan's (1986) book on metaphors of organizations. It has been extremely useful in the field of social organization because in applying a series of different metaphoric lenses it offers powerful insights into the dynamics of organizations and the history of organization theory that are missed by use of the standard metaphors.

There are many voices in the family field speaking about the value of turning to frameworks other than family systems theory (e.g., Handel, 1985; Lowe, 1990). They speak about what seems to them to be the sterility of family systems theory or about its empty generality. They speak about family systems theory imposing a theoretical view on a family that discounts, transforms, or ignores how family members understand their family. They speak about family systems theory as being not necessarily attuned to cultural diversity, to the diversity of family ecologies, or to the diversity of perspectives, experiences, standards, values, abilities, and personalities within the family. They speak about the value of feminist theory, discourse analysis, social constructionism, phenomenology, narrative analysis, cognitive–behavioral approaches, and other perspectives. The family systems framework seems to some family scholars and practitioners to miss important elements of family functioning and to be a poor base for effective family therapy. Obviously, there are alternative realities that family systems theory has masked. There is quite clearly a crisis in family systems work in that there is considerable dissatisfaction with the theory. What I hope to show with this book is how the standard metaphors of family systems theory structure thought, creating certain realities and obscuring alternative realities. Identifying the problems with the standard metaphors does not make the crisis go away, but it can be seen that some of what the theory seems to have missed is still consistent with the theory and can be revealed by exploring alternative systemic metaphors.

This book is written in sympathy with the critics who seem to be saying that we must move to other ways of thinking about families, yet I am not arguing that we should abandon family systems theory or that an alternative framework, such as social constructionism, is necessarily inconsistent with family systems theory. A view of theory as metaphor is like social constructionism in leading us to see that any reality is cooked up and maintained socially, that the world can only be partially and selectively known, and that what is selected is shaped and maintained by social processes. In any case, selectivity is inevitable; people inevitably miss some of what could be apprehended and believed to be true (cf. Keeney, 1983; Spender, 1983).

Even if our theoretical metaphors lack the rock-hard solidity of what may still be longed for but what many social scientists now agree does not exist—objective truth—these metaphors lead to discovery, insights, and understandings. The theoretical metaphors we use are provisional and do not invalidate alternative metaphors. However limited, they are all that we have in theorizing about the world. From this perspective the question to be asked in evaluating a theory based on a particular metaphor is not whether it is true but whether it is useful (Brown, 1977). And the usefulness is enhanced if we recognize that the theoretical metaphors we use are social constructions, because with that recognition comes an openness to alternative perspectives, questions about the social construction process itself, and curiosity about what might be missed by the particular metaphors chosen (McNamee, 1992).

Campbell's comparative psychology of knowledge processes (1956, 1959a, 1959b, 1966, 1974) provides a parallel perspective on working with theoretical metaphors. From that perspective, a theoretical metaphor provides a way of knowing, one of many different ways, all of which are fallible. A theoretical language can be understood, from the Campbellian perspective, as a random variation that may or may not survive the test of time, depending most of all on the winnowing provided by experience. Thus, new theoretical metaphors give us new experiences to look at, new lenses for seeing things, new ways of organizing events, and new alertness. At the same time, they are tested against an experience that is not fully engulfed, fooled, overpowered, or overcome by the new lenses. From the perspective of Campbell's comparative psychology of knowledge processes, there is no alternative to the continued development of new theoretical conceptions and tests of experience in the evolution of theory and knowledge. From the perspective of Hoffman's (1990) account of the lens of second-order view in family therapy, a lens such as the one on theoretical metaphors offered in this book can help the reader take a step back and think about alternative systemic approaches rather than continue to work with one that seems to be engraved in stone.

There are dangers in writing about a metaphor as though one understood it fully and could explain it to others so that they would know the whole truth about it. A metaphor is a living thing; it changes as we consider and discuss it, and it changes as our experiences change. It is quite likely different for each of us. Applying it changes it, and thinking about it changes it. It is never quite what one thinks it is, never only what one thinks it is, and may never quite be what one would like it to be.

It is also important to recognize that the metaphors of social science theory and the metaphors of experience arise out of the same culture. In that sense the metaphors of social science theory are a codification of everyday metaphors known widely in the culture. The penetrating insight of a social theory typically arises from common-place cultural conceptions. A theory of family systems from a culture other than the one in which much of the published work on family systems theory has been written might yield startling new and original ideas about families. But it might well be based on metaphors and metaphoric referents that make so little sense to people from the culture in which this book and much of the family systems literature has been written that it would seem irrelevant to what people in this culture try to understand about families.

That does not mean that there is a culturewide monolithic uniformity in conceptions of family phenomena. American society is a mosaic and blend of many different cultures. The culture has so much complexity and internal contradiction that it is quite possible to generate mutually inconsistent social theories (e.g., family systems theory versus individual psychological theories). Moreover, everyone has unique experiences within the culture and brings unique perspectives and filters to that experience and to language. Between any two persons' use and understanding of a metaphor that is widely known and deeply rooted in the culture, there may be a great deal of difference arising from subcultural, gender, class, racial, occupational, educational, regional, and other experiential bases. We are all affected by experience. Quinn (1981, 1987), for example, reported that people's models of marriage in American culture reflected the cumulative idiosyncracies of their own marital experiences overlaid on the common metaphors of marriage as, for example, a couple and a person. The

idiosyncracies of experience partially explain why a theoretical meta
phor that seems brilliantly illuminating to one family professional
seems trivial to another. Nonetheless, there will be enough shared
experience to make it likely that some theoretical metaphors will be
perceived in rather the same way by different professionals.

The metaphors of everyday experience can be said to shape
people's behavior, understandings, thoughts, and feelings. Similarly,
the metaphors of social science theories shape the behavior of practitioners, researchers, teachers, policymakers, and others who work with the
theories as they act on what they believe is true. However, the
metaphors of social science theories select truths and realities from all
truths and realities that can be entertained. All of thought is selective.
We are captured by what is at the focus of our thought and can only deal
with a small range of all that might conceivably be dealt with. Theories
help us to organize and focus, which is valuable, but they do so at the
cost of blocking out a great deal of what we might profitably attend to.
This book is an attempt to open up new possibilities of behavior,
understanding, thought, and feeling about families by reminding the
reader of parts of the cultural experience that the standard metaphors of
family systems theory obscure.

DEFINING FAMILY SYSTEMS THEORY

The published works on family systems theory are so diverse that it is
misleading to write as though there is a single family systems theory
(Broderick & Pulliam-Krager, 1979; Merkel & Searight, 1992). The
books, chapters, and journal articles on family systems theory provide
a universe of maps. There are commonalities, but there is considerable
diversity (cf. Burr, 1991).

Perhaps one reason for the diversity is that the metaphors of
family systems theory come from many different sources; there are, for
example, metaphors of the biological organism, machines, stage plays,
and competitive games. Perhaps another reason for the diversity is that
in this age of postmodern criticism, relativism, and social constructionism, it has become ever more legitimate to read a text in ways
that others do not. The texts of family systems theory, no less than
other written texts, are open to many different readings. As they are

read differently by different people, the differences in readings lead to a diversity of new writings, each of which, as it is read in multiple ways, leads to still new diversity in writings. (See, e.g., Beavin, Black, Chovil, & Mullett, 1990, p. 21, on the proliferation of understandings of the family systems theory concept of transactional disqualification.) The field is not chaotic; there are limits and patterns to the readings that are given, and there is a great deal of in-group discipline in the choice of the texts on which to base next steps and on how to read those texts. Still, there is considerable diversity.

I think the key reason for the diversity in versions of family systems theory is that it is difficult and perhaps often not even very productive to work with a total systems perspective. As therapists and other scholars think about the peculiarities of specific cases or specific family issues, they write (and perhaps think) about only fragments of family systems. At times they may even claim to be writing about something in a systemic way, but what is written seems to be an account of individuals, of linear causality, or of system fragments, not of systemic interactions.

In all this diversity, there is no clearly delineated canon of texts, no single set of readings, that defines the field (Merkel & Searight, 1992), although for some people who work with family systems theory there is a basic set of texts that is a kind of personal canon. I have read widely in family systems theory, talked to others who teach and write about family systems theory, and reviewed what is cited often and seems influential. From all that, I have chosen the concepts represented in this book as the key metaphors in family systems theory. The way I have laid out family systems theory is only one of many ways of characterizing the theory; there are alternative canons (e.g., Ackerman, 1984, chap. 10). I believe my choices are legitimate. I do not want to write a treatise on the diversity of family systems theories but, rather, to present a way of thinking about family systems theory that could be applied to that diversity. I think my choices represent the field fairly and are an adequate foundation for delineating the key metaphors of family systems theory. I believe I have included the metaphors that others who work with systems theory recognize as key metaphors. However, there are riches in the family systems literature far beyond that with which I deal in this book. Particularly in the family therapy area, there is an enormous diversity of systems analyses. There are also innumerable metaphors for families that provide insight but are not systemic, for example, the family as a haven in a heartless world (Lasch, 1977), or the family is falling apart. These metaphors might possibly be contextualized in ways that would make them systemic, but they fail to highlight the emerging properties and the focus on family connections and pattern that are the hallmark, I think, of family systems thinking.

Family systems theory has been the foundation of many important developments in family therapy and a respectable share of the published research dealing with families. The theory is arguably the greatest contribution of the family field to social thought. Understanding families as systems allows transcendence of the limits of the dominant mode in Western society for understanding human life—individual psychology. In Western thought, explanations of what goes on in people's lives, even in the context of their families, typically are couched in terms of individual psychology. Understanding is considered to have been achieved when there are plausible words about individual motivations, intentions, needs, feelings, and thoughts. If family members have a place in an explanation, it is typically as a cause of individual dispositions. Family systems theory, by contrast, provides an understanding of the family. It focuses both on the mutual interplay of family member dispositions and on supraindividual family properties. Thinking in terms of family systems can provide striking new realities and perspectives on what had been taken as reality; it is like being able to use microscopes and telescopes when previously one could only see things with the naked eye. Family systems theory provides insight into the ways in which family members create a system of mutual interlock, the intergenerational carryover of patterns, the patterns that arise and persist without written or voiced agreement, and much, much more. The metaphors of family systems theory have been precious tools for seeing what would otherwise be missed. However, like all metaphors, the metaphors of family systems theory are limiting. Exploring alternative approaches to conceptualizing family systems requires exploration of these limitations. An analysis of what family systems theory highlights, how it structures phenomena, and what it obscures can open up new avenues of theoretical thinking. It can make it easier to understand how the specific metaphors of the theory facilitate and block certain kinds of thought, and it can make it easier to use the theory with metaphoric substitutions that will enable creative new applications and insights.

CHAPTER TWO

The Metaphor of the Family as an Entity

THE ENTITY METAPHOR

In all family systems theories the family is an entity. Like a rock, an automobile, or a stamp collection it has reality, definable boundaries, and an essential character. The entity metaphor is a central metaphor in American culture for the family (Gubrium & Holstein, 1990, pp. 6–8), so using a metaphor that is so much a part of the culture makes family theory one that is not incongruent with the realities of many of the people to whom the theory is applied.

In family systems theories the essential character of the family entity includes culturally defined family roles and role interactions that differ by age and gender. It includes culturally defined family identity markers as, for example, a name, a dwelling, genealogical relations, commitments made by members to each other, or legal rights and obligations to one another. The essential character of the family as defined by family systems theories also includes a family development process, one that arises from the development and aging of each individual family member and from the accumulation of experiences of family members with one another.

The present chapter explores what the entity metaphor in family systems theory highlights and obscures. As part of the exploration, the family is likened to two other entities, a house and a river. The metaphoric analysis of the family as house and river helps to show how specific entity metaphors can uncover some of what is obscured by the more generic entity metaphor, suggesting, for example, alternative ways in which an entity may exist through time, interact with its environment, and have an identity.

WHERE THE ENTITY METAPHOR LEADS THOUGHT

The Family Exists Independently of Its Members

The metaphor of the family as an entity leads people to think of the family as existing independently of its members. Once the family is defined as an independent entity, it can be thought of as having its own needs and a life of its own (Gubrium, 1992) and as something that can be benefited or harmed independently of its members. Thus, family professionals, family researchers, and family policy makers may worry about what is best for the family independently of its individual members. As a consequence, actions can be taken that are "for the good of the family" but that are experienced as unwelcome or even harmful by some or all family members.

As an independent entity the family is another player in the family system. Family members can bring the family in for therapy, claiming that they have no problems as individuals but that the family is in trouble. With the family as a separate player in the system, people can try to save it when it seems in danger and mourn it when it is gone, even though the changes that put it in danger or that led to its end might be perceived as beneficial to some or even all individual members.

As a separate entity from individual family members, the family, rather than individual members, can be blamed when things go wrong and credited when things go right. The family can thus be blamed for individual unhappiness, individual moral failings, and family communication gone awry. Personifying the family in this way obscures individual responsibility. Obscuring individual responsibility may be an unintended consequence of thinking of the family as an entity, or it may be an intentional defense against taking or granting responsibility. One can make a case that even in family systems therapy it is challenging to treat the family as a whole while respecting, allowing, and encouraging individual responsibility.

(Although it can be very useful to recognize when the metaphor of the family as an entity obscures individual responsibility, I am not arguing that morality and causal analysis should necessarily be based on individual considerations. A case can be made, though it goes against the individualistic grain of Western thought, that moral considerations and causal attributions should always be at a collective level. In that way of thinking, family members are held collectively responsible for the actions of individual family members.)

The bias for family members and others to perceive the family as an entity sets goals for the family. These goals have to do with working toward a family with the characteristics of a group that can be perceived as an entity (cf. Campbell, 1958; Quinn, 1981), through, for example, exclusive interaction, proximity, and shared experience. These goals are appropriate for any social group that is to continue as an entity. However, striving for such goals may disadvantage individual family members and the larger society. It may, for example, lead social service agencies and the courts to put an inordinate amount of energy into keeping an abused child with an abusive father or an abused wife with an abusive husband. It may lead all of us to underestimate the importance of all that is not familial in social life—for example, friends, neighbors, and community. In focusing policy-making, legislation, social service, and education on the family, we may fail to acknowledge and support relationships that are for many, if not all, people vitally important and perhaps even crucial in grounding them, meeting their needs, and sustaining them.

Generalizing from Quinn's (1981, 1982, 1987, 1991) work on metaphors for marriage, the metaphor of a family as an entity also highlights how the family endures through time. Once one thinks of the family as enduring, it is an easy next step to value the longevity of the family. Thus, the entity metaphor may bias people—judges, human service workers, therapists, family members themselves—to value the continuation of what is perceived as an entity even if that continuation is not desirable by some standards.

The entity metaphor may also make it harder to recognize how the family is repeatedly transformed over time. Family members move away, separate, divorce, or die; they are added by birth, adoption, fosterage, marriage, or moving in. Perhaps each change in membership destroys the family that had been existing and creates a new family, but the metaphor of family makes it easy to think that there is continuity. Broderick and Smith (1979) point out that the idea of a system that persists though membership changes leads conceptually to the view of a system as having roles. Thinking in terms of roles that persist though group membership changes leads to a systems theory in which key system dynamics center on how roles become vacated and filled. This approach is counter to a systems theory in which new systems emerge out of old and in which key dynamics include emergence processes and processes of transforming past roles, rules, precedents, and patterns with each new emergence. It is also counter to a systems theory in which roles are constantly negotiated and changing (Berger & Kellner, 1964) and are inevitably linked to changes in membership.

Finally and obviously, the metaphor of the family may obscure the individuality of the members of the collective called a family (Lowe, 1990). It is their individual feelings, individual thoughts, and so on that must be perceived, understood, and dealt with. Using the article "the" in referring to family helps to make family more of an entity, but "the family" is an abstraction. It cannot communicate, feel, or think. Family therapy may deal usefully with the family, but it must deal with, build on, and influence individual feelings, thoughts, perceptions, understandings, and actions.

Obscuring the Ways There Is No Family Entity

Seeing the family as an entity focuses attention on the ways the family forms a unit. Attention is drawn to the ways family members are similar, the times they interact together, the times they are in proximity to each other, and the ways in which they exclude people who are not members of the family. Attention is drawn away from evidence to the contrary, evidence that there is no clearly definable family entity. Thus, attention will be drawn away from the ways family members are dissimilar, the large amount of time in which they do not interact together or are physically distant from each other, the difficulty of meeting individual needs for family-like experiences within the family, and the vital importance to each family member of connections with people outside of the family.

Because the entity metaphor leads us to think of a family as a distinct system, it obscures the extent to which each member of a specific family is likely to be considered by self and others to be part of some family in which no other member of that specific family is counted. A married woman with children, for example, may consider herself to be part of two families, the family of her husband and children and the family of her parents and siblings. Her husband may also consider himself part of two separate families—his own family of origin and the family he shares with his wife and children. To complicate matters still further, according to Schneider's (1980) research on whom people count as relatives, Americans often do not count people linked to them through marriage as relatives. Thus, a woman may count her children as relatives but not her spouse. If either partner has children from a previous marriage, those children may constitute yet another family to which the partner belongs. Partners with parents who have divorced and remarried may consider themselves members of still other families. On one level, what this means is that it does not make sense to think of people as belonging to a single family; if we do, we will miss a great deal about their family life. A network view of relationships may make more sense than a punctuation of relationships into distinct families (Erickson, 1988). Multiple family membership requires us to think not of single families but of linked families. And what goes on in a single family may not be understandable without reference to those linkages (Gluckman, 1956); systemic analyses must take those linkages into account.

Differences among family members as to who is considered part of the family arise not only from differing kinship relationships to people whom somebody in the family may count as a relative but also from the differing criteria they use in defining kinship. These issues come to the fore when there is a divorce or remarriage; when children are adopted, fostered, produced without the biological parents being married to each other, or produced through some means for dealing with infertility that requires genetic material or child bearing from a third party; when fictive kinship occurs; and when there is family estrangement. Use of the metaphor of the family as an entity may reduce the likelihood that family professionals or researchers will be aware of the differences among family members about who to count in the family and of the implications of those differences.

The entity metaphor also obscures how families and family members differ on whether any of the following can be considered family members: pets; people who are not yet born or who are dead (Rosenblatt & Elde, 1990); people who are not related by blood, marriage, or adoption (e.g., lesbian or gay partners of a family member, servants, close friends); and God. Differences between families and between family members on who should be counted in the family arise in part because the concept of family implies certain attitudes, feelings, and behaviors (Gubrium & Buckholdt, 1982). One may, for example, refer to somebody as not much of a parent when that person seems to be just going through the motions of parenting. On the other hand, a neighbor, friend, health care worker, or influential teacher may be so important, helpful, caring, and in other ways like a family member as to be spoken of as "sort of," "just like," or "truly" a family member.

The entity metaphor also obscures the extent to which some families are, by the standards of their members, more family-like than others (Gubrium & Buckholdt, 1982; Gubrium & Holstein, 1990, pp. 13–16). It is this quality to which people refer when they talk about how often family members get together, how much they support each other when a death or some other disaster occurs, or how interested they are in one another. In other words, to the extent that the metaphor of the family as an entity implies a thing that one is either part of or not, it misleads by obscuring the cultural and experiential ambiguities that make it possible for people to say how much of a family a given family is.

By treating the family as a distinct and freestanding entity, the family metaphor obscures how families exist and are defined in transaction with other systems (Maddock, 1992b). Families come into existence and form their boundaries and rules through transactions with other systems and are defined in distinction from other systems. In talking about a given family, the transactional connections with other systems may be unvoiced, but to fully understand what a given family is, why it is the way it is, and how it changes and remains stable requires an understanding of its relation to other systems.

Obscuring Family Competition, Difference, and Disunity

The metaphor of family as entity obscures the extent to which family members may compete intensely for resources, may have extremely different values and needs, and may experience the family (and much else) differently. Feminists who write about the family (e.g., Thorne, 1982) have emphasized that to treat the family as an entity is to obscure the differing needs, values, concerns, and experiences of individual family members. To the extent that treating the family as an entity gives greater voice to the family member with the most power, the voices of women and children in a society in which many factors operate to give men more power are muffled or silenced. Moreover, treating the family as an entity creates the illusion of equal participation in family life by women and men, an illusion that hides the extent to which childrearing and other family responsibilities have been much more the work of women than of men. Although women may receive a disproportionate share of the blame (e.g., for child schizophrenia) in some family systems theory writings, they do not necessarily receive a disproportionate share of the credit (e.g., for child educational achievement) (Smith, 1987, pp. 21–22).

By obscuring family competition, difference, and disunity, the metaphor of family as entity may make it more difficult to see the systemic connection of competition, difference, and disunity within a family to that family's connection with other families (Gluckman, 1956). Competition, difference, and disunity in individual families may be part of the dynamics of a system of linked families with overlapping membership. Partial or temporary estrangement in any specific family may be part of what keeps the linked families linked, and their linkage may be part of why there is estrangement (Gluckman, 1956).

THE FAMILY AS AN ENTITY

If there were no metaphor of the family as entity and no prior identification or labeling of the groups that people now identify as families, the identification of those groups would be a matter for inference. In inferring the existence of a social entity people might attend to the members' common fate, similarity, exclusive interaction, or shared identity (Campbell, 1958). Remaining aware of the inferential processes used to decide that a social entity exists would make it harder for one to be captured by an entity metaphor like family. There might be debates about the "familyness" of different constellations of individuals and about how to characterize groups of people in which some members consider the entire group to be a family and some do not. There might develop an array of different family systems theories for "families" characterized in different ways, including theories for unbounded, ambiguous, and recurrently transforming social entities. In addition, if one could look at a particular family and ask how it is and is not an entity, one might be able to get beyond what the family metaphor obscures, to see the extent to which family members are similar, interact exclusively, share identity, share economic and health statuses, and so on.

Thinking of entitivity as something to be inferred from a number of indicators also makes it possible to think of a continuum of entitivity. Some families can be seen more clearly as entities than others. They might differ, for example, in how much they submerge individuality or in how much family members interact with one another to the exclusion of others. With a continuum of entitivity, one might resist applying the same standards to all families and consider the possibility of different theories, public policies, therapeutic approaches, and descriptive language for families differing in entitivity.

At their most abstract, entities are interchangeable. A thing is a thing. But entities differ in what makes them entities. It may be helpful in thinking about the family to consider different ways in which an entity may exist through time, interact with its environment, or have an identity. Considering alternative entity metaphors for families may help us to think about how the meaning of the term *family* carries a package of metaphoric implications. It is possible to think of families in other ways; the world is full of potential metaphoric models for entities. In what follows, I explore two different metaphoric models of the family as an entity: the family is a river and the family is a house.

The Family Is a River

Rivers and Families over Time

Thinking of the family as an entity like a river emphasizes the long-term continuity of the family. No particular person in the family is necessary for the family to exist, just as no particular water molecule is critical for the river's survival. Rivers are relatively timeless, so thinking of the family as a river emphasizes the timelessness of families and their supraindividual nature. One may not know the names of ancestors even a few generations back. Even knowing the names of ancestors one may still know little or nothing about their character, identity, or activities, and one certainly knows nothing of future descendants. Yet there is a sense in which everyone is part of a family river. We are at any moment a point in a flow that started far earlier than our memory and knowledge can reach and that may continue far into the unknowable future. Just as a drop of water that began its flow in the headwaters of the river may still be present at the mouth of the river, aspects of a long-forgotten family past may still be with a family—facial features, traditions, speech mannerisms, beliefs, reactions to threats, ways of expressing emotion, and so on. Thus, thinking of the family as an entity like a river gives one a sense of something that both reaches back and extends forward in time. Analyzing a family system only in terms of the people in a single household at one point in time misses the existence of the family through time.

Thinking about the family only in the present also misses how through time the family is ever-changing in its thingness. Recall the observation of Heraclitus that one cannot step twice into the same river. It could be argued that similarly one cannot make contact twice with the same family. Although the players may appear the same today as yesterday, they will have been affected by a day's worth of individual and family experience, a day of aging and of contact with their environment. From this perspective it is easy to question case reports of families that are written with a kind of confidence in the comprehensibility of families. To characterize a family system as though it is and will continue to be what it has been, as though it is constant, is to accept how the entity metaphor obscures the "ever-changingness" of families.

Thinking of the flow of the family through time makes it clear that much of what is observed now in a family has origins in the past, sometimes in a past so remote that it cannot be traced. From this perspective, one could argue that individuals are not solely responsible for who they are and that much of what can be observed in a family member, both the bad and the good, has distant origins. The praise and blame belong not only to the individual but also to the individual's antecedents. The Nobel prize and the prison sentence should be shared with others. In a sense, then, change requires not merely a personal change but some sort of divorce from the family of the past. And taking full credit for personal successes and achievements is a form of cheating, a way of being dishonest with oneself and others about how one reached those successes and achievements. Of course, a case can be made for free will in the here and now. As individuals we each have the freedom to change some of what we do, think, and feel, but the river metaphor draws attention to the distant origins and the long-held traditions and patterns that have led to our current actions, thoughts, and feelings. For a person to give up being abusive, being a victim, being an alcoholic, or being a narcissist requires not only a shattering of well-established personal patterns but a break with antecedents. Change can thus be seen as an act of disloyalty—and, to the extent that we act as a piece of a collective entity, as an act of self-destruction as well. No wonder people resist and grieve change and may feel empty during the change process. A family systems theory with a long view of family systems would have to attend to family history and family archeology and would deal with processes for maintaining and transforming connections with the past.

Replenishment

To maintain continuity of flow, a river requires replenishment. Rivers lose substance to the earth through which they pass, to the air, and to those who draw water from it. The family that is a river also loses substance as it flows; family members move away, die, or are lost in other ways, and family energy and enthusiasm are dissipated. For the family to continue, new members must come into the flow, through birth, adoption, fosterage, marriage, or some other way, and energy, enthusiasm, time and other intrinsically necessary resources must be replenished. From this perspective replenishment is crucial to family existence, and family systems theories must address replenishment processes. They must include the assumption that replenishment is so important that it influences a great deal of what goes on in families. For example, the existence of an apparently pathological interaction pattern in a family or the way a family struggles with a dilemma may be influenced in important ways by issues of replenishment.

Thinking of families as needing replenishment makes it easy to think of families, like rivers, as confluences of material from many different sources. Each family is the confluence of other families and of various sources of energy and enthusiasm. Thus, even though we might think of a family as representing a unitary flow and directionality, it, like a river, also draws its substance—genes, traditions, social patterns, identity, work efforts, members, involvements—from many different sources. Understanding where and how a family draws its substance and becomes a confluence might be an appropriate task for a family systems theory attuned to the "riverness" of families.

In thinking of confluence in family life it is a simple next step to think that with rivers there is usually a joining with other waters—another river, a lake, an ocean. In the merging there is blending or even disappearance of identity. With a family, there is always a flow toward joining with other families, toward a blending that may make it difficult or impossible to recognize the original genetic material, identity, commitments, and so on that were the family's. So a family systems theory that is sensitive to the riverness of families might deal with how families blend and join with others.

The Paths of Rivers and Families

A river's course is in part a product of its previous action; it cuts its path, and that path constrains it. Similarly, a family exists within forms it creates for itself. Commitments to friendships, involvements in religious congregations, decisions about where to live, educational choices, and so on, lay out the streambed for the family as it operates now and constrain the family's future. Changing the families course requires members to engage in the challenging and painful task of giving up the easy route of flow in favor of a new one that may require enormous effort before it becomes as easy as the path being abandoned. Moreover, the riverbed in which the family travels now originated in part in actions, choices, and accidents generations back. Thus, change is not merely a break with one's own past but a break with actions by parents, grandparents, and more distant ancestors. A family systems theory that is attuned to the riverness of families would deal with these and other riverbed dynamics.

The Family Is a House

The Family as a House-like Structure

Thinking of a family as a house leads to a rich set of metaphoric implications. The house metaphor implies a stable structure that protects, keeps inhabitants warm in cold weather and perhaps cool in hot weather, and separates those on the inside from the outside. Like a house that can be either built on strong and firm foundations and assembled competently with sound materials, or built on weak or shifting foundations and assembled in a shoddy fashion with substandard materials, a family can be built well or poorly, given the abilities, motivations, resources, needs, actions, and interactions of family members. Like a house, a family can be understood to persist though individuals come and go. By highlighting the ways in which a family may be an entity that is stable, protecting, and potentially well built, the metaphor of the family as a house can lead to family therapy and family policy designed to maintain families as stable, persisting entities. By contrast, metaphors that emphasize the ambiguous and ephemeral nature of families might lead to family therapy and family policy with very different aims.

Location

All entities have a location. Houses are safe or not depending on where they are—on a geological fault, under a freeway, on an unstable mountainside, next to a river that might flood, in the shadow of a factory that emits toxic fumes. The safety of a house is also dependent on its neighbors and the others who pass through the neighborhood. Houses must be built or modified to fit their location; heavy insulation is required for extremes in weather, bars on the windows and heavy locks on the door are needed for areas with high crime rates, and so on. The house metaphor, by leading us to think about location, focuses our attention on the environment of the family as well as on the family. In doing so it leads us to concerns about how the family does or does not fit its location and what the costs of fitting or not fitting the location are.

Houses and Families as Places of Confinement

Families, like houses, can be places of confinement. In some countries house arrest occurs. Confinement during pregnancy means confinement to the house. Teenagers grounded by their parents are confined to home. Quarantine for contagious illness is typically a confinement at home. Some people who are ill or handicapped are confined to the house. Just as the house may be a place of safety, so too can it be a place of confinement. Similarly, the family may be either a place of safety or a place of confinement. People may feel jailed in their family, or they may feel that their freedom is restricted by family demands and standards. They may feel confined by the requirements of family life (e.g., to attend family events; to stick to family schedules; to care for ill, infirm, or younger family members). The confinement entailment of the family-as-house metaphor thus helps us to think about families in ways that the generic entity metaphor does not.

The confinement entailment also leads us to think that just as there are occasions for unlocking a house, there are also occasions when families become no longer confining (Friedman, 1989). One such occasion, according to Friedman (1989), is a rite of passage. As a family becomes involved in a rite of passage—a birth, a bar mitzvah, a wedding, a retirement, a major geographical move, a death—it is more open to change and more likely to change. What has been taken for granted is now open to examination. Confining relationships, rules, and patterns may be changing. A major change in a family entity opens the entity to other changes. It is a challenge to any family systems theory to deal with the processes of entity transformation. Conceivably, a house-based family systems theory could facilitate the analysis of transformation.

Choice of Entity Metaphors

The discussion of the family as a river provides new views on the metaphor of entity by emphasizing issues of entity that are not salient with a generic entity metaphor, issues having to do with the existence of the entity over time, with replenishment, and with the paths the entity travels. Similarly, the discussion of the family as a house provides new views on the metaphor of entity by leading to issues of protecting and enclosing; location and paying the costs of fitting or not fitting that location, and confinement. The metaphors of river and house are not the only interesting and useful entity metaphors that can be applied to the family. If one route to creative thinking about the metaphor of the family as an entity is to recognize all that the entity metaphor obscures, another route is to choose from among the variety of alternative entity metaphors. With different concepts of entity we have the power to acknowledge, perceive more clearly and fully, and think more creatively about the family as an entity.

SUMMARY

The metaphor of the family as an entity is perhaps the foundational metaphor in family systems theory and in cultural conceptions of families. This chapter has explored how the metaphor is a metaphor, what it implies, and what it obscures. Among the things obscured by the metaphor are individual responsibility, how much of what is real and perceptible in the family is due to the presence and action of individual family members, the extent to which each person in the family is considered by self and others to be part of another family, and the way family members and others may differ on who and what can be counted in the family. Also obscured by the metaphor are the extent to which some families are more family-like than others, the extent of competition and diversity among members, and the "ever-changingness" of each family entity.

Although the metaphor of the family as an entity should be used cautiously, because it may obscure what is important to apprehend, it also organizes and facilitates thinking about families. And it makes it possible to draw on other entity metaphors to expand thinking about family systems. The metaphor of the family as a river-like entity was developed in this chapter to draw attention to the enduring nature of the family (cf. Hoffman, 1990, p. 3), the relationship of the family to its members, the importance of replenishment of the family's membership, the flow of family life, and the ways families create the paths they follow. The metaphor of the family as a house-like entity was developed in this chapter to draw attention to the ways families, like houses, are built well or poorly and are or are not unchanging, to the fit of the family to its environmental location, to the ways families may confine their members, and to the importance of life cycle events in ending confinement of family members.

CHAPTER THREE

The Metaphor of System

ROOTS OF THE SYSTEM METAPHOR

This chapter examines the metaphors of "system" in family systems theory, exploring what the metaphors highlight and obscure. The word "system" is rooted in Latin and Greek words that mean "to place together," so a system can be thought of as an entity made out of other entities that are placed together. The system unites and organizes its separate entities into a whole. The unity of a system means that its separate parts can be interdependent. The organization of a system means that an observer can see order and pattern in it (Boulding, 1985, p. 9).

There is no single basic system in human experience that forms the foundation for the metaphoric application of the word "system." Nor does "systemness" seem to be as fundamental in human experience as "hard," "big," or "hot." There are, however, many uses of the word "system" in American English that together might form a metaphoric base for the application of this word to families. Among the systems that Americans speak of are the solar system, a transportation system, the digestive system, the nervous system, the circulatory system, the reproductive system, the body system, an irrigation system, a school system, the justice system, a sewage system, a water system, and a system of government.

As a metaphoric base, each of the referents of the concept of system is a whole with connected elements that can be said to operate in a predictable and recurrent pattern. These characteristics of the referent systems imply a family system theory that deals with the joining of individuals in predictable and recurrent interaction (cf.

Kantor & Lehr, 1975, pp. 9–12). Another characteristic of the referent systems is that each is often discussed as though it were a freestanding system not connected in any way to more or less parallel systems or to the larger systems in which it is embedded. Extending this characteristic to family systems implies that an analysis of family systems removes families from their connections to other families and to the larger systems in which they are embedded. Thus, systemic analysis often ignores contextual information that could be useful in understanding what is going on in families and that could also lead to questions about the central importance of family in a person's life (cf. Merkel & Searight, 1992).

Finally, with the probable exception of the solar system, all the aforementioned examples of referent systems can be said to accomplish goals that serve the needs of individuals or of the system and that maintain other systems to which they are connected. Thus, the metaphoric bases for thinking about families as systems lead to thinking about how families meet the needs of individuals and maintain other systems (economic, governmental, community, religious, occupational, educational, etc.) to which they are connected.

Meanings of the System Metaphor in Family Systems Theory

The system metaphor may be applied to families in two ways. Bateson, whose books *Mind and Nature* (1980) and *Steps to an Ecology of Mind* (1972) have been influential in stimulating family systems thought, directed attention to the larger system that connects all of nature. In that perspective, the focus is on a common system, a metapattern, that can be applied to families and to all of nature. It is that larger system, that broader metapattern, that makes families like other components of nature. In Bateson's thinking, the metapattern for families, as for other parts of nature, includes internal communication, transference from past relationships, and interactions with the environment that hinge on biology, for example, patterning in and across human families related to the need for food and sleep, to the processes of human reproduction, to physical growth, and to the death of human organisms. These patterns recur over time and yet are expressed in changing ways.

The second way the system metaphor may be applied to families focuses on the patterned interaction of family members with one another. These patterns are also, in the Bateson view, recurrent and yet ever changing, intimately tied to human biology and of a piece with other patterns of nature. In this metaphor the system is a whole in which interactions create something that is much more than the sum of the individuals in the system (Constantine, 1986, p. 54; Jackson, 1965a). This second metaphor has been employed in virtually all of the creative work of family systems theoreticians, work that involves labeling and describing internal family patterns and delineating interventions that might alter internal patterns that seem pathological or that family members might want to change. As the family theoreticians who imported systems thinking into the family field made clear (e.g., Constantine, 1986; Hill & Klein, 1973; Kantor & Lehr, 1975, chap. 2; Minuchin, 1974, chap. 1; Watzlawick, Beavin, & Jackson, 1967, chap. 1), with this second metaphor there is an attempt to be sensitive to context, both the family context of the individual and the larger social, institutional, and physical context of the individual, the family, and the family's presenting problem. Yet the focus remains on the family, which sometimes makes it difficult to perceive the context.

In this second view, a family system consists of a set of people and their relationships with one another. What distinguishes systems thinking from the view of families taken in individual psychology is the emphasis on interaction processes, on the dynamics among the people in the system (Jackson, 1965a; Watzlawick et al., 1967, chap. 1). Models that emphasize family interaction processes are sometimes labeled "structure and process models" to emphasize the notion that the structure of the system is not necessarily stable (cf. Buckley, 1967, p. 41). Of course, the processes that lead to change or stability are themselves subject to systemic analysis.

Focusing on the interaction of elements, rather than on the elements themselves, might be appropriate for any of the metaphoric roots of the concept of system. For example, one could think of the human digestive system or of the solar system in terms of the interaction of their elements, but one might also think simply in terms of the elements themselves. Thus, a hazard in thinking about systems is that one might come to think about the things of the system and not about their interaction. Perhaps it is true of any theoretical metaphor that there are multiple meanings, but a slide from thinking about interaction of system elements to merely thinking about the elements of the system is especially a hazard in thinking about family systems. To think about families as simply the individuals in them and to ignore their interactions is to retreat to an individual psychology, which misses all the sensitivity to family dynamics of family systems theory and misses all that is beyond the sum of the parts.

What the Metaphor of the Family System Obscures

When applied to families, the system metaphor may prevent people from perceiving and acknowledging randomness in relationships (cf. Handel, 1985). Humans are so good at seeing pattern that they impose pattern on events that are actually random (Bruner, Goodnow, & Austin, 1956); for example, we can perceive pattern in a list of random numbers. Since the perception of pattern when there is none is something everybody does, it seems easy enough for researchers, theoreticians, policymakers, clients, and family therapists to perceive pattern where there is none and to persuade others to perceive that pattern, thus missing the disorder and uniqueness of family events (cf. Gubrium, 1992, on the processes of imposing a therapeutic reality on client families). The misperception of pattern when there is none may have its uses, for example, getting a family therapist into a position to try something when trying almost anything may help to move a family stuck in difficulty. But there is also the possibility of mischief. For example, clients' random choices about where to sit in a therapy office may be taken erroneously as valid indicators of family patterning (Gubrium, 1992, pp. 55–60). Or random moodiness might be perceived as patterned, suggesting the need for a family system intervention; when the intervention seems ineffective, everyone may feel frustrated and discouraged. Moreover, focus on a misperceived pattern may draw attention from a genuine pattern that could more productively be the focus of attention.

The emphasis on pattern may also lead to a focus on whatever is patterned, even though what is patterned may be trivial in comparison to what is not patterned. For example, focusing on recurrence makes it less likely that researchers and clinicians will recognize the significance of such once-in-a-lifetime events as the first serious bereavement, the death of a pet, a miscarriage, the birth of a first grandchild, an angry threat, a sexual assault, a heart attack, a betrayal of trust, a moment of great spiritual intensity, or a near miss of what could have been a fatal accident.

Focusing on recurrence may also lead people to miss the special significance of relationship precedents. When people first do something that subsequently is patterned, there may be special awarenesses, bargains, understandings, misunderstandings, and anxieties. For example, in a relationship where physical violence has occurred, the first time a blow was struck in the relationship might have been an especially significant event. The first time a couple has sexual intercourse, the first time a specific family member is quite sick, the first time a gift is given in a relationship, or the first time a family member slams a door in an argument—all such events may be especially significant to the people involved and especially influential on the relationship dynamics that follow. Focusing on the pattern of these behaviors may miss very telling things about precedents. However, there are family systems theory analyses that do take precedents into account. In particular, Montgomery and Fewer (1988, pp. 134–138) pointed out that recurrence and pattern are always an expression of precedents. In fact, precedents may not simply be echoed by what comes after but may profoundly influence what comes after. For example, Montgomery and Fewer implied (1988, p. 135) that some precedents make systems relatively closed or relatively open and give a character to all other aspects of a family's system.

The family system metaphor can also lead to a failure to recognize the unique elements that happen in conjunction with what is patterned (cf. Handel, 1985). For example, family members may recurrently argue over expenditures. An emphasis on system will lead to an interest in understanding the recurrence of the arguments and the recurrence of money as a topic of argument. Perhaps focusing on arguments over money may be the most productive thing for a clinician or researcher to do in the situation, but it may be that extraordinarily important information will be missed. Imagine, for example, that in a couple's most recent argument over money, an issue never raised before comes up, say, whether a comfortable reading chair should be purchased. Perhaps this single event tells crucially important things about how a family member feels, for example, that she has no place that is hers or that her intellectual and emotional interest in reading is constantly discounted.

Focusing on patterned interaction may also obscure the importance of what does not occur and therefore has no pattern. For example, what might be most important to know, if it is true, is that people do not communicate with anyone in the family about much of their deepest and most important feelings and thoughts. Family therapists and researchers may have implicit templates for family patterns so that they can detect patterned absence, but the templates may be inadequate for detecting certain significant nonoccurrences— for example, of events that have received little or no attention in the family literature and of events that are common to humans but rare in the observer's culture.

As might be inferred from the discussion in Chapter 2 of the family as an entity, when the system metaphor is applied to families, it obscures the unboundedness of families. The members of the family supposedly united in a given system are each connected to other family systems in linkages that are chained beyond comprehension. Moreover, the system metaphor obscures the extent to which each individual in a family may be embedded in a set of systems that is different from that of every other family member. An adult woman in a family consisting of herself, her husband, and their child, for example, may be linked uniquely to families of her parents, her grandparents, her siblings, her siblings-in-law, her cousins, her closest friends, and her ex-spouse. And each individual in these families will be linked uniquely to still others. The typical characterization of family systems masks this chaining of relationships far beyond the limits of any group of people that can be classified as a family and ignores the unique locus of each individual in the chaining (cf. Erickson, 1988). The typical characterization of family systems also masks the fact that family systems exist not in isolation but in dialectical relation with subsystems, ecosystems, and other systems (Maddock, 1989).

Despite the notion of family systems as dynamic, the system metaphor obscures the fluidity of family composition (see Anderson & Goolishian, 1988). Who is in the family changes as a result of births, deaths, marriages, and divorces. It may also change as people become distant from other family members or resume relationships. Yes, the system is dynamic, but its constituents change so much that the notion of dynamism may not capture how much it is not even the same system from one time to another. And "in" and "out" may not be the way to think about family membership and linkage. What may be more appropriate is to think in terms of degree of "inness" and "outness," with the possibility of a continuum of "in" and "out" and many different continua of connection, so that one may be more "in" the family on some dimensions and less "in" on others.

Even in the recognition that families change there may still be a lack of awareness that there is a perceptual fluidity to what is going on in any given moment, a fluidity arising from the multiple ways in which the reality of the moment can be perceived and characterized. Yes, the system is dynamic, but perhaps what seem like dynamics arise in part from our limited capacity to know or make sense of what is going on at any given moment.

From another perspective the fluidity of family processes may be beyond our capacity to know. It may, for example, be appropriate to think about a rule-based recurrence of family interactions or a need-driven recurrence in family communication, but the rules and needs may change in dynamic processes that we have not come close to understanding. Moreover, each family interaction is a foundation for future family interactions. Rather than thinking about family patterns as renewed expressions of a basic template, it might be more appropriate to think of each interaction as based on all that came before and involving cumulative change processes and enough newness of content and context for there often to be new twists and turns to the system.

Using the systems metaphor makes it seem as though there is a real system—in the sense that as we write or talk about family systems we may lose the vague and hypothetical quality that is present when we are working carefully. The system metaphor may lead to a reification of family systems (Gubrium, 1992; Merkel & Searight, 1992). The phenomena of family interactions are not the same as the terms we use to characterize what is going on in the family (Montgomery & Fewer, 1988, p. 29). Accepting the metaphor as a reality obscures the ways in which systems are matters of inference and social construction (Gubrium, 1992). The family system that one observer sees may be very different from the system seen by another. And if the two observers interact, they may arrive at still other conceptions of the system, and these conceptions may change with further interaction and further contact with the family. Moreover, family members may not see the system observers see. They may see no system or may disagree among themselves about whether there is a system or what the system is.

The system metaphor obscures those crucial aspects of family life that are taken by theorists as individual dispositions rather than relational processes. Raush, Greif, and Nugent (1979), for example, pointed out how strange it is that theories of family communication systems should give so much attention to power and virtually none at all to love, affection, and other dimensions of affect. Power, according to these authors, can be taken as relational, whereas love and affection are apparently more likely to be constructed as individual emotional properties. Nevertheless, Raush, Greif, and Nugent made a case for the possibility that affective terms could be thought of as relational.

The family system metaphor may also obscure how much it privileges the clinician's or researcher's experience at the expense of the clients' or research subjects' experiences (cf. Erickson, 1988). I do not deny the validity and value of systems analyses generated by clinicians and researchers, but it may be worthwhile to consider the ways in which people are much more expert about their own lives than any outside observer could be. In fact, some of the standard clinical and research approaches to thinking about family systems may be based on an awareness of the limits of even the most sophisticated observer. Consider, for example, that family systems clinicians and researchers are not in a position to say who started a family pattern or how it developed. Consequently, to clinicians and researchers issues of cause and effect may seem generally useless to pursue. However, family members may have clear memories and great certainty as to how a pattern started, and for them the idea of theirs being a circular system may not make much sense. Of course, it is a mistake to compare a view of the ongoing operation of a system with a view of the origin of the system. Nonetheless, the system metaphor may deny the validity of the nonsystemic view of the historical origins of family patterns that is held by the members of a family. And the family members' views may be well grounded in experiences that are fully valid for them.

Finally, the family systems metaphor obscures the ways in which the characteristics of individuals—their biology, ways of understanding things, separate histories, and so on—are an important part of understanding what goes on in the family (Merkel & Searight, 1992; Searight & Merkel, 1991). By focusing so much on the family, we can miss much (Merkel & Searight, 1992)—for example, the needs of the individual, the capacity of the individual to change, the uniquely individual dispositions and history that a family member brings to the apparent family system, the possible uses of individually focused treatment, the biological limits and capacities an individual and the people around the individual must deal with. Focusing so much on the family also obscures how much the cultural context, including the American legal system, emphasizes individual responsibility, individual rights, and the welfare of the individual (Searight & Merkel, 1991).

THE METAPHORS OF SYSTEM CIRCULARITY AND LINKAGE

Perhaps qthe key idea in systems thinking is the metaphor of system linkage. It is the piece of the structure and process models of family systems theory most responsible for giving family therapy a power to transform family problems that individual therapy lacks. If the metaphor of system linkage is not understood, no other metaphoric element of the structure and process models of family systems is very interesting or useful.

In systems thought, system elements are linked so that each piece affects all others. With a system of elements A, B, and C, saying that A causes B to do something is inconsistent with what might be called a strong version of systems thinking. In the strong version if family member A seems to control family members B and C, the apparent control only comes because of systemic processes. The systemic processes might be that B and C choose to let it happen or that they communicate to A that they would prefer A to do what A does. Thus, one could as validly say that B and C make A do what A does as that A makes B and C do what they do. All family members are involved in the control aspects of the system, though that does not mean there is a simple and smooth coordination of action. Nonetheless, the causal linkages can be said to be circular, with no start and no end and with no possibility of concluding that things started with this person or that event. The system does not operate with a linear chain of cause and effect (Jackson, 1965a).

Family members and outside observers often "punctuate" (perceive boundaries, perceive causality, and divide up wholes) the circle of the system so as to talk about one element affecting the others (Watzlawick et al., 1967, pp. 54–59), but with an awareness of family system dynamics one can always trace the action of the "causal" element back to the action of the affected element and other elements. The circle can be artificially broken by an analysis involving punctuation, but, as the strong version of the theory characterizes reality, the system operates as a circle. That people punctuate their analysis of their own relationships and those of others says something about their causal thinking. It may also say something about power dynamics and the politics of responsibility and blame. The choice of punctuation is a choice about the ascription of power, responsibility, and blame. Once people have punctuated a system, their punctuation may have a profound effect on their perceptions and actions (Keeney, 1983, pp. 25–27).

Punctuation is itself a metaphor (Keeney, 1982). It highlights how people see family action and interaction as resulting from specific events and actions. It obscures how what is called punctuation may vary enormously in how definite, confident, or open to changing perceptions the punctuator is about a given punctuation. It obscures the family situations that people ordinarily do not punctuate and the situations in which punctuation only arises because a therapist or researcher seems to ask for it. In fact, to the best of my knowledge we lack a thorough exploration of the ways people in families think about families. We may find that many people are as reluctant as systems theorists to punctuate what goes on in their own or another family.

In what might be called the weak version of the idea of the family system as a circle, the possibility of mutual influence and issues of punctuation are granted, but the case is also made that some family members are more influential than others (Constantine, 1986, p. 84). The family members who have more influence may be in a stronger position to impact others and may have greater control of resources and more capacity to monitor what others do, to provide a variety of communications to others, and to modulate how they interact with others. But the weak version of the idea of the family system as a circle does not grant any family member control of the family and does not deny the place of any family member in the circle of influence.

Systems thinking goes against the phenomenal experience of lineal causality, so it is a difficult and not particularly believable kind of thing for many people; but that does not make a theory of systemic linkage any less valid or useful (see Dell, 1986). Jackson (1965a) pointed out that people often do not even have time-sequenced information (they only have information gathered at one point in time) when they infer a time sequence of cause and effect. He also pointed out how the belief in cause and effect in families ignores how psychological events seldom occur only once but recur and overlap one another. More generally, as Jackson developed the idea of the family system, the belief in cause and effect ignores how complex the antecedents for an event or behavioral pattern in a family might be, and it leads, in families and in therapy, to a blaming mentality. Thus, for both therapists and clients, a search for causes can lead to historical explorations that miss the dynamics of what has gone on and what is still going on.

Because systems thinking attributes so much of what goes on in families to family system dynamics, it makes the individual seem less clearly (than in popular individual psychology) to be an independent and relatively constant entity. In systems thinking, in contrast to popular individualistic thinking, a person is not a freestanding, constant entity but achieves her or his nature of the moment through interaction. In different relationships the individual is different and is defined by others—and defines himself or herself—differently. To know and understand oneself, one must be known and understood by others (Watzlawick et al., 1967, p. 36).

The Metaphor of a Circle

Graphic metaphors have been influential in systems thought. Visual imagery can be powerfully persuasive, and when the imagery is geometric, it can import powerful notions of symmetry and regularity. In Chapter 5 the graphic metaphors of the circumplex model will be discussed. What follows is a discussion of perhaps the key graphic metaphor in systems thought, the circle.

The metaphor of a circle is a metaphor of wholeness, continuity, perfection, and homogeneity. When applied to family system dynamics, the metaphor of the circle highlights mutual causal links and the impossibility of identifying final causes or knowing with certainty what causes what in a relationship with a substantial history. The metaphor of circularity challenges simplistic notions of responsibility and blame, making all in the system potentially responsible for the actions of each individual in the system. The metaphor alerts us to the possibility of any action or statement coming back to its source in some fashion.

The metaphor of a circle obscures how the apparent circular patterns are not a whole but are embedded in a vast sea of other relationships. The circle of experience and events is not closed, even if the circle of theoretical analysis is closed; that is, the patterns within the family may reflect processes extending far outside the family. The metaphor of circular linkage also obscures how challenging it is to decide what linkages exist among family members, to define what family members are doing. Family members may disagree among themselves about what is going on; and systems observers too may disagree about what is going on. One family member may seem to control another, but there may be many other ways of defining that interaction. The metaphor of circularity, implying continuity and homogeneity, also obscures, as does the systems metaphor, the variations in the apparent pattern. What A does in relationship to B may be different in crucial ways at different times.

The circularity metaphor obscures real differences among family members in strength, power, ability to control family resources like money, and status ascribed by the community (Imber-Black, 1986). By obscuring these differences the metaphor also obscures how the differences affect the interactions and experiences of family members. The concept of circularity may be taken to imply something like equal power to make things happen, equal control of the situation, and equal moral responsibility. But the part of the circle representing a large, combative husband/father is very different from the part representing a small and gentle wife/mother or a tiny three-year-old.

By highlighting wholeness the metaphor of the circle obscures what cannot be easily perceived when looking at the whole—individuality, subsystem quirks and details, and the influence on each person in the family system of events, individuals, and institutions outside of the family. In a sense, the metaphor of circular system linkage is inconsistent with and obscures the metaphor of the family as an entity. If the family is an entity, it functions as an entity. To look at elements of an entity, as one does when looking at circular causality and systemic linkage, is in some way to deny the entity. To move from talking about the family as a whole, its rules, its boundaries, its identity, is to change the metaphor without explicitly saying so.

The Metaphor of Linkage

In dictionary etymology, the root metaphor for linkage is the chain. However, the more appropriate metaphor for the linkage implied by family systems theory is mesh, a physical array in which each element is interconnected with many others. (The interconnections involve a variety of mechanisms discussed in later chapters, e.g., feedback and communication.) Combined with the metaphor of the circle, the implication of the metaphor of family system linkage is of an interlock that cannot easily be broken and of connections that are relatively homogeneous. The linkage in family systems theory represents all that might occur when people in a family have an impact on each other.

The metaphor of systemic linkage obscures the lack of connections among family members. This includes the ways members do not know what other members feel, think, or do because members are insulated from one another, secretive, uninterested, or unaware. The metaphor obscures their errors in communication and understanding (see Campbell, 1959b). Given that there are inevitable errors in communication among family members, what happens at any given step in system process is not neatly predictable from what went before. By implying relatively homogeneous internal family linkages, the linkage metaphor obscures how some links, both internal to the family and with the outside, may be far more significant than most internal family links. It also obscures what might be, from the perspective of ethics or effective therapeutic intervention or on some other grounds, best understood as linear and not as a matter of circular linkage. A commonly cited example of this sort involves the adult male family member who sexually abuses a young child. A circular construction of the abuse would obscure the ethical responsibility and physical dominance of the adult in the abuse situation.

THE METAPHOR OF SYSTEM GOALS

The metaphor of system goals expresses a sense of underlying direction and purpose to the family system. Satir (1972) defined the goals of a system as the reasons why the system exists (p. 113). For her the goals of family systems were "to grow new people and to further the growth of those already here" (p. 113). For Wertheim (1975) the key system goals were "autonomy, or an optimal balance of intra- and extra-systemic interpersonal control" and "competence, or an optimal balance of control in dealing with the relevant intra- and extra-systemic physical environment" (p. 288). Although one can conceive of system goals that family members can and do verbalize together, I believe that most of the writings on system goals assume that the therapist or other system observer/analyst is in a far better position than family members to know and articulate system goals. Thus, the goal metaphor obscures the role of the observer in defining the system. Even for a family in which all members articulate the same goal, it seems to be up to the system observer to decide whether that goal is truly a system goal. And the system observer may claim to detect many other goals that family members do not articulate in common. It is always the observer (Satir, 1972, p. 113) who decides what the system goal is.

When systems theorists or clinicians identify system goals, there may be a plausibility rooted in cultural obviousness to the goals they identify. Yet anything they name as a goal is a product of their subjectivity. However profound, however documented, however much that goal fits common sense in the writer's and reader's social class and culture, it is still a product of observer subjectivity. The goals are those defined by an outside observer, based on the observer's culture, experience, wisdom, and learning. But why privilege the observer more than the members of the family, or one observer more than another? What independent ground is there for deciding whether a system has a given goal? The goal of growth for members of the family sounds like a goal of middle-class, achievement-oriented Americans. The goal of survival is rarely used as an example in the literature, though that seemingly would be a goal of higher priority for a family living in a world of famine, warfare, or random violence. And why assume that systems have goals? Systems are not rational entities with purposes. How does a goal become established, embodied, and maintained in a system?

I may be helpful to examine family goals, regardless of who articulates them, as metaphors. The goal of individual growth in the family setting, emphasized by Satir, can be understood as a biological metaphor that highlights the ways in which people need not be static in the family setting and the possibility of family support for individual striving. The individual growth metaphor obscures how what is considered individual growth is not biological or natural but a product of contemporary middle-class values. The metaphor of individual growth as a family goal also obscures how the metaphor privileges an individualistic view of families at the expense of a view that subordinates the individual to the family or the community. There are many cultures— for example, the Hong Kong Chinese (Salaff, 1981, pp. 57, 225) or Eastern European Jews prior to World War II (Zborowski & Herzog, 1952, pp. 201–203)—in which striving for family or community good has been a goal of far more significance for most people than family support for individual growth. Furthermore, the metaphor of a family goal of individual growth supported by the family obscures the ways in which one family member's growth may be at the expense of the growth of other family members.

From another perspective family systems may be said to have many simultaneous, overlapping, and ever-changing goals, perhaps more goals and in more complexity than can be enumerated. The goals that must be met to keep people alive and healthy, reasonably connected to one another and to all the institutions of their society, and safe for people around them may be more than can be counted. Thus, the metaphor of family goals obscures the complexity and unknowability of what goes on in family systems. Statements like Satir's, that family systems have as their goal to grow new people and further the growth of those already present, may be usefully articulated in therapeutic work, but such goal statements obscure how families exist to meet individual physical and sexual needs, satisfy societal "shoulds," pay taxes, and meet thousands of other goals that are not necessarily family goals. The goal metaphor may thus obscure the complexity and impenetrability of what families are up to, the multiplicity of goal sources, and the complex processes that legislate among goals when they are in conflict. The metaphor of family goals also obscures the situations in which family goals are an impossibility because there is no way to legislate among conflicting individual goals in the family (Searight & Merkel, 1991). All this does not mean that a simple statement of goals is unhelpful to family members, to people who might try to help families, or to family theoreticians or researchers, but there is much that is obscured by the metaphor of family goals.

THE METAPHOR OF SYSTEM DYNAMICS

The word "dynamics" derives from Greek roots having to do with power and ability. In the physical sciences the concept of dynamics refers to the motion of bodies, the action of forces in producing changes in motion, or the interaction of forces or energies. More generally, in the English language, the concept of dynamics refers to action, as opposed to inaction.

Extended to families, the metaphor of dynamics in family systems theory commonly refers to family interaction, the interplay of influences in a family, and family change. Family dynamics are most commonly written about as internal family processes. A family system can be understood to begin with properties derived from the previous experiences, preferences, and expectations of the individuals who have come together to form the system (Minuchin, 1974, p. 27). The system then can be understood to develop as family members accommodate their pasts (if any), their preferences, and their expectations to one another, to each individual's development, and to myriad contextual forces. The dynamics of the system must also accommodate major changes in family context and membership. An important aspect of family dynamics is understood to be the members' accommodation to one another's differences (Satir, 1972, p. 123), an accommodation that is ongoing as these differences develop and are expressed. As Satir conceptualized family dynamics, it is crucial to the accommodation of family members that they find meanings together. The process of reaching shared meanings is complicated because family members may differ about what constitutes meaning and about how they find meaning and because these differences may change over time.

Hundreds of articles and essays in the family therapy literature elaborate the concept of system dynamics, providing insight into the dynamics of families dealing with an enormous variety of issues—for example, divorce, child asthma, unemployment, a family member's death, changing residence, a grown child leaving home, infertility, and family sexual abuse. Although the focus of a systems analysis may be on a specific family system, there is almost always a sense of the family's dynamic interaction with other systems, an interaction involving give and take, action and interaction, sources of information and assistance, barriers to dealing with problems, and processes that are capable of being recognized and comprehended.

The metaphor of system dynamics implies that the system researcher, theoretician, clinician, policymaker, or educator is an expert with considerable capacity to know what is going on. To know that there are dynamics and to identify them requires knowledge and acuity. The metaphor of system dynamics may, as a consequence, mask the ignorance and limitation of those who claim knowledge about a system's dynamics. What seem to be dynamics may be illusory. The illusions may have many sources. They may arise, for example, from shifts in the awareness and perspectives of the systems theoretician.

The systems theoretician may not be able to apprehend all that is going on at one time and so may believe that there is process in a family when there is merely a shift in his or her focus.

The system dynamics metaphor may also obscure a shift in theoretical stance from a circular model to a punctuated or linear model. Consider, for example, the dynamics of a hypothetical divorcing family in which one spouse leaves, a child then acts out, the parent who stays behind acts helpless to deal with the child, and the leaving spouse then returns to help the helpless spouse deal with the acting-out child. It is easy to tell the family's story in a way that makes it seem that there is a dynamic arising out of the act of leaving. But all of these pieces of the process may have been present for quite a long time. The divorcing stage may only make more obvious to an observer things that were present in the first minutes the couple met.

THE METAPHORS OF SUBSYSTEMS AND LARGER SYSTEMS

A family system may be thought of as including subsystems (Kantor & Lehr, 1975, chap. 3; Minuchin, 1974, chap. 3). Individual family members may be perceived as subsystems of the family. Family members may also be perceived as grouped in subsystems, for example, the marital subsystem, the parental subsystem, the generational subsystem, the gender subsystem, the mother–child subsystem, or a coalition of two or more family members who agree about something, act together, are treated similarly, or take the same side in opposition to another family member. The family, in turn, may be seen and may function as a subsystem of a larger system. Particularly in the therapy literature, the family may be seen as a subsystem of an extended family or of a larger system that includes the therapist or the therapy agency. In Minuchin's thinking, subsystems have functional significance (1974, p. 52). A subsystem works as a unit to carry out some function, for example, the parental subsystem works to nurture the children of the family.

Subsystem is a metaphor in that it draws on the roots and referents of the prefix "sub-." The root refers to something that is beneath, less than, imperfect, secondary, nearly, or subordinate with regard to something else. Thus, the "sub-" piece of the word "subsystem" calls attention to the superiority of the total system, which is above, more than, perfected, primary, complete or superordinate with regard to the subsystem. Similarly, the referents that come to mind when considering the prefix "sub-" include words that bring to mind things that are beneath, less than, etc.—like submarines, subcommittees, subcontractors, subcultures, subdivisions, or suburbs. The metaphoric usage of the prefix "sub-" obscures the ways in which what is called the subsystem may be dominant, more important, primary, or higher ranking than the family system as a whole. Thus, the metaphoric root "sub-" tends to close questions that should remain open, about which relations in a family are the most important, the most primary, and so on. It may be that family system subsystems are often the crucial relationships in a family system, with the entire family system being a tag, being dependent on subsystem processes to continue to exist as a system or being dominated by the subsystem.

From another perspective the prefix "sub-" obscures the fact that "sub-" is not an absolute term. Any given system is both a subsystem with regard to something higher in a systemic hierarchy and is an ecosystem with regard to something lower in a systemic hierarchy (Maddock, 1989). Thus, the unit called family can be thought of as a subsystem of an extended kinship, a community, and other ecosystems. Moreover, the units called family subsystems become systems when the family composition changes (e.g., the parental subsystem becomes the family system when the children are gone), and the units called family subsystems can serve as ecosystems for their own subgroups (e.g., all the children in a large family can be counted as a family subsystem, but this subsystem can serve as the ecosystem for sibling coalitions).

The metaphor of subsystems also obscures how the system analyst decides what the system is. The system analyst punctuates groups of people in order to decide what is a system and what is a subsystem. One could, for example, decide that a mother–child pair is the system and that the larger group of coresident people, including mother's adult partner and other children, is an ecosystem.

The metaphor of subsystem may also obscure the fluidity of connections in a family. The concept of subsystem may imply more reality, cohesion, and constancy for connections within the family than can be seen from moment to moment or day to day. Who is connected to whom may change rapidly and how any subgroup of people is connected may change often.

Family systems may be thought of as subsystems in an ecology of larger systems that either intersect the family or engulf it. There are systems of the culture, of the work world, of societal politics, of religion, of adolescent peer culture, the community, and so on. Some systems theorists have written about the family as not in systemic interaction with larger societal systems but as reactive to them (Minuchin, 1974, p. 50). However, one can think of all societal systems as reciprocally influencing one another.

The metaphor of larger system (or exosystem) highlights the ways in which the environment of a family may be understood to be systemic and in dynamic interaction with the family system. It thus highlights the possibility of systemic linkage and patterning of relationships between a family and the larger systems. However, the metaphor of a larger system may, like the metaphor of subsystem, obscure how it is the system analyst who decides how to punctuate social relationships in order to define systems and exosystems. In important ways the family may not be separable from perceived entities that are labeled as larger systems. For example, the dynamics of a family may be inseparable in crucial ways from the dynamics of the political and economic system. The metaphor of a larger system may also obscure how chaotic and unsystemic the surroundings of a family may be, with parts working at cross purposes to other parts or working with no purpose or with no shape, form, or pattern.

THE METAPHORS OF FAMILY SYSTEM INPUT AND OUTPUT

Drawing from control system theories, family systems theory metaphors include the concepts of input and output (e.g., Kantor & Lehr, 1975, p. 13). The input is seen as coming from outside the family, with the family operating as an input-processing system. The input can be anything entering the system, for example, information about the economy and about the safety of the neighborhood. The output is seen as anything returned by the family to the external environment, for example, working longer hours at a job, making more frugal purchases, or having an adult accompany a child to the bus stop.

The metaphor of family system input and output privileges the system analyst, who decides what things are input and output and characterizes them, ordinarily without taking into account the realities of the members of the family. The metaphors of system input and output thus seem to obscure the subjectivity of evaluating what can be called input and output and to imply that the system analyst has objective knowledge of what those things are. Further, the metaphor of family system input and output obscures the fluidity and subjectivity of what constitutes the system. As the metaphor is used, it seems to imply a constant system, yet some inputs might affect who is in the system and what the system is. The metaphor often seems to imply a system with definite membership and structure, yet, as has been indicated previously in this book, the idea of a family system with clearly defined membership and structure can be challenged. Thus, what appears to be system output might be a transformation, still within the system, of the input. For example, a system analyst who sees information that close friends need assistance as input and childcare assistance given to the friends as output might miss how the childcare and the child cared for are within the family system.

If we are loyal to systemic thinking, the distinction indicated by the metaphors of input and output will break down at least some of the time. The distinction makes little sense when both input and output can be seen as processes of a macrosystem. Moreover, the punctuation that separates input and output is open to question to the extent that input only has reality in terms of system output and output often is entangled in input. That is, many inputs are as much output as input, and many outputs are as much input as output. For example, that a family receives information—commonly considered an input— that it is in a dangerous environment might be a matter of family member perception and selective attention to news reports, and perception and selective attention can be considered outputs. Similarly, family members accompanying a child to the bus stop may be considered as much input (into family and community perception of danger) as output.

THE METAPHOR OF FAMILY TYPES

Some family systems theory writings focus on the analysis of one or more types of family systems. A family type is a category of family whose characteristics a family theoretician, researcher, or therapist considers significant, for example, the family in which one of the marriage partners is defined as far less competent than the other (Pittman & Flomenhaft, 1970) or the family in which someone has a psychosomatic illness (Wood et al., 1989). The metaphor of type highlights the similarity of problems and patterns in families that have a significant characteristic in common. It also highlights what seems, in clinical experience, research findings, or theory, to be a dominant pattern in certain families.

The metaphor of family types obscures the variability in pattern, dynamics, character, and origin of the families classified as a given type. For example, there may be many different patterns that could be labeled alcoholic, and families in which someone is labeled alcoholic may differ widely on many dimensions associated with alcohol use.

Paradoxically, the metaphor of family types obscures the typological complexities of families. Any family is simultaneously of many different types; it may be a family with an alcoholic, but it may also be a family with teenagers, a blue-collar family, an ethnic family, an urban family, a Jewish family, a family of readers, and so on.

The notion of types may seem objective, but it always seems to imply a value-based stance. The values are present metaphorically in the labels chosen for the types and in the clinical, theoretical, or empirical indications searched for and imputed to the types. With other metaphors, there might be very different understandings and implications. For example, one can speak of chaotic families, with the label *chaotic* implying lack of organization and a pathological and destructive pattern of nonsupport and unpredictability. One indicator of a chaotic pattern is that frequently everyone in the family speaks at once; too often it seems that there is no sequencing or turn taking in family conversation. That pattern may be experienced by people in one culture (including the culture of therapists or researchers who label the pattern as chaotic) as truly chaotic and disruptive, yet in another culture the pattern may be what most people grow up with and value. In this latter culture, people know how to listen and to communicate in that seemingly chaotic situation. Instead of the simultaneous communication being disruptive, it is experienced as a way for all to participate at once, to have a voice, to enthusiastically join in the family, with no one relegated to a subordinate position. Instead of each voice being drowned out by others, all voices contribute to meanings, and what is assimilated is the truth of multiple inputs and perspectives. Rather than chaos, the family pattern can be experienced as a polyphonic, beautifully patterned, yet fully improvisational chorus. Similarly, one may speak of an angry and conflictful type of family, implying a pattern that is best eliminated or escaped. In other cultural contexts, however, angry conflict may be associated with intense expressions of family love and support, with minimal threat of physical and emotional harm, and with a sense that angry conflict is proper in a healthy family.

THE ACHIEVEMENT OF FAMILY SYSTEMS THOUGHT

The family system metaphor has been central in the family field, providing conceptual challenges to the dominant individualistic thinking of what is sometimes called Euro-American culture. The family system metaphor enables researchers and policymakers to conceptualize family phenomena creatively, and gives educators provocative material to challenge student definitions of reality. Perhaps most importantly, the family system metaphor has been central to the invaluable innovations of family clinicians. It has enabled at least temporary or partial escape from the binds and limitations of clinical thought focused on the individual. It moves us from notions of individual responsibility and individual pathology to notions of family as context and family expression, from notions of individual agents who by themselves affect the course of something to notions of complex family interactions and of the limitations of cause-and-effect analysis. Systems thinking has been responsible for new and effective ways of dealing with family problems (and with individual or couple problems as well).

The discussion in this chapter of what the system metaphor highlights and obscures should not be taken as a denial of the fundamental value and importance of family systems thinking. I think family systems theory is an extremely important conceptual resource. I believe, however, that just as the language of individual psychology can lead to a pseudoreality in which relational processes such as leadership and dependency are misunderstood (from a systems perspective) as properties of individuals (Watzlawick et al., 1967, p. 27), so too can the language of systems lead to pseudorealities that miss what is important from nonsystemic perspectives and from alternative systemic perspectives.

CAN ANY METAPHOR BE A SYSTEMS METAPHOR?

Onceq one thinks in terms of systems, perhaps anything can be viewed as a system. Perhaps all entities can be seen as made up of parts in patterned interaction; and all systems have isomorphisms that can be dealt with in a common systems language. However, it seems to me that different kinds of systems (e.g., galaxies, economies, and single-celled organisms) are conceptualized with very different descriptive and theoretical languages. This diversity of systems languages means that there is a diversity of systems metaphors available for thinking creatively about any system. We can, for example, use the vocabulary, concepts, and methods of analysis of astronomy, economics, or biology to develop novel ways of thinking about family systems. There may be something to be gained from almost any system metaphor for family systems. Part of the excitement of systems thinking is that systems principles apply to such diverse phenomena while the languages for different kinds of systems are different enough to make creative metaphoric transfer an interesting possibility. When there seems to be a homology between one system and another that is used as a metaphoric description of it, there is a likelihood of insight into the general system characteristics of the first system (Bertalanffy, 1968, pp. 84–85). Because there is something telling in using the most implausible of family system metaphors, consider as an illustration the metaphor: the family is a rock.

The Family Is a Rock

Systems are organized; there is a pattern of information flow in them. By definition, one can identify in a system patterns of action and organized transactions occurring both internally and with the environment. Using a rock as an example, one can argue that there is a structural organization, a pattern of information flow, action, and organized internal transactions. This patterned interaction is carried out through the molecular and structural relationships within the rock. Rocks may seem amorphous, to have no structure at all, yet there may be very tight and regular internal relations, predictable on the basis of the physical principles of crystal structure, chemical bonds, and mechanical forces. For families, what seems amorphous and chaotic may also belie comparatively simple patternings, predictable on the basis of a few social principles.

Rocks, like other systems, are interacting parts of larger systems. A rock is a part of systems that involve gravity, chemical interactions, and mechanical forces. Families too live in a world where they are part of a larger system of something like gravity, a social inertia that draws families together and holds them in place. Families, like rocks, have "chemical" interactions with their environment in the sense that a family can be dissolved by caustic environments and can be caustic to other families. One can also say that families apply mechanical forces to other families and are affected by the forces other families apply.

A rock may seem solid and yet a rock, like an apparently solid family, may be destroyed or broken by the action of a great force, such as a blow from a much heavier rock or the crush of an avalanche. In the case of families, even seemingly stable and solid ones, the action of war, political terrorism, or a freak accident can destroy what once seemed solid. But even with destruction, what remains still has material solidity and a chance for continued existence.

There are even metaphors for family types when one thinks about rocks. For example, rocks may be solid or crumbly and so may be families. The solid family endures over long periods of time and weathers the bumps, bangs, and even crushing forces of the environment. The crumbly family seems friable even without external influences. It does not seem to hang together well, and once external pressures are applied, even rather mild ones, it falls to pieces. The pieces may remain in proximity and may well retain some sort of common identity, but the initial unity will is gone.

One example proves nothing, but there is a suggestion in the discussion of the systemic nature of rocks that the world is full of systems. Looking in even the most unlikely of places, one can find systems, and even the most unlikely of systems can metaphorically enrich our understanding of family systems. Finding systems in unlikely places is consistent with the work of general systems theorists (e.g., Bertalanffy, 1968), who have identified systems throughout the natural world. However, the analysis of rocks also suggests that the systems concept is like an enormous shroud that can be thrown over anything and seems to fit, while masking a great deal. A system theorist would take the homology of systems of various types as a basic conceptual achievement of systems theory and an argument that multilevel systems analysis, not metaphoric analysis, is the wisest and most productive approach to understanding systems. However, from the perspective of metaphoric analysis, the ability of the system metaphor to apply to unlikely things suggests that the world is filled with potentially useful sources of family metaphors. It also suggests that the capacity of the system concept to apply to so much may obscure important realities that are inconsistent with systems thought. We must be alert to the ways that rocks are useful or interesting for properties that seem nonsystemic (e.g., when they are missiles, paperweights, gems, symbols of solidity) and the important ways that families are unlike rocks or any other systems.

SUMMARY

This chapter has continued the analysis of the metaphors of family systems theory by exploring the metaphor of system and the major systemic metaphors—system circularity, system linkage, system goals, system dynamics, subsystem, larger system, system input, system output, and family types. The analysis has shown that these verbal expressions are metaphors, that they highlight certain things and obscure others. The highlighting these metaphors provide is crucial in making family systems theory useful and powerful. However, the analysis of what these metaphors obscure indicates that the standard metaphors of family systems theory have important limitations. There are important nonsystem views and important alternative ways of thinking about family systems that are loyal to systems thinking but different from the standard ways of talking about and conceptualizing family systems. One of the most obvious things that seems to be obscured by the various system metaphors is the extent to which systems analysis involves observer subjectivity (e.g., in punctuating social relationships in order to say what is and what is not a family system), a subjectivity that may overlook important aspects of the uniqueness of events and impose pattern where it might be more useful to keep track of ambiguity, uniqueness, and difference. The system metaphors may make it harder to detect the randomness of family events, the importance of precedents in families and of one-of-a-kind events, the ways in which the individual functions in isolation from the family, the unboundedness of families, the embeddedness of each family member in different families, and the variability and fluidity of families and of what goes on in them. Moreover, systemic metaphors obscure the situations in which it might be more useful or more ethical to see linear cause and effect instead of system circularity. The chapter concluded with a discussion of the ubiquity of systems and the possibility that the language and concepts used for analyzing any system other than a family can provide useful metaphors for thinking about family systems.

CHAPTER FOUR

Metaphors of
Family Boundaries

Consider the metaphor of family boundary and the closely related metaphors of family subsystem, family boundary permeability, family boundary ambiguity, and the metaphor of gender differences in boundaries. What do these metaphors highlight and obscure?

THE METAPHOR OF FAMILY BOUNDARY

The dictionary defines a boundary as "something that fixes a limit or extent." A boundary marks off one territory from another; it marks off difference. The word "boundary" has Latin roots referring to a field with limits. For English speakers, the referents for the metaphor of boundary include the boundaries of political entities like school districts, cities, states, and countries. In the United States, where ownership of real estate involves very precise measurement and records of property lines and where trespassing is a legal violation, the referents for the metaphor of boundaries suggest all that defines pieces of real estate. Also implied in the referents for the metaphor of boundaries are the rules for sports that separate what is good and proper because it is inside the boundaries from what is not good, is improper, or doesn't count because it is outside the boundaries (e.g., a tennis ball served out of bounds, a foul ball in baseball, a step over the line while in possession of a football or basketball, a volleyball hit out of bounds).

All boundaries are sociocultural constructions. The boundaries people think of as circumscribing families can be understood as metaphoric extensions of the concept of boundary as it is applied to political entities, real estate, and sports. For families, the things that establish and maintain boundaries may be said to be rules (Minuchin, 1974, p. 53), rules that say who can and should do what, where, how, and with whom. The rules for a family are generally unwritten and derive from the culture and the family's cumulative experience. A family's rules are constantly challenged and modified through interaction with the outside, through the members' interaction, and through attempts to adapt the rules to new contingencies. The Kantor and Lehr (1975) version of family systems theory characterizes the continuing family process involved in establishing and maintaining boundaries with the term "bounding" (pp. 68–70).

The metaphor of family boundaries has been central in family systems thinking because it has been helpful both in understanding specific families and in therapeutic intervention with families (Ryder & Bartle, 1991). The metaphor of boundaries is important in family systems theory partly because it is such a clear entailment of the metaphor of the family as an entity. In the ordinary categorical thinking of American culture and social science, an entity must have a boundary separating it from things that are not it. Thus, a newly married couple can be said to have strengthened the boundary around themselves by the act of marriage; as a legal unit they are separated off from others, and they can be seen as now separated from certain former contacts, activities, and relationships (Minuchin, 1974, p. 30). A case can also be made that similar boundary strengthening occurs for lesbian and gay couples; even if the boundaries are not legally sanctioned, they are sanctioned by the couple and the members of their community.

What the Boundary Metaphor Highlights

The metaphor of boundaries is useful in highlighting heterogeneities in the family world, both the ways the members of a family may be more connected with one another than with outsiders and the ways some family members are more connected with one another than with other family members. The boundary metaphor is used with the metaphors of family system and family subsystem to highlight, explain, and persuade that there truly are heterogeneities in the family world, that those within a boundary are in some sense connected more strongly or more comprehensively to each other than to others.

The boundary metaphor highlights the processes by which people organize and control those around them and are organized and controlled by them. In highlighting the processes of organization and control, the metaphor also highlights what is gained by organization and control, for example, limits on obligations, the ability to limit who knows what, and predictability in relationships.

The boundary metaphor is used to show how systems and subsystems must have some autonomy from other systems and subsystems in order to function properly (Minuchin, 1974, p. 54). For example, parents, as a family subsystem, must be at least somewhat free from interference from their children, their own parents, and their employers in order to function as parents.

The boundary metaphor highlights what bounds families. It directs us to the ways housing arrangements; legal definitions; customs in using last names; insurance rules; culturally defined obligations, loyalties, and affections; interaction patterns; sleeping arrangements; resource sharing; and much else bound some people into families. Even in families that are not currently sanctioned in law (e.g., gay and lesbian families), there is still much that bounds them—for example, housing arrangements, interaction patterns, sleeping arrangements, resource sharing, obligations, loyalties, and affections. Further, for gay and lesbian families, a shared orientation toward defending against the homophobia of the larger community also has the effect of bounding them.

The boundary metaphor highlights margins and edges. It leads us to pay attention to the people who are at the edge of the family, for example, the young adult offspring who is almost out of the family or the family member who is most peripheral in terms of interaction with other family members. The boundary metaphor also highlights the interactions at the edges of the family, such as the way the family interfaces with neighbors, governments, the schools, the medical system, and so on.

The boundary metaphor implies confinement. If we are bounded in our families there are also ways we are confined. Thus, the boundary metaphor alerts us to the ways in which people may feel trapped or be trapped in the family, how the trapping may work, and what might be lost in being trapped.

The boundary metaphor also highlights regulatory matters (discussed in Chapter 6) that have to do with boundaries. Boundaries are not merely barriers. They are matters for defense and enforcement, for dealing with intentional and unintentional violations of limits. In fact, one can expect boundary violations to be a normal part of relationship development (Ryder & Bartle, 1991); hence, part of relationship development is the establishment and enforcement of boundaries.

Obscuring That Family Boundaries Are Not Real

The boundary metaphor draws so strongly from sources that have a cultural reality (national borders, property lines that are a matter of surveying, the boundaries of a ball field, etc.) that using the boundary metaphor obscures that family boundaries are not real. As Minuchin (1974, p. 9) pointed out, the notion of family boundary is artificial. One indicator of the artificial nature of a family boundary is that the actual location of a family boundary is unclear. Is a family's boundary in the observer's thinking, in the minds of family members (their perceptions, judgments, identities, definitions of things), in their interactions with each other, in their environment, or in their interactions with the environment? What do we make of situations where family members have different perceptions of the family's boundaries or where various outside observers see a family's boundaries differently? What if family members differ in their thoughts and behaviors that are boundary setting?

A related ambiguity that may be masked if we think of family boundaries as real has to do with what could be called the ownership of the family's boundary. If boundaries exist only in interaction with people or social entities outside the boundaries, whose boundaries are they? If, for example, two adults work at keeping from outsiders knowledge of the physical abuse suffered by one of them at the hands of the other, is the boundary impermeability theirs? Or have outsiders partial or even full responsibility for creating that impermeability? One way to think about the metaphor of family boundary is that a family boundary, like a border between two countries, has two sides. Either side could make it difficult for anything or anyone to cross the boundary. Without clear evidence, it would be presumptuous to assume that because the border seems closed it is the fault of one country rather than the other or of both of them. It would be equally presumptuous to assume that if the border seems closed to traffic from one direction, it is closed to traffic in the other.

Once family boundaries are reified, it is easy to ignore or to fail to seek out information inconsistent with the boundary metaphor, for example, evidence that someone who seems to be in the family in some respects is not a member in many other respects. Recognizing that boundaries are sociocultural constructions frees observers of the system, as well as the players in it, to construct the family's boundaries in many different ways. It frees us to explore whether, for example, a unit we label a family should be the systemic unit of analysis, whether we should change the label or apply it to a different group of people, or whether a smaller or more inclusive unit that we do not call a family might be the most productive unit to analyze. Nor is the analysis necessarily a matter of either-or. A productive systems analysis may involve exploration and simultaneous imaging of several different conceptions of boundaries.

Obscuring the Ways the Family Is Not an Entity

The metaphor of boundaries, like the metaphor of the family as an entity and the metaphor of a family system, obscures how each member of a family may be a member of another family. From this perspective, claiming that there are external boundaries to a family leads us to miss the individually centered uniqueness of family systems. A married woman living with her husband and children may be bounded not only with them but with her sister and parents who live in different households. Her husband may be connected in a similar fashion to both his family of procreation and his family of origin. The couple's children, while in a different family of origin than either of their parents, may àlso be counted as members of the families of both of their parents, as grandchildren, nieces and nephews, and cousins. When the children grow up and enter or help create a new family, each will be in a different family. So every family member may be embedded in at least one other family that is different from every other family member.

The metaphor of family boundaries highlights the division between public and private and makes a family seem to be a relatively autonomous unit, but it obscures how thinking in this way supports an ideology of family self-sufficiency (Rapp, 1978) that promotes some political perspectives at the expense of others. By obscuring the ways the family is not autonomous, the metaphor of family boundaries makes it more difficult to see the ways the family is linked to the economy and to family-relevant public policies. It becomes more difficult to see how public values are imposed on the family's private realm, including both the values most people would endorse (such as proper care of children) and values they would not (such as the valuing of privacy for family matters even to the point of concealing physical abuse). Obscuring the ways the family is not autonomous also obscures the enormous social class differences in the capacity of families to sustain a separation of their public and private lives (Rapp, 1978). Families in poverty are, for example, more likely to have police and welfare authorities intrude upon their lives, are less likely to have good visual and auditory privacy, and are more likely to have children taken to foster care. Highlighting the division between public and private also seems to close off what is an open question about any particular family or family member—whether a split between public and private is actually experienced (Thorne, 1982).

Obscuring That Boundaries Are Fluid and Processual

Another way in which the boundary metaphor obscures stems from the fact that, in ordinary English, boundaries are generally static. The boundaries of a field, of a city, of a ballpark, of a house lot are generally unchanging. As a consequence, the boundary metaphor obscures a point that systems theorists often try to emphasize, namely, that family boundaries are processual rather than static. The external boundaries of families exist in their transactions with the external environment (Maddock, 1992b). To the extent that interaction process is always fluid and responsive to the variability of situations, family boundaries are never fixed. They are different from interaction to interaction and not perfectly predictable from previous transactions. Moreover, any family transition is potentially a time for boundary reorganization (Wood & Talmon, 1983).

Obscuring That Family Boundaries Are Multiplex

There have been ambiguities and confusions in the use of the boundary metaphor (Wood, 1985; Wood & Talmon, 1983), concerning, for example, the differences between interpersonal boundaries and generational boundaries and the diversity of expressions of family boundaries (what Wood and Talmon, 1983, have called "contact time, personal space, emotional space, information space, conversation space, and decision space"). Wood and Talmon have helped us see how the family boundary metaphor obscures the complexity of family boundaries. Even if boundaries for contact, personal space, emotional space, information, and so on, are at the same location, the boundaries may be quite different in permeability for the many possible things that might potentially cross the boundary. Even within a category like information or emotional intimacy, boundaries might be very different for different things within the category. For example, members of a family may be quite willing to tell stories about a family vacation but quite unwilling to tell anything about family finances. Or they may be quite willing to share their joys but very unwilling to share their sorrows.

Another way of looking at the multiplex nature of family boundaries is to identify situations in which a boundary that seems to accomplish one thing accomplishes quite another. Ryder and Bartle (1991) have discussed situations in which a boundary ostensibly understood or designed to do one thing did another, for example, when a barrier to a romantic relationship facilitated the development of a romantic relationship or when a barrier to leaving a relationship helped to create a disposition in someone to do just that. Hence, one thing that may be obscured by the boundary metaphor is how boundaries may encourage what they seem to be intended to prevent.

Obscuring That Boundaries Are Perspectival

Different people may experience and understand a given family boundary in very different ways. A therapist or researcher may appear to have some sort of objective standing in saying that a boundary is present, that it circumscribes a defined group of people, and that it has a specific degree of permeability, but there may be quite different and equally valid ways of assessing that boundary. It may be that what a therapist or researcher judges to be a clearly defined boundary is based on inadequate information about what goes on within and across that apparent boundary. Family members may see the family boundaries differently from the outside observer; moreover, family members may not even agree among themselves on what the boundaries are. I do not want to say that it is possible to arrive at a correct view of a family's boundaries, but it is certainly possible to detect differing views, many or all of which have some sort of validity.

Alternative Metaphors for Interfaces

Use of the boundary metaphor makes it harder to recognize the ways other metaphors for interfaces may be more useful. In speaking, for example, about the contact of a family with other social groups or with social institutions, it might be more productive and useful to use not a structural concept like boundary but an energy concept like synergy. ("My spouse and I find it easy and joyfully productive to work together because the excitement of each of us infects the other, but with a former colleague any attempt at working together was deadening.") Or it may be more useful to speak not of structures at the edge but of whole structures. For example, it might be better to focus not on the boundary between family A and family B but on the ways in which their structures, rules, and processes become more similar when they·come into contact. ("When we get together with the Jones family, we feel dragged toward the gender segregation and distancing of children that is characteristic of their family life, and they feel dragged toward the everybody-is-more-or-less-equal-and-in-contact approach that is true of our family life.")

The boundary metaphor characterizes links between people. When we look at family, family subsystem, or individual family member boundaries, we are looking at links. In fact, some of the early systems writers (e.g., Satir, 1972) wrote about links rather than boundaries. And the emphasis on communication in the literature from the Mental Research Institute (the source of much of the early writings by Satir, Jackson, Watzlawick, Bavelas, and others) is in part an emphasis on links rather than boundaries. In a sense, the boundary metaphor obscures the links—the connecting of individuals and of families, of subsystem and system, of system and ecosystem—and emphasizes the separations. Because it focuses our attention away from the qualities of communication, we become less sensitive to what goes on through the links.

THE METAPHOR OF SUBSYSTEM BOUNDARIES

The boundary metaphor is used not only to denote the separation of the family from entities outside the family but also to denote separations of subgroups within the family and the separation of the individual from others in the family. Although the metaphor of subsystem has been discussed extensively in the preceding chapter, it adds to the analysis of boundaries to discuss subsystem boundaries here as well. When the boundary concept is used to denote separations within the family, those separate divisions of the family are called subsystems. Subsystems may be seen to act independently of one another in some situations and to interact as though part of the same system in others (Watzlawick et al., 1967, p. 123).

The metaphor of a subsystem boundary highlights the heterogeneity and differentiation of connections in the family, the existence of family coalitions, the barriers between generations in the family, and the fact that each individual in the family has some kind of separation from other family members (and thus the limits of knowledge family members have of each other). The metaphor of subsystem boundary highlights the limited extent to which anyone can speak for a whole family and the ways that the form and strength of family connections may not be uniform throughout a family. The metaphor of subsystem boundary also highlights how identity, which can be taken as a marker of boundaries, can involve identification with a family subsystem (e.g., identity as a parent or identity as one of the more adventurous members of the family).

People who come to the boundary concept from a systems viewpoint may be drawing on the family boundary concept metaphorically when applying it to subsystems and individuals. The metaphoric use of the concept of boundary highlights similarities between boundaries of the individual family member or of a family subsystem on the one hand and the boundaries of the entire family on the other. To the extent that the metaphor of subsystem is rooted in the concept of system, the metaphor obscures how the nature of individual and subsystem boundaries and the maintenance of those boundaries may be different from the boundaries of an entire family system. For example, it may be a sense of self that is crucial in separating an individual from other family members, but there may be nothing quite like that to separate a family subsystem from the family or an entire family system from what is outside it. A family is separated from others outside of the family by legal rights and obligations, but there are far fewer legal rights and obligations that separate some kinds of family subsystems from the remainder of the family or that separate an individual from the family. A family subsystem may be less likely than a family system to be able to use family identity markers or separate residence to separate itself off from the family as a whole. It thus might be better to have different terms to describe the bounding of family systems, family subsystems, and individual family members. With different terms, our attention would be called to the importance of understanding the different motivations, processes, and dynamics involved when each of these entities establishes and maintains what could be called boundaries.

THE METAPHOR OF BOUNDARY PERMEABILITY

In family systems theory, boundaries are not defined as binary, that is, as either present or absent. Rather, they are understood as varying in permeability on a continuum from relatively open to relatively closed (Broderick & Smith, 1979; Constantine, 1986, p. 67; Satir, 1972, chap. 8; Watzlawick et al., 1967, pp. 123–129; Wertheim, 1973). Boundary permeability has to do with how much the family lets things in (people, information, energy, material, etc.) and how much it lets things out. The members of a relatively closed family may feel that they live in a dangerous world, or they may feel embarrassed or ashamed. They may want, for religious or other reasons, to keep external influences out. They may find input from the outside distracting, disruptive, offensive, confusing, or otherwise undesirable.

A family that is relatively closed to outside influences will also be relatively closed to manifestations of outside influences on the inside. In such a family, members must be cautious about what they say; they may have to act as though all have the same feelings, opinions, and desires (Satir, 1983, p. 237). Nonetheless, even the most closed of families is a somewhat open system—it must bring in some resources from the outside (information, nourishment, etc.)— and virtually all families engage in some sort of social contact with the outside. Even acts excluding others can involve some sort of interaction with them.

Family boundaries may be understood as interfaces between what they bound and what surrounds what they bound (Kantor & Lehr, 1975, chap. 3). Rather than being simply barriers, they are gates, sieves, and windows that open or close. They also are devices for engaging the boundaries of other individuals, family subsystems, and other social entities. The engagement with others will involve, among other things, rules about how to approach them and when and how to negotiate matters related to the crossing of boundaries.

Like the family's external boundaries, the family's internal boundaries can be understood as more or less permeable and as differing in permeability at different times. A subgroup of family members may, for example, want more privacy at times when they are highly stressed or when their interactions are embarrassing or require minimum distraction.

Whether a family system's boundaries are more or less permeable is said to be related systemically to much else. Satir (1972, chap. 8; 1983, chap. 15), for example, wrote about the association between family boundary permeability and individual self-esteem; family flexibility in dealing with emergent problems; the ways power and authority are exercised in the family; family openness to change; family communication that is indirect, unclear, unspecific, and incongruent; and family rules that are covert and inhumane.

The metaphor of boundary permeability draws on meanings of the term "permeable" that have to do with the degree to which a substance is open to things that might pass through it, with the passing through involving entry through such things as pores or interstices between cells. The metaphor of permeability also draws on a second meaning of permeability—the capacity to absorb a great deal of liquid material, to become saturated. With metaphoric application to the family of either meaning of permeability, the metaphor makes a family seem reactive on the basis of physical or biological principles rather than on the basis of conscious choice and social dynamics. Moreover, since a cell wall or a piece of fabric has a certain uniform permeability, the metaphor pushes us to think of the family system as uniform in permeability. The metaphor thus obscures how family members or family subsystems may differ in their openness. The metaphor, particularly to the extent that it draws on the second meaning of permeability, also implies a one-way passage of whatever crosses family boundaries. That is, even though the metaphoric application of the concept of permeability to families typically involves examples of the two-way passage of something across a boundary, the metaphor may lead us to think more about entry (e.g., of information) into the family rather than exit from the family.

A fact emphasized by Anna Hagemeister (personal communication, October 29, 1992) is that in the dynamics of membranes (a primary referent of the boundary permeability metaphor) materials flow across membranes from areas of higher concentration to areas of lower concentration. Extending that concept metaphorically to families, we might look for the flow of violence, energy, happiness, information, and anything else to be directional across the family boundary. The violent family, for example, might spill over its violence into social situations outside the family and experience the spillover of nonviolence into the family. By contrast, the nonviolent family in a violent environment might find violence moving across the family boundary into the family or might transfer some of its nonviolence into the environment.

The metaphoric extension of the concept of permeability to families was developed to highlight features of two types of disturbed families: (1) families that seem particularly closed to input from the outside and closed to giving information to therapists and other outsiders and (2) families that seem so unbounded that just about anything can go in or come out. Similarly, the extension of the boundary permeability metaphor to individuals was intended to highlight pathological extremes. As a result, the terms used to describe family and individual boundary permeability were initially (and often still are) terms that imply pathology, for example, rigid or blurred boundaries. The implication of pathology makes the metaphor of boundary permeability less useful than it might otherwise be (Wood & Talmon, 1983). For example, pathologizing the metaphor of permeability tends to discourage questions about the connection between certain forms and levels of boundary permeability and various aspects of the sociocultural environment. The permeability concept becomes a way of labeling pathology rather than a way of generating questions about what makes for more or less open pores or lattices. We may thus miss cultural understandings that make individuals and families in some cultures (e.g., the Balinese; see Wikan, 1990) relatively closed about giving off certain emotional expressions. For example, the north Balinese described by Wikan work at being very closed about individual and family grief in order to reduce vulnerability to culturally defined dangers to health and well being. Similarly, we may miss how a climate of racist hostility can make an individual or family oppressed by racism inclined to defend against the racism by closing boundaries to the outside (Pinderhughes, 1982); in this case the closed boundaries are a matter of protection, not family pathology.

THE METAPHOR OF
BOUNDARY AMBIGUITY

Boss (e.g., 1977, 1980) and colleagues (Boss & Greenberg, 1984) have written about an extension of the metaphor of family boundaries, namely, family boundary ambiguity. Their point is that when family boundaries are ambiguous because a family member is both in and not in the family (e.g., because of illness or prolonged absence), families may have problems. Although Boss (1992) does not see family boundaries as real and static, the boundary ambiguity metaphor plays off of the metaphoric implication that family boundaries are real and static, like boundaries of countries and pieces of real estate. The metaphor of boundary ambiguity highlights how individual family members may be confused about how to deal with certain family members, how treating a family member as "in" who is not really able to be can create trouble, how treating a family member as "out" who still is in some way in the family can create trouble, and how family members may disagree about who is in or out in ways that make trouble.

Although Boss (1992) is clear that boundaries are perceptual and subjective, the boundary ambiguity metaphor is applied often with an outsider's judgment that a certain boundary is ambiguous. It is the outsider who says that having a family member who is in prison, missing in action, kidnapped, or demented creates an ambiguous boundary. To the extent that it is outsider "objectivity" that defines what is an ambiguous boundary, the boundary ambiguity metaphor obscures what the boundary metaphor obscures, that family boundaries are abstractions, ever changing, only inferred, multiplex, perspectival, and always indefinite. The metaphor of boundary ambiguity may thus be said to obscure that all families have ambiguous boundaries. Granted there are social situations that may make it more likely that boundary ambiguity will exist for family members (e.g., when a family member is serving a long prison sentence), but there are uncertainties for all families in how to count deceased relatives, close relatives living elsewhere, coresident family members who are emotionally distant, pets, infants, family members who are even temporarily absent, visitors, and others. There may be societal or familial conventions about how to talk or even feel about the common ambiguities, but members of all families may struggle recurrently with questions of who is in and who is out and how to deal with those who are sort of in but also sort of out.

The boundary ambiguity metaphor, centered as it is on a specific family, also obscures how the ambiguity is a multidirectional problem. Not only is it true that there are ambiguities for a woman who must deal with such matters as whether to count as a family member her son who is away at college, her widowed mother who lives in a distant city, or her estranged and emotionally distant sister, but her son, mother, and sister also face the uncertainty of whether to count *her* in *their* families. The multidirectionality of the ambiguity may mean that people in these other families do things that draw the woman toward them and that may affect how she interacts with other people in her own household. Thus, the boundary ambiguity metaphor may mislead if in applying it we do not see that we must often look simultaneously at processes in more than one social grouping.

THE METAPHOR OF GENDER DIFFERENCES IN BOUNDARIES

Analyses of boundary permeability within lesbian relationships as compared to heterosexual relationships (Roth, 1989) and of permeability in mother–daughter relationships as compared to mother and son (Chodorow, 1978, chap. 6) suggest that the genders may differ in boundary permeability. Women, compared to men, are seen to be more willing to reveal their feelings, perceptions, understandings, and experiences (Cozby, 1973) and more open to outside information and influence. Chodorow (1978) sees the gender difference as arising from differences in attachment to mother during childhood and from existence in a society where many women will mother (pp. 169–170). To the extent that these gender differences in boundaries exist, they can account for tensions between women and men in a family about such things as the appropriate level of self-disclosure of feelings within the family or in relationships with outsiders. They can also account for differences in such phenomena as information sharing and emotional contact between family subsystems consisting exclusively of women and those consisting exclusively of men. And they can account for differences between women and men in the frequency and importance of their emotional sharing in friendships.

Comparisons of boundary permeability between women and men, to the extent that they focus us on gender and not on the context of gender, obscure the sociocultural, gender politics, which are central to understanding gender difference in the family (Weingarten, 1991). If we look at the boundaries and not the larger environment, the gender comparisons obscure the societal homophobia that pushes lesbian partners together (Meyer, 1988). They obscure how sexism in the family, community, and society may force women to have more permeable boundaries (Taffel & Masters, 1989), for example, by allowing them less privacy in the home so that they have no choice about boundary permeability or by more often causing them to feel intense sorrow, frustration, and anger, which must be processed in a friendship relationship. And they obscure how the context of sexism may unite women friends, sisters, or mothers and daughters because they share a common set of burdens.

Comparisons of boundaries for women and men, by implying some objective outside basis of comparison, obscure the ways in which what is experienced as a boundary may be experienced differently and have different meanings for the two genders. What constitutes a highly permeable boundary for a man may be rather impermeable by the standards of a woman. And yet the information that crosses the boundaries may be so often different for women and for men that it may make no sense to try to characterize gender boundaries comparatively. Even when the information crossing the boundary is the same, it may have such different meanings for women and for men that their reactions are not comparable.

THE FAMILY IS A CONTAINER

If we can think about the family as bounded, we can think about the family as a container. Lakoff and Johnson (1980, pp. 29–32) have suggested that the container is a primary metaphoric root in human thought. Exploring the container metaphor may help to reveal some of the ways the boundary metaphor organizes thinking about family systems and some of what it obscures.

Containers have physical walls that hold things in and keep things out. Container metaphors have in common an inside and an outside. If the family is a container, it contains the family members in an inner world, limited by the container and separated from the outside. The surrounding world, not contained, is limitless. With an inside and an outside there is the opportunity to define the inside in terms of its difference from the outside (Rosenblatt, 1964). In that sense, container metaphors always involve a duality, an "us versus them" or an inside versus an outside.

The Family Is an Aquarium

One kind of container that might be a useful metaphor for the family is an aquarium. Like an aquarium, the family contains its members and separates them from the outside. Like the walls of an aquarium, the safety and nurturance of the family boundaries are also limiting; the family's aquarium, like the fishes', is a small world. Like an aquarium, the family boundaries contain not only the creatures who belong in it but also the sustaining medium necessary for life. Thus, it would be potentially useful for family systems theory to deal not only with the family within the boundaries but with the qualities of the sustaining medium within those boundaries—nutrition, air quality, water quality, sanitation, appropriate temperatures, and so on. It is not stretching the aquarium metaphor too far to say that a family, like an aquarium, can lose the capacity to sustain its members. Perhaps, as with aquarium boundaries, family boundaries that are not sufficiently open to what must be brought in from the outside to sustain family members (food, oxygen, fresh water, etc. and their emotional and cognitive equivalents) are dangerous. Moreover, once a family, like an aquarium, becomes hazardous, members may be irreversibly damaged if they are not quickly removed. For example, alcohol addiction, incest, and physical violence may be permanently damaging to family members.

Anna Hagemeister (personal communication, October 29, 1992) has suggested that families, like aquariums, may have glass-walled boundaries; people can see in and out, but the boundaries still block most transactions. Perhaps the families of well-known politicians and entertainers have the glass-wall quality in that they have very little visual privacy but may still be closed to many kinds of transactions across the boundaries. Of course, the glass can distort vision or become smudged, but perhaps the radical change for a family with a glass boundary happens when the glass cracks or breaks. When the glass cracks, transactions may occur across the boundary that previously were blocked and whatever seemed to sustain the family behind the glass boundary may be lost.

If boundaries isolate a family in some ways from the outside, the boundaries may facilitate illogical deductions—for example, about the uniqueness of the family situation or the degree to which the family is the best place for each family member. Similarly, by highlighting those within the family, the boundary metaphor obscures how a researcher or clinician can come to erroneous conclusions. A family is not necessarily very helpful in understanding itself. Focusing on a family and attending to the family's boundaries as the family depicts and enacts them, a researcher or clinician may have no understanding of how the family is like or unlike families in general and no understanding of larger forces that are crucial in making things happen in the family.

SUMMARY

This chapter has extended the analysis of the metaphors of family systems theory to the metaphor of family boundary and to the closely related metaphors of family subsystem, family boundary permeability, family boundary ambiguity, and the metaphor of gender differences in boundaries. The chapter has shown how these are metaphors and has explored what each metaphor highlights and obscures. The boundary metaphor, which has been helpful in conceptualizing families and in intervention, highlights heterogeneities in the social world, patterns of connection, family barriers to all sorts of things that might go into the family or leave the family, ways of organizing and controlling interactions, limits on autonomy, bounding processes, what goes on at the margins and edges of families, the ways families are confining, and the regulation and enforcement of family barriers. The metaphor obscures the artificiality of the boundary concept and of any apparent boundary. It obscures the ambiguous location of family boundaries, the two-sidedness of any boundary, the perspectival nature of boundaries, the ways public versus private is a false dichotomy, the fluidity and the processual nature of boundaries, and the multidimensional nature of what might be called boundaries. The chapter has offered suggestions about alternative metaphors for the interface of families with other things. The chapter has also discussed what each of the metaphors related to boundaries highlights and obscures, and it concludes with a discussion of the metaphor of the family as a container. By developing a particular container metaphor, the family as an aquarium, the chapter has explored some of the implications of the notion of family boundaries, for example, the importance of the sustaining medium that contains the family, the possible lack of perspective for people confined within the family boundaries, and the potential for missing the larger context of a family, which is realized when there is an exclusive focus on the container and the contained.

CHAPTER FIVE

Metaphors of Family Structure

STRUCTURAL METAPHORS

The present chapter explores the metaphor of family structure and the closely related metaphors of family role structure, family differentiation and cohesion, generational structure, gender structure, and structure through coalitions. The chapter shows how each is a metaphor and explores what each metaphor highlights and obscures. In doing so, the chapter helps to show the possibility of alternative ways of thinking about family systems. Included in the discussion and in the effort to expand our ways of thinking about family systems is the exploration of an extended structural metaphor for the family, the family is a tapestry.

The word "structure" is rooted in a Latin word having to do with arranging and constructing. Perhaps the most common use of the word "structure" in everyday language is in reference to buildings, bridges, and dams, all of which are relatively intricate, functional, solid, engineered or carpentered, and enduring, with predictable attributes. The word "structure" is also commonly used to refer to other organized arrangements of interrelated parts—for example, the structure of society, an atom, government, a biological cell, a plant, a geological formation, a storm system, a molecule, a political party, and a university. The metaphor of family structure draws on these notions of structure. Without these metaphoric roots for the term "structure," the idea of a family structure would be meaningless.

Constantine (1986) has defined system structure as "the sum total of the interrelationships among elements of a system, including membership in the system and the boundary between the system and its environment" (p. 52). Thus, the metaphor of family structure is linked to the metaphor of family entitivity (entities have some sort of structure in order to be recognized as entities) and to the metaphor of family boundaries (boundaries delimit structures and substructures and contain family structures). The metaphor of family structure highlights the systematic arrangement of family members in terms of roles, interaction patterns, attachment relationships, and other perceptible, orderly, and at least somewhat enduring patterns. All structural metaphors for family systems highlight the ways family relationships remain at least somewhat stable over time and the similarity of those stabilities across families. The structure metaphors imply that some sort of construction has taken place and that the patterns and arrangements of the family have been constructed by the family members themselves, by other people, or by social institutions. The metaphors of family structure thus imply that families are somehow of a piece with buildings, atoms, governments, and so on, and that as a consequence the family, just like these other structures, can be known, researched, observed, diagrammed, analyzed, rebuilt, and strengthened.

All structural metaphors applied to the family obscure the insubstantial, ever-changing, situation-bound nature of what might be called family structure. All obscure the uniquely different ways in which what seem to be the same patterns are played out across apparently similar families. All structural metaphors applied to families obscure the extent to which the construction of the order and other aspects of family structure involves the imagination, subjectivity, selective perception, and inference of theorists, researchers, clinicians, and other observers (see Constantine, 1986, pp. 52–53). In obscuring those things, the metaphor of family structure also obscures how much we have every reason to expect different family members and different nonfamily members to see the structure of a family differently. Further, the metaphors of family structure obscure how, in contrast to buildings and many other structures, the structure of the family is never complete.

STRUCTURE THROUGH FAMILY ROLES

Family structures may be conceptualized in terms of family roles, using a metaphor drawn from the theater. The dramaturgical metaphor has been an influential one in the social sciences (Brown, 1977, pp.

153–160) as a result of the notions of roles, actors, acts, and role playing; Goffman's (1959) analysis of everyday life; and other developments of the idea that "all the world's a stage." The metaphor implies that all people play parts in interaction with others. The playing of parts may most often involve role behaviors that are sincerely intended, but it may also involve role behaviors that are deceitful and manipulative (cf. Manning, 1991).

Unlike theatrical roles that are written in advance of performance, family roles are developed and played out in interpersonal transactions. Family roles are contextual; they are situated in a here and now of who is present, surrounding events and recent interactions, and the physical setting and other specifics of the moment (Minuchin, 1974, p. 51). In systems theory analyses, the patterns that are labeled "family roles" involve recurrent patterns of action considered by a systems observer to be in role. However, the patterning may be more that of an abstract overlay than of the details of what is going on. For example, the systems observer typically does not pay attention so much to the minutiae of what somebody does as parent or child as to generic relationship patterns. This does not mean that the patterns considered to be in role are static; they may well have a quality of emerging rather than of being (cf. Minuchin, 1974, chap. 3). Despite the emerging quality, there still may be a predictability or constancy to family role enactments. For example, Kantor and Lehr (1975) indicated that a "four-player model" fits how families differentiate roles with regard to each other and to collective family interaction, the four roles being mover, opposer, follower, and bystander. They argued that every family member may at times play every role or a combination of roles. Although there may be preferences for certain roles, that family members can and will play various roles is one way families achieve flexibility in dealing with problems (Constantine, 1986, p. 124).

What the Role Metaphor Highlights: The Family as the Cast of a Television Comedy Series

The structural metaphor of family roles draws so much on the culture's standard theatrical metaphor that family systems writings about family roles typically do not develop family role concepts systematically but merely use aspects of the theatrical metaphor that are widely known in the culture. To explore the metaphor of family roles, it seems helpful to explore the root cultural metaphor. What follows is an analysis of one expression of the root metaphor, the interplay of roles of the cast of a television comedy series.

As an actor playing a part, one may typically have several layers of consciousness. One may be aware of what one is doing in the role, how well one is doing it, and how much the audience seems to think one is doing it properly. Even for such intensely focusing family experiences as going through a wedding ceremony, giving birth, or being with a loved one who is dying, the metaphor implies that there will be, at least some of the time, all these levels of consciousness plus the sense of playing a part. The characters may experience intense feelings and yet they are also outside of themselves, looking at their role enactment and evaluating how they are playing their parts.

Family roles are inherently social. They are not played in isolation but with regard to others who are also playing social roles (Turner, 1962). Thus, there is a systems nature to family roles. One cannot be a parent without someone in the offspring role. One cannot be a domestic partner without another person also playing a domestic partner role.

With television comedies there is for the actors a sense of playing to an audience, in some cases an audience whose reactions can be heard and seen but in all cases a viewing audience that cannot be heard or seen but whose reactions are important. With families too there are seen and unseen audiences whose existence may be crucial to role enactment. In fact, it is a continuing challenge to family therapists to determine whether what family members do and report is in some sense the playing out of roles tailored to the therapist as the audience or whether what the therapist sees and learns has trans-situational validity.

In playing to audiences, much that is taboo is hidden in both television family comedies and in the public functioning of ordinary families. Also, in television comedies and in the public presentation of ordinary families, there is often not even a hint of what the audience might consider out of character or discrediting to the parts being played.

People in television comedies are typically trapped in their roles. One person is a buffoon, another a cute child, another a competent woman who must deal with a buffoon husband. In families too people may be trapped in their roles, finding it difficult to leave a role, finding themselves pressed to return to a role whenever they are in the family context, and being defined by others as belonging in the familiar family role. For example, an adult returning to visit parents may slip or be pushed into old patterns of dependency or rebellion (Rosenblatt, Johnson, & Anderson, 1981).

In television comedies characters almost never question their parts. They do not speak up, on screen, for an altered characterization. On "The Cosby Show," for example, Cliff Huxtable never demanded of the other characters that he be allowed to give up being responsibly and playfully connected with them and become a character who speaks eloquently of his own spiritual needs. Similarly in families, people may rarely question aloud their roles or work toward negotiating role changes.

One can say that family life operates on the basis of love or commitment, but just as actors in television comedies play their parts because they are employed to do so, so too do family members play their family parts because those are the parts they have. Love, caring, loyalty, dependency, and much else may draw or hold family members together, but at another level members continue to interact because they have been interacting; they play their parts because those are their parts. They may play them even if they do not feel love, compassion, loyalty, or other connecting feelings. They may play them and may even feel connecting feelings, but they may also wonder (at a level perhaps never voiced) whether they have those feelings only because they are supposed to have them. They may be trapped, at least as much as an actor with a contract who wants to remain employed and employable.

Television series are trapped by their ecology (e.g., "All in the Family" in a working-class neighborhood). The ecology provides a set of problems, resources, a meaningful context for interaction, and shape to the characters. It is also eventually limiting, and it makes it hard in the long run to keep things interesting. Families too may be trapped by their ecology of community, jobs, dwelling, extended kin, culture, and so on.

In television comedies, gender is typically important. A gross and undocumented generalization about gender in sitcoms is that gender relations are considered a very important source of humor, perhaps because gender is a very important source of ambivalence, conflict, power battles, confusion, and fear in many families. Thus, it may be useful to take a closer look at gender as it is dealt with in television comedies. Typically, characters play relatively stereotypical gender roles or play off of the stereotypes. Not infrequently, there is a battle between the sexes, though the battle may be playful and may be only one of a number of relationship dimensions between the sexes in the show. In a television comedy the person in charge of casting and the writers cast the performers in gender roles and write the lines that deal with gender. In real life the casting of persons in gender roles and the lines dealing with gender are built into our sociocultural conceptions of gender and gender relations, which are embodied in virtually all social interactions. However, the sociocultural context is rarely depicted in any detail when gender and gender relationships are portrayed on television (cf. Livingstone, 1987, p. 253). Thus, if a woman in a television comedy is portrayed as relatively empathic or as deferring to her husband or as having problems with her husband because of her career, there is little discussion of how there is a larger societal context that could produce the story line, that could make all this seem plausible and interesting to an audience, or that could be associated with events like those in many families. Similarly, family members may have little sense of the sociocultural context that leads to the gender role interactions that go on within the family. For example, a wife's demands for a husband to be more actively involved in child care or the pressure exerted by a husband and a mother on a woman to become pregnant may be contended with as matters of personality and preference, not as matters of larger sociocultural forces. Matters as personal as gender identity and one's relationships with people of one's own and the "opposite" gender arise in a context that pushes women and men to differ and to relate in certain ways.

A big problem for a successful television series involving children is that in appearance and personality a child actor grows up. In some comedy series (perhaps reflecting the situation in some families) there are attempts to continue to write scripts for the actor as though he or she were still a child; the actor (or family member) who is age 27 continues to play the part of a 16-year-old. In other television program series (as perhaps in some families) new young children are brought in to allow the part of a younger child to continue to be played.

What the Role Metaphor Obscures

Brown (1977, p. 154) cited Edie (1967) on a number of ways in which the dramaturgical metaphor misses what goes on in everyday life. In drama there is an author; an authored work that exists, at least in the minds of the audience, as a complete, inevitable whole; and a defined script known to the actor, who performs as though living spontaneously. The script may be unknown to the audience, who may even feel that there is spontaneity in what they witness. By contrast, in life, to which we metaphorically apply the model of drama, there is unpredictability as events unfold, and the play is always unfinished. There is no script, no way of knowing how things will end, and no certainty to anticipated consequences of action. In drama, time is condensed; we may live through one or several lifetimes in an hour. This makes theatrical expressions of role much more significant and much less mundane. There is no possibility in the theater of representing in accurate dreariness the endless hours people put into such mundane routines as sleeping, watching television, and putting on clothes. Thus, the theatrical role metaphor obscures how much of life is ordinary and how little life has to do with the grand schemes implied by theatrical roles—or by the roles people may be assigned by a family systems therapist or researcher. Finally and obviously, in drama we never actually enter the world depicted, even if we are intensely gripped as audience members or even if we ourselves are playing the parts. Thus, the theatrical metaphor may obscure how much there are life-and-death consequences with no possibility of replay to what people do.

As was said earlier, the family role concept highlights how much roles are played in relationship to roles played by other people. However, the metaphor obscures the extent to which what may be played to is not another person's actual role performance but a player's view of the other's role performance. In other words, two family members playing opposite each other in complementary role relationships may be playing out very discrepant views of each other's role. A father may, for example, understand his daughter to be in a child role of sweet obedience without understanding that what the daughter thinks she is up to is cleverly self-indulgent, resistant, and disobedient.

The role metaphor also obscures the extent to which the metaphor makes no sense to some or all members of a family. Thus, the metaphor obscures both that it may be entirely an outsider's construction and that by applying the role metaphor we can actively suppress how the members of a family understand what is going on in ways that are at odds with the role metaphor.

STRUCTURE THROUGH DIFFERENTIATION AND COHESION

Differentiation and Cohesion as Metaphors

In family systems theories family structures are often conceptualized in terms of the pattern of internal family differentiation and cohesion (Olson, Sprenkle, & Russell, 1979). Although theorists do not necessarily agree with one another and are not necessarily self-consistent over time (or over the course of an article) in how they define differentiation and cohesion, there is a common core of thinking about the two concepts. It is possible to think of differentiation and cohesion as separate dimensions. Thus, family members can be said to be both differentiated from other family members and joined with them (Minuchin, 1974, pp. 47–48). Most often, however, it seems that differentiation and cohesion are conceptualized along a single continuum.

A family thought of as relatively differentiated might be described as having clear individual boundaries, family members who have a reasonable degree of individual autonomy, and a reasonable degree of physical and emotional family apartness or interpersonal distance. Extreme differentiation might be described as disengaged, unconnected, or emotionally divorced.

A family thought of as relatively cohesive might be characterized as having high levels of connectedness, physical togetherness, or emotional togetherness. The extreme of cohesiveness might be described as an undifferentiated family ego mass, as a family that is emotionally fused or enmeshed, or as a family that has diffuse or blurred individual boundaries with very little tolerance for family members' autonomy.

The extremes of cohesion and differentiation are seen as pathological (Minuchin, Montalvo, Guerney, Rosman, & Schumer, 1967, chap. 5; Olson et al., 1979). Extreme differentiation is thought to be a problem when it means, for example, that family members are not bound together enough to function as a family, that children are neglected, that family members do not feel cared about, or that family members lack the support that would come with even modest levels of family cohesion. Extreme cohesion is thought to be a problem when it means, for example, that one individual requires a certain relationship with another in order to have an identity, that people may be emotionally smothered, that disagreement or criticism can be taken by a family member as attack, that separation or even difference may be inhibited or not allowed, that family members too closely monitor one another, or that there is not enough flexibility for individual needs to be met.

Theoretical examples of cohesion (or what, at the extreme of cohesion, might be referred to as enmeshment or fusion) may deal with physical contact or frequency of communication, but they especially address the dimension of psychological unity. Highly cohesive families are said to have members who use each other as reference points, relying on cues from one another about what to do, believe, and feel. Highly differentiated or individuated families (see Anderson & Sabatelli, 1990, for an approach to differentiating the two terms) are said to have members who behave relatively independently of one another. Family members may be in less physical contact than in most other families and—more important in applying the concept of differentiation—are relatively free to agree or disagree, to be like or unlike one another, and to have different values, goals, interests, and so on. At the extreme of differentiation, family members may seem to be indifferent to one another.

The word "differentiation" stems from a Latin root meaning "to carry apart" or "to be different." The metaphor of family differentiation may rest in part on the developmental psychology concept of individual differentiation with increasing physical, social, and emotional maturity. The metaphor of differentiation has biological origins: Cells of a multicellular organism differentiate through development yet are functionally and structurally integrated. Thus, cellular differentiation is necessary for organismic function but does not lead to a separation of cells.

The metaphor of differentiation in families highlights the normality and developmental inevitability of separation and differences among family members. It highlights the reality of being in a family and yet in some ways separate from it. It also highlights how common it is in some cultures of the United States for a young person, with development, to move to greater physical and emotional distance from family members and often, in many senses, to move out of the family.

The word "cohesion" stems from a Latin root meaning "to stick together." The metaphor of family cohesion highlights the ways in which family members seem to stick together and the processes of family interactions that lead to and maintain this sticking together.

What the Metaphors Obscure

Family systems theory metaphors focus so much on the family that they obscure the impact of the larger society. It is a matter that is brought up in this book when discussing a number of family systems theory metaphors, but it is particularly pertinent when considering the metaphors of differentiation and cohesion.

In American society, in contrast to many other societies, individuality is more highly valued, and offspring are typically expected to leave home in their late teens or early twenties and to live independently of their family of origin. Feminist critics of American society point out that individual differentiation is more often highly valued by men in American culture than by women and that because of male power and privilege individual differentiation has been a relatively dominant societal value (see Hare-Mustin, 1987, and McGoldrick, Anderson, & Walsh, 1989, for a discussion of gender role concepts in family therapy theories). The valuing of individuality in social science theorizing is thus seen as an advocacy of values that are more male than female. Thus, therapy that attaches notions of pathology to the relatively undifferentiated family is aimed at making one cultural group's and one gender's values apply as general standards of family well-being.

The metaphor of cohesion/fusion/enmeshment, used as it is to define a pathology, may obscure how much cohesion, fusion, and enmeshment may be comfortable for the members of many families. A therapy literature that is based on clinical cases may give a skewed picture of cohesion, fusion, and enmeshment. There may be many nonclinical families with apparently high levels of cohesion, fusion, and enmeshment in which everyone is satisfied and functions well enough by personal standards, and perhaps even by the standards of many family therapists. Similarly, the metaphor of differentiation/individuation may obscure how much families that seem to be extremely differentiated may function in a way that is comfortable and satisfying by the standards of all family members, and even by the standards of many family therapists.

By highlighting differentiation/fusion or any other structural characteristic of a family, the importance of existential issues to the family may be obscured (Wright, 1985). Focusing on structure may obscure the "big questions" that the members of a family are struggling with and must deal with in order to get past their relationship difficulties (Wright, 1985). These questions may be about such existential issues as multigenerational accountability connected to existential guilt (Boszormenyi-Nagy & Spark, 1973), mortality, the meaning of life, the relationship of the family or of individuals in the family to God, or personal authenticity. As Wright (1985) has said, the struggle with the big questions may be observed through their impact on family structure. People may deal with their existential issues through a family pattern of differentiation or fusion. Thus, therapeutic focus on family differentiation or fusion without consideration of existential issues may be unhelpful. In fact, Wright suggested that "all persons or families in therapy should be guided into an intense confrontation with existential issues" (p. 42).

As with all other family systems metaphors, a problem with the structural metaphors of cohesion and differentiation is that they obscure the internal diversity of families. Characterizing families in terms of cohesion/enmeshment/fusion or differentiation/individuation obscures how much the members of a family may differ in the extent to which they are tied to or differentiated from the family. Even in a family dyad, there may be considerable asymmetry—one person may act, think, and feel much more enmeshed, the other much more individuated. Similarly, as with all family-focused metaphors, the metaphors of differentiation and cohesion obscure the differences among family members' individual perspectives as well as the differences between the family's and outsiders' views about how integrated or differentiated the family is. The metaphors also obscure how much a person's connectedness and separation from the family may vary from time to time.

With any metaphor, what is obscured may be at a different level of reality from what is in focus. Characterizing families as enmeshed or differentiated may require a focus on some levels—for example, behavior in the therapy office or self-report of feelings and actions during family conflict or in everyday family life—that obscures what goes on at other levels (e.g., the levels that bubble up in dreams or that appear when a family member dies). Thus, characterizing a family as differentiated or cohesive may oversimplify and may miss important contradictions. Families who appear to be at the extreme on differentiation or enmeshment may actually function well in part because of these contradictions.

Finally, by focusing on the family we lose track of how integration and differentiation are not solely in relationship to one specific group, the family. A given family system may appear to be enmeshed, but the individual players in that family may all be members of social groups that are important in their lives and that provide them with a reasonable amount of differentiation from family members and from others in the social groups. A given family system may appear to be fragmented and emotionally divorced, but the individual players in that family may be members of social groups that are important in their lives and that have a reasonable degree of cohesion. Despite variations in regard to any one group, most people may be part of primary groups that are not at the extreme of cohesion or differentiation.

The Circumplex Metaphor

A circumplex model for the family, a highly influential graphic metaphor of family structure, has been developed by Olson and colleagues (e.g., Olson et al., 1979; Olson, Russell, & Sprenkle, 1980; Sprenkle & Olson, 1978; Walsh & Olson, 1989). The model has continued to evolve since first being published. Recent versions have included the three dimensions of cohesion, adaptability, and communication (Olson & Lavee, 1989). There is also an alternative version, developed by Constantine (1986), that builds on the idea of family paradigms (Reiss, 1981) and emphasizes four fundamental family types and the processes of family change and stability within that typology. Figure 5.1 depicts one version of Olson's circumplex model.

The circumplex is a metaphoric representation. It incorporates the metaphor of cohesion versus differentiation already discussed in this chapter and the metaphor of open versus closed communication discussed in Chapter 7. Using the graphic presentation of concentric circles overlaid on two equally long lines bisecting each other at right angles, the circumplex draws on notions of balance and symmetry.

Balance and symmetry, metaphors that can be traced to geometry and aesthetics, are compelling in the sense that they are cultural values representing good form, neatness, completeness, and order. In visual materials, imbalance and asymmetry typically violate cultural standards of appearance. Moreover, balance is a metaphor drawn from basic kinesthetic experience. That is, we humans feel balance, know what it means to keep our balance, and know the unpleasantness of losing our balance (kinesthetic balance is an achievement in difficult situations—for example, while walking on a narrow beam or walking on ice). The graphic circumplex metaphor, drawing on cultural standards and physical experiences, thus provides a compelling endorsement of the view of families that is advocated theoretically by the circumplex model.

Drawing on these powerful metaphors, the circumplex highlights the potential clinical use of simple schemes for characterizing families. In doing so, it highlights the risks of unbalanced (extreme) family life and the benefits of balanced family life. Not only is unbalanced family life (the extremes of cohesion, of open and closed

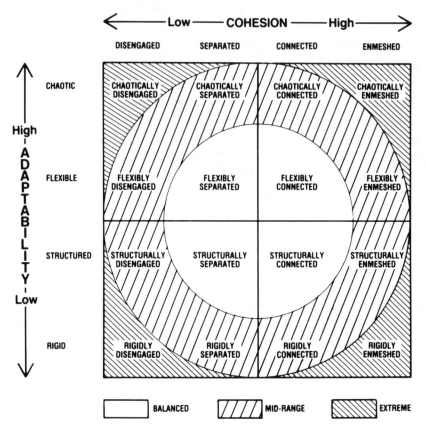

FIGURE 5.1. Circumplex model: Sixteen types of marital and family systems.

communication and of adaptability) aesthetically unpleasing, but it represents a kind of fall from balance. Not only is balanced family life aesthetically pleasing, but it represents an achievement in the face of the many potential unbalancing forces in family life.

The circumplex model also draws on the metaphor of being in the middle versus being on the periphery. The model provides a graphic sense of middle and periphery, drawing on metaphors of group membership (which stress the security of being in the middle of groups versus the insecurity of being deviant or at the edge of the group) and on metaphors of normality (those individuals who are considered statistically normal and functioning well are in the middle of the frequency distribution, not at the tails).

The graphic metaphor obscures the possibility that what is good for one family is bad for another. In different environments, in different cultural settings, or with different values, different ways of family functioning may be preferable. Olson has made clear how families move to extremes on the circumplex when stressed (Olson, in press), but in relying on the circumplex graphic we can still lose sight of how the stressed family that seems extreme compared to what it and other families are like when not stressed is not extreme compared to other stressed families.

The circumplex graphic also obscures the diversity of family member experiences; different family members may have very different experiences of the family and may provide very different descriptions of it. It obscures the ways in which asymmetry and imbalance on the dimensions represented in the model and with the metric used in the model for characterizing families might be sensible and functional. The extremes on any dimension might work best for some people, given their needs, preferences, histories and so on. In fact, the choice of dimensions and of terms for the endpoints and the middle of the model, though quite possibly appropriate for the language and culture of many Americans, still represents a language-bound and culture-bound view of what is important and what represents the optimum in family functioning. (See Olson, 1990, for his account of possible cultural and experiential origins of his approaches to thinking about intimate relationships.)

A paper-and-pencil measure called FACES (Family Adaptability and Cohesion Evaluation Scales) was developed along with the circumplex model. Currently in the process of moving to a fourth version, the third version (Olson, Portner, & Lavee, 1985) has been widely used in research and clinical work. FACES gives clinicians and researchers a ready means of assessing families and has the trustworthiness that comes from frequent usage in the family research and assessment community and from assurances of validity and reliability through conventional means of test construction and evaluation. It is perhaps also attractive to use because of what may be the typical complexity, subjectivity, and haphazardness of coming to an understanding of a family system (Gubrium, 1992). So much of what goes into an assessment of a family in a therapy office or in a research interview is mundane, casual, nuanced, fleeting, selective, and accidental (Gubrium, 1992). It is not surprising that many therapists and researchers are eager to use evaluation instruments that are supported by frequent use and published validation studies.

Like the dimensions it assesses and like the circumplex model, FACES is also a metaphor. As is discussed further in Chapter 8, paper-and-pencil measures are always metaphors. Their metaphoric roots include the labels used to characterize the measures, the concepts to which those labels are linked, and the meanings imparted to the criteria used to validate the paper-and-pencil measures. Thus, the metaphoric roots of FACES include the labels (cohesion, etc.), the theoretical texts, and the graphic (Figure 5.1) that accompanies FACES. The items of FACES are not themselves the concepts but are only metaphoric representations of the concepts. Nor are they the stuff that Minuchin, Jackson, Bowen, Satir, and other family systems theoreticians reported as their documentation for family assessments. Paper-and-pencil measures such as FACES are also metaphors in that they draw meaning from all other paper-and-pencil measures in common use, (e.g., intelligence tests and personality tests), that meaning being scientific precision and respectability.

Paper-and-pencil family assessment measures highlight the possibility that simple self report measures can be of great use clinically. They also stress the importance of the family characteristics they are designed to assess. However, each paper-and-pencil measure obscures the crucial importance of trying to understand any specific set of dimensions not assessed. Each obscures, in its printed neatness, how the process of test construction inevitably sifts out items that on face look like they should tap the dimensions being assessed. So paper-and-pencil measures obscure the fact that they are an unusual subset of all items that might tap the dimensions of interest. A measure like FACES, which was developed along with a graphic, also obscures how much it was designed to support the graphic, that is to create a pattern of scores that allows the theoretically specified phenomena to appear in terms of balance, orthogonality, and center versus periphery differences.

Paper-and-pencil family assessment measures obscure how much the items ask people to be aware of phenomena that the theories connected to the measures say people may be unaware of. That is, the items of a measure like FACES ask people to characterize their family life on dimensions that many clinicians believe quite a few family members would miss, deny, overlook, defend against, deceive themselves about, or not understand. Furthermore, items on paper-and-pencil family assessment measures typically ask respondents to assess actions, feelings, and perceptions of all members of the family. A family clinician would not assume that individual family members have such awareness and would not take an individual member's statements of what others do, feel, and perceive as truth. They might even take a person's readiness to make such statements as suggestive of family problems.

The content of the specific items of paper and pencil measures such as FACES are metaphoric in that they transfer their meaning metaphorically from the theories to which the measures are linked. Consider the following item from FACES III: "We like to do things with just our immediate family." Individual respondents are asked whether that applies to their family on a 5-point scale from "almost never" to "almost always." The item is metaphorically, not directly, connected to cohesion in family systems theory. It is a metaphor because meaning is imparted to a verbal expression made by an individual in the family. Response to the item is not a direct expression of the family pattern to which the theoretical concept of cohesion refers. The theoretical concept refers to family patterning, not pieces of information from individual family members.

The content of the specific items of paper-and-pencil measures such as FACES are also metaphoric in that they import meanings for family members. Take the hypothetical item "In our family we stick together." The language is metaphoric in importing the concept of "sticking together" from other places. It is also metaphoric in that it draws meanings from other applications of the concept of "sticking together" to social groups, as, for example, in the expressions "a couple who sticks together through adversity" or "United we stand, divided we fall." But perhaps the most important way family assessment items are metaphors is that they provide respondents with a chance to speak to the pain, concerns, and frustrations of their family life. Thus, the items enable respondents to communicate metaphorically whatever they are inclined to communicate about family experiences. A person who is feeling defensive about the family having serious conflicts may be influenced by his or her sense that "things are not as bad as they look" and may respond accordingly to the item "In our family we stick together." A person who wants to communicate how alienated or oppressed his family life seems might import the meanings of alienation and oppression into his response to the item, indicating how little people in the family stick together. Assessment items, partly because they are so general and decontextualized, are excellent media for the transfer of meanings from feelings, concerns, and frustrations.

Finally, paper-and-pencil family assessment measures obscure how much they are metaphors. They obscure how different they are from what the concepts they represent refer to. They obscure how different the processes leading to responses to the items are from the processes the items are supposed to tap (e.g., individual cognitive processes requiring memory, generalizing, and pattern matching versus family interaction dynamics). And they obscure how much it is the rhetoric of social science measurement that makes the measures seem relevant and useful.

GENERATIONAL STRUCTURE

One dictionary definition of "generation" is "a single stage in the succession of natural descent, hence, the people of the same genealogical rank or remove from an ancestor" (*Webster's*, 1956). By this definition, a person is inevitably in a different generation from that of her or his parents and children.

One of the ways the family systems literature makes use of the concept of generation is in addressing what is seen as inappropriately adult behavior by a child, coupled with inappropriately childlike behavior by the child's parents (e.g., Penn, 1983; van Heusden & van den Eerenbeemt, 1987, chap. 3). Theorists write, for example, about "parentification" of a child, a situation in which the child is asked to give too much care to the parent or to take on too many of the parent's responsibilities (possibly including care for other children in the family) while the parent gives too little to the "parentified" child (Minuchin et al., 1967, p. 11; van Heusden & van den Eerenbeemt, 1987, p. 48).

The use of the concept of generation in deciding what is generationally appropriate metaphorically extends the concept of genealogical status into matters of morality and pathology. The metaphoric extension of a descriptive term into such matters is a metaphoric leap that bears close examination. On what basis can it be decided that certain patterns are pathological or not moral? If one turns to the cross-cultural literature on the activities of children (e.g., Weisner & Gallimore, 1977), it is clear that young children in many societies are what Western therapists would consider parentified. Does that mean that families in these societies are pathological or that families from these societies who have moved to the United States are pathological? To define them as pathological seems ethnocentric and fails to appreciate the moral logic and the social and economic forces that underlie parentification.

It may be easier to appreciate how the concept of generation is used metaphorically in family systems theory writings if one thinks about generations of fruit flies or apple trees. When the term "generation" is applied to species that greatly differ from humans, there is no sense of a continuing intergenerational relationship or of norms of appropriate or inappropriate intergenerational behavior. It is only when there is concern about the appropriateness of generational patterns in human family systems that the descriptive term, genera-tion, is extended metaphorically into areas of morality and pathology.

A second metaphoric usage of the concept of generation in the family systems literature is to translate the concept of genealogical distance into a statement about a hierarchy of power that spans the generations (e.g., Goldner, 1985). Thinking of generations as ranked hierarchically makes it seem crucially important that parents have authority over minor children. A reversal of that pattern or a lack of parental authority is seen as inappropriate and perhaps pathological. The hierarchical rank means that a parent has the right and the duty to influence a child and that the child must respect the parent. At the level of moral authority and at the level of family and societal consensus about linear causality, the hierarchal concept of generation is easily understood and a matter of common sense. However, from a family systems theory perspective it is a superficial view of what goes on in families. In a family systems theory view, A may give B orders but whether B follows them is as much the doing of B as of A. In fact, B may do as many things to influence A as A does to influence B, though the form of influence may be different. In a systems view of hierarchy, the higher-ranking person may use more direct, overt, formal, and recognized forms of influence, for example, requesting, ordering, and instructing. The lower-ranking person may use more indirect, covert, informal, and unacknowledged forms of influence, for example, going through third parties who have more influence, appearing helpless, pleading, and crying.

The generational metaphor has also obscured gender dynamics in the family by creating the illusion that women and men in the family are more or less equal players (Goldner, 1988). The obscuring of the ways in which women are made sex objects, scapegoats, and unequal bearers of the work of the household and are subject to male threats and violence has made the generational metaphor in family systems theory a device for devaluing women.

Another way the family systems literature makes use of the concept of generation is in looking at the replication of family-of-origin patterns (e.g., Penn, 1983). In analysis of family of origin family systems, people bring patterns into their current family that were learned in their family of origin. For example, a parental pattern of nagging offspring, learned in the family of origin, may be reproduced in one's relationships with one's own offspring. The metaphor of genera-tion used in this way stresses the ways in which what is learned in the family of origin may influence or even dominate a certain domain of activity. It highlights the debts owed the family of origin that are paid through interaction with one's own offspring, and it also accents the family-of-origin embeddedness of a person's current behavior and the ways that a person is still participating in the family of origin even if appearing to be involved in a new family. The metaphor obscures the ways in which the family of origin may have had many different patterns to offer, so what is carried over may be a small, selected fragment of all that could have been carried over. The metaphor also obscures the ways in which the expression of carryover in patterns from the family of origin may be different in form, meaning, and context from what is taken as the family-of-origin pattern. Yes, one may nag one's child as one was nagged by one's parents, but the nagging may have a different tone, be set off by fewer things, and be different in effectiveness because of how it is contextualized. Thus, the metaphor of intergenerational transmission of patterns obscures how much may change from one generation to the next.

GENDER STRUCTURE

Gender structure is a metaphor. To claim that there is something like a gender structure is to import the concept of structure, with implications of stability, complexity, and so on, into discussions of gender. Looking for a single gender structure or reinforcing a single gender structure in a family would be slighting the diversity of families and of the individuals within families. Even expecting to find gender structures, no matter what their form, may be a step toward blocking families from dealing with gender-related matters flexibly and in a way that is fair to all family members.

Early (and even recent) writings about family systems theory were clear that gender is a major structural attribute of "the" family and were notoriously biased in the ways they treated gender (Meyer & Rosenblatt, 1987). These writings seemed to lock people into stereotypical roles and to reinforce arrangements, values, and perceptions that disadvantaged women. The early writings also were notorious in taking on gender matters at the family level, rather than exploring, explicating, and challenging the gender biases of the larger society.

Feminists who write about family systems have justly criticized many of the early and even recent theoretical writings about family systems for ignoring gender and the sociohistorical context that creates gender-based contradictions, power relationships, and hierarchy in family life (Avis, 1986; Goldner, 1985). The feminist critics have argued that the writings they criticize have trivialized gender and obscured the reality of women's oppression by focusing on gender roles and gender issues within the family (Avis, 1986). They point out the myriad ways in which male privilege is expressed in many families, for example, the extent to which men are able to get away with and make use of physical threats and violence against women, the ways in which women are overburdened (in comparison to men) with responsibilities for children and household work, the ways in which the societal bias to pay men wages higher than those of women for comparable work influences power in the family, and the extent to which women do not have as much control of family financial resources as do men. Feminists have criticized family systems theories that deal with gender (notably, Bateson, Jackson, Haley, & Weakland, 1956) in blaming mothers for the mental illness of their children (Spiegel, 1982) and in treating certain divisions of labor by gender (including mother/wife as primary nurturer of children and father/husband as the adult family member who works outside the home) as more desirable or more normal. They have also criticized family systems therapists for holding stereotypical male values and traits in higher regard than stereotypical female values and traits, for too often siding with male privilege in family battles, and for failing to recognize or to attempt to neutralize the societal forces that advantage men and disadvantage women (Hare-Mustin, 1978).

The patriarchy metaphor is often used by feminist critics of family systems writings to emphasize the significance of gender in families and the ways in which women are disadvantaged in families and in the larger society (Goldner, 1985). This metaphor was not used in any of the early canonical writings about family systems. Indeed, no metaphor dealing with gender was central in those writings. The patriarchy metaphor highlights what gender-neutral systems metaphors obscure (see, e.g., Goldner, Penn, Sheinberg, & Walker, 1990): It draws attention to the cultural and societal factors that permit, enable and promote male privilege in family life and stresses how much the dynamics of the family arise from cultural understandings of gender and from norms for female and male that shape the relationships of spouses and of parents with their children.

What the patriarchy metaphor highlights is very important, insightful, and useful. Nonetheless, like any other metaphor, the patriarchy metaphor also obscures. One approach to recognizing what it obscures is to look within feminism for other gender metaphors that highlight what the patriarchy metaphor obscures. Two such metaphors are the metaphor of the goddess and of sisterhood.

The goddess has powers that transcend those of mortals, powers to transform reality. Goddesses may come among mortals disguised as ordinary people, but their powers are still great. In families the goddess metaphor can underscore the ways in which women, even women who seem quite constrained by patriarchal forces, may transform their own situation, that of other family members, or of the whole family. The power to make things different may arise from a woman's capacity to feel love and other feelings, to know her feelings and experiences, or to relate to others. From this perspective one may say that the patriarchy metaphor, with its grounding in men's oppression of women, obscures the possibilities for women to overcome or transcend patriarchal oppression.

The sisterhood metaphor emphasizes how much women's relationships to other women are a source of strength, knowledge, support, healing, and groundedness. The metaphor highlights how much women's friendships may be the important element in society, arguably even more important than their family relationships (to the extent their friendships are with people outside of the family). In contrast to the patriarchy metaphor the sisterhood metaphor stresses how much families are linked to one another through the friendships of women; how crucially important same-sex relationships are in the lives of many women; and how women who are subordinated in the family may be sustained by their links outside the family.

THE METAPHOR OF TRIANGLES

Triangulation (Ackerman, 1984; Bowen, 1978; Friedman, 1989) is a metaphor that refers to a three-person relationship in which one person is adversely affected by the relationship of the other two. The term "triangulation" is perhaps most often used when somebody is caught in the competition or conflict of two other people. The person caught in competing pressures is presumably distressed and has little room to maneuver. In addition, catching somebody in a triangle tends to stabilize the relationship between the other two people. When, for example, a young woman who is marrying is caught in a triangle between her divorced parents who are in continuing conflict, their conflict and feelings of antipathy toward each other are expressed in their relationship with her, with each putting pressure on her in ways that make her relationship with the other parent more difficult. The triangulation of the daughter tends to sustain the conflict and hard feelings of the parents. One way for a person who is triangled to cope with the triangle is to duck out of the trap, for example, by changing his or her relationship with one of the other two people in the triangle or by becoming disengaged from the triangle and the relationship of the other two.

Triangles may be linked to and may sustain other triangles. For example, in the hypothetical example of the young woman with divorced parents, the mother may be triangled between the demands of a business and the demands of her current housemates. The young woman's father may be triangled between his mother and a second wife. In part because of the interlock of triangles, any triangle may be very resistant to change.

When applied to families, the metaphor of triangulation highlights how a given family member may be affected by the relationship of two others and how subsystems may interlock. But it obscures how any triangle is linked to a universe of individuals and social institutions. Beyond triangles, there are always other players. The young woman and each of her parents interact with many other people beyond any analysis of a specific triangle or of interlocked triangles. It may be a serious mistake to reduce what is going on in the lives of any of these people to the dynamics of a specific triangle.

The metaphor also obscures how much the triangled person is not a passive victim of another relationship but a player who also has a part in whatever happens in the relationship of the other two. Maddock (1992a), in discussing the possibilities when a therapist is triangled between perpetrator and victim, wrote about the potential of the triangle to lock perpetrator and victim in their roles or to make the therapist a victim. But he also wrote about the possibility of the therapist destabilizing the perpetrator/ victim dyad in ways that enable the two parties to begin to play different roles. The triangle metaphor also hides the fluidity of relationships. Even if the triangle is there at some moments, it may not be at others.

STRUCTURE THROUGH COALITION

The final major metaphor in the structural analysis of family systems is the family coalition. In the most common usage of the term "family coalition," two or more family members join together to achieve a goal or to oppose someone else in the family. The word "coalition" has a Latin root meaning "to grow together." Despite the Latin root implying that coalitions achieve some sort of fusion, coalitions in family systems theory writings are often described as temporary and shifting. For example, a mother and daughter may unite to persuade a husband/father to retire, or the parents may unite to persuade the daughter to end a love affair. Coalitions may also be described as long-standing (see Haley, 1967, on "perverse triangles"); for example, a mother and daughter may remain united on virtually all issues, jointly opposing the husband/father whenever his position is different from theirs and communicating more with each other than with him.

Coalitions are seen not only as structures perceived by therapists and theoreticians but also as structures perceived by family members. The husband/father in a family with a wife/mother and a daughter may often treat them as a unit; for example, he may express his anger at his wife by attacking the daughter (see, e.g., Minuchin, 1974, p. 51).

A long-standing comprehensive coalition may be seen as disadvantageous not only to the family members not in the coalition but to those in the coalition as well. It may be that no member of the coalition has the experience of personal efficacy in family conflict or of self-reliance in important areas of decision making. Being in a long-standing coalition may block some forms of intimacy or closeness with people not in the coalition. Moreover, to the extent that people in a coalition are in some sense equals, family members who are in other ways not equal (e.g., because they are of different generations) risk confusion over their relationship and may lose benefits that stem from the unequal relationship.

The metaphor of coalition highlights heterogeneity in family relations and the ways in which family members do not function as individuals in relation to one another. It stresses the alliances that arise in family conflict or that fuel family conflict, the affinities that underlie apparent individuality in families, and how at the same time there is conflict in a family there may also be cooperation.

The metaphor of coalition obscures the complexity of family relationships. Underlying an apparent coalition may be a great deal of opposition and nonconnection. Although a family coalition may highlight opposition or difference in the family, it may also obscure how much connection there is between the coalition and those not in the coalition. It may obscure how much the coalition exists only because of the attitudes, actions, acceptance, and even active encouragement of those not in the coalition. Furthermore, the coalition metaphor, by focusing on the union of those in the coalition and the schism between the coalition and those not in the coalition, obscures how much there is a broader dynamic in the family of which the coalition is a part. A coalition may be linked dynamically with other aspects of a family system. For example, coalitions exist when other family members want them to exist, when the family rules do not allow adequate respect for individual wishes and needs, or when the family operates democratically, meaning that one always needs the votes of others to make something happen. In such cases focusing on the coalition obscures the larger and possibly more significant dynamics.

THE FAMILY IS A TAPESTRY

> Tapestry: "A heavy, hand-woven, reversible textile, commonly figured and used as a wall hanging, carpet, or furniture covering; also, a machine-made imitation of it, of different weave and not reversible."
> —WEBSTER'S NEW COLLEGIATE DICTIONARY, 1956

The metaphors of structure discussed so far in this chapter all obscure the fact that there are many potentially valuable sources of structural metaphors outside of the family systems literature. Models for structural metaphors abound in the culture. In this section of the chapter, I want to show that structural metaphors from outside of the social sciences can highlight aspects of family systems that are not highlighted by the standard systems theory structural metaphors. To illustrate how systems thinking can be facilitated with structural metaphors distant from family systems writing, consider the metaphor of "the family is a tapestry."

The Nature of Tapestries and Families

Belenky (1986) and her colleagues developed a tapestry metaphor for family connectedness, a metaphor of webs and nets:

> Webs and nets imply opposing capacities for snaring or entrapment and for rescuing or safety. They also suggest a complexity of relation-ships and the delicate interrelatedness of all so that the tension and movement in one part of the system will grow to be felt in all parts of the whole. In the complexity of a web, no one position dominates over the rest. Each person—no matter how small—has the potential for power; each is always subject to the actions of others. It is hard to imagine other ways of visioning the world that offer as much potential for protection to the immature and the infirm. (p. 178)

Once we think of a tapestry as a web or net of linkages, it is easy to think of family ties, the links among family members. Any one person in the family is like a part of a tapestry and is linked to others in the family, who in turn are linked to still others. From this perspective, it is a simple next step to think of families as the weaving of the webs of different families (Trinh, 1989, p. 55). A marriage or other connection between what were once separate families links them together. And typically it is not simply the connection of a person in one family with a person in the other. For example, when a couple marries there is often a buildup of multiple linkages between their families of origin as people from the separate families participate together in family rituals, develop friendships, and share in kinship links with the children and eventually the grandchildren of the married couple. In that sense, a family is not a tapestry made whole but a uniting and perhaps even blending of separate tapestries. To the extent that most families are linked in some way to more than one other family, one can conceive of a single enormous tapestry that spreads across much of society and even the human species. This is a very different picture of the structure of family systems from what is commonly found in the family systems literature.

Centers and Edges

In thinking about specific families as tapestries, it may be helpful to remember that tapestries have centers and edges. Are some family members in the center and others at the edge? Perhaps almost everyone sees himself or herself at the center. Or perhaps the center includes all of one's immediate family, with those kin at the edge who are defined as distant by oneself or by one's immediate family. Seeing oneself and being seen by others at the center may have important implications for identity, responsibility, and frequency of communication with other family members and influence over them. Perhaps someone in this position has a clear identity linked to the family, important responsibilities (including the obligation to communicate frequently), and is in an influential position in the family.

Difference

Thinking of the family as a tapestry emphasizes how differences are necessary for the whole. Tapestries are usually figured; there is some kind of pattern made out of differences in color and perhaps texture. With families there are differences in gender, age, health, energy, and much else. The differences among family members may be taken for granted, but in the American image of family those differences are necessary for what is a common stereotypical view of the family. A group of people of the same age and gender and of virtually identical physical and psychological attributes might make for an interesting-looking dance line or athletic team, but they would not resemble what quite a few people think of when they think of a family. The family is built on differences. The dynamics of the family are in part responsible for the differences, and the differences are responsible in part for the dynamics of the family. From the differences in the family come division of labor, differential inputs into decisions, interesting conversation, sexual dynamics, and much more. (And from division of labor, etc., come the differences.)

Warp and Woof

A tapestry has a warp and a woof at right angles to each other. This structuring of pattern and elements is necessary for the whole. With families too one can identify a warp and woof. The interactions of family members involve reciprocal relationships among various elements of family life that can be understood as warp and woof, with one element providing a foundation structure on which the other plays back and forth in constructing the whole. It might be useful to think of the warp, which provides the foundational structure, as properties of individual family members, that is, individual development, genetics, or individual personality. Or it might be useful to think of the warp as properties of the family, for example, more or less constant family rules, beliefs, and attitudes. Similarly, it might be useful to think of the woof, which plays back and forth across the warp to create the tapestry, as something like individual experiences. Or it might be useful to think about the warp as something shared among family members, for example, family interactions or shared activities.

From a distance the structure of warp and woof in a tapestry may not be seen. Even close up, with a cleverly woven tapestry, it may be difficult to see the structure. So too with families. One may miss the underlying pattern and interlacing of individual characteristics, family rules, family interactions, and so on, that keep things together and produce what is seen. Underlying even apparently chaotic families there is structure. An individual in the family would not have as much meaning and character and his or her personality would not make as much sense if he or she were abstracted from the underlying pattern and from the whole.

The Underside

As with the underside of tapestries, the underside of family life may be very different from the display side (Rosenblatt & Wright, 1984). It may be in some sense a mirror image of what is displayed: For example, sweet relations in public may belie nasty ones in private; high energy in public may mask the low energy of private relationships. Or the underside may not be nearly as smooth, free of knots, and gracefully formed as the display side.

The Aesthetic

In families, as in tapestries, there is an aesthetic unity to the whole. The aesthetics may be appreciated by some or all of the family members and those who know them. There may be a sense of aesthetic form in how people entertain, vacation, coordinate their morning routines, eat dinner together, argue, deal with shared anxieties, make love, celebrate specific holidays, and so on. The aesthetic may be recognized in the similarity of family patterns across situations, and its absence may be inferred from the confusion and conflict that arise when new social relationships or a new context must be faced.

In families and with tapestries any one element of the whole contributes but is not necessarily crucial to the aesthetic whole. However, the strands that were laid down in the beginning tend to constrain the color and texture of later ones. There is a kind of heredity of aesthetics such that in tapestries we do not usually move abruptly from one motif or texture to another. Similarly with families, what has gone before may constrain what can occur now.

The Making of a Tapestry and a Family

A tapestry is a manufactured product. Similarly, one can think of relationships that endure as manufactured (Quinn, 1981, 1987). People engage in activities to make family relationships strong and durable. They may speak of it as being a lot of work to make a good family life. With tapestries, the manufacturing processes that make for longevity include artful weaving and the choice of strong materials. With relationships, the manufacturing processes that make for longevity may be in the choice of partner and in-laws and in the artful weaving of commitment, communication, caring, love, attention, decision making, compromise, and goal setting.

With a weaving metaphor comes a sense of a weaver. Who weaves families? One can think of a family as its own creation. Children are pushed in directions parents want them to go, and children are also very much their own agents. Adults work out the way they want to live, given their resources, values, environment, and abilities. But always what is taken to be the family is a product of shared processes—shared choices, family communication, shared family experiences. The great medieval tapestries were made by groups of artisans, each with specific skills and specific assignments. Perhaps families are similar in that a family, over all the years of its existence, is made by many people, each with unique skills and abilities, each making specific contributions to the whole. Even an infant contributes, for example, by being there to teach people to love, to nurture, to be playful, and to be unreservedly delighted.

Tapestries may more often be thought of as made by women, created by the touch of women. What is there in the touch of women that creates families? Babies come from women, and in the contemporary United States women more than men are involved in the day-to-day activities of rearing children. Also, in most households in the United States where there are adult women and adult men, women have more responsibility for most domestic work. In those senses, the family tapestries are creations of women.

The Family Is a Tapestry in Process

Think of families as still being made, still emerging in pattern and texture, still capable of surprising changes (though with limits on transformations dictated by what has already been laid down). The metaphor of the family as a tapestry in process gives us a sense of recurrent shuttling as a family unfolds. The same things happen again and again—laundering, grocery shopping, preparing meals, making and receiving phone calls, opening the mail, paying bills, saying hello and good-bye, laughter, anger. Yet out of that recurrence comes the weaving of additional family material.

SUMMARY

This chapter has explored the metaphor of family structure and the closely related metaphors of family role structure, family differentiation and cohesion, generational structure, gender structure, and structure through coalitions and has explored what each metaphor highlights and obscures. All structural metaphors for family systems highlight the systematic arrangements that exist in the family, the stability of families, and their knowability. All obscure the tenuous, ever-changing, situation-bound nature of family relationships, the impossibility of observing a great deal of what is called family structure, the subjective/perspectival nature of assertions about family structure, and the ways in which family structures are never complete.

The role metaphor in family systems theory highlights the inherently interactional nature of family roles, how family members play to audiences, how things that are out of role are hidden or suppressed, how family members are trapped in roles and role situations, how people may unquestioningly play their parts, and how family member feelings, commitments, and actions may be epiphenomenal to the parts they play. The family role metaphor obscures how what family members do, think, and feel may be unpredictable, how family roles are in process, the consequences of playing roles where time is never condensed, how family members play their parts to their perceptions of the roles of other family members, and how role analyses are outsider perceptions that make it more difficult to know or to value how family members understand what is going on in their family.

The metaphors of family differentiation and cohesion highlight the ways that separation and distance are normal and inevitable in family relations and important in enabling family members to stay together. The metaphors obscure how the larger society influences what is seen as family differentiation and cohesion, the implicit valuing in systems theories of differentiation, the possible family member preferences for what might be classed in systems theories as the pathological extremes of differentiation and cohesion, how families can function well while seemingly at pathological extremes of differentiation or cohesion, the internal diversity of a family in terms of differentiation and cohesion, how a family may be simultaneously differentiated in some regards and cohesive in others, and the importance of looking at membership in many groups besides the family in order to understand the place of differentiation and cohesion in an individual's life.

The circumplex model, a particular approach to family assessment that includes consideration of family differentiation and cohesion, has been discussed as a metaphor drawing on notions of balance and symmetry. The fact that the circumplex model was developed along with a family assessment instrument, FACES, provided the opportunity for discussing the ways in which family assessment measures are metaphors and what such measures highlight and obscure.

The metaphor of generational structure obscures how the metaphoric transporting of the concept of generation into family systems theory transforms the concept into a matter of morality and pathology. These imposed culturally based standards seem risky to apply. Moreover, the family systems theory uses of the concept of generational hierarchy are inconsistent with system-sensitive analyses of how power and influence operate in hierarchies.

The metaphor of gender structure in family systems theory has been criticized by feminist critics for the many ways in which it has been used to disadvantage women and to turn attention away from the gender biases of the larger society. Feminist critics have offered the metaphor of patriarchy as a useful corrective metaphor. Of course, that metaphor also obscures. Among the crucial things that can be obscured by the patriarchy metaphor but that can be highlighted by other feminist metaphors are the transformability of oppressed lives and the importance of women's alliances with other women.

The chapter has also offered an analysis of the metaphors of triangulation and of family coalitions and has then explored how alternative structural metaphors can highlight what the standard structural metaphors obscure. It has done this by developing the metaphor that the family is a tapestry.

CHAPTER SIX

Metaphors of System Control

S ystem control is a basic concept in family systems theory. This chapter analyzes the metaphor of system control and the closely related metaphors of family rules and of negative and positive feedback, exploring what each metaphor highlights and obscures.

THE METAPHOR OF SYSTEM CONTROL

The metaphor of system control is central to family systems theory. The cultural referents for the metaphor include the body's control of its functions (e.g., through the nervous system, genes, and hormones), the thermostatic control of heating and cooling systems, the control of a vehicle in transit, self-control of emotions and actions, and government control of citizens. All referents have in common a sense of monitoring and regulating a process in order to keep it within limits. The control metaphor thus highlights the regularities in family functioning and the ways in which family process involves monitoring and regulating what goes on in the family in order to keep it within limits.

The family systems literature is rich in accounts of specific system control metaphors (e.g., family myths are explored by Ferreira, 1963, and transactional disqualifications are the subject of a paper by Sluzki, Beavin, Tarnopolsky, & Verón, 1967). Two system control metaphors seem to have received more attention in the literature than any of the others—the metaphor of rules and the metaphor of negative and positive feedback. Each of these metaphors has been elaborated in a number of ways and highlights certain aspects of family functioning while obscuring others.

FAMILY RULES

The Metaphors of Family Rules

The metaphors of family rules are used to explain and highlight regularity in family life. Why do family members recurrently deal with each other and with whatever is outside the family as they do? One answer is that they are following family rules (Ford, 1983; Jackson, 1965a, 1965b). A family rule may be defined as a spoken or unspoken prescription that operates within the family to guide action. Jackson and Ford used the family rule metaphor to explain regularities in family behavior. Family rules might deal with anything: for example, quid pro quo exchange in the family, emotional expression, which topics can and cannot be aired in various situations, which issues are fair or not fair to bring up in family arguments, or ways to spend family leisure time. Rules can be thought of as guides, but they can also be thought of as laws backed by sanctions. The sanctions might include disapproval, criticism, rage, deprivation of affection, being labeled "sick" or "crazy" or "disloyal," threats to terminate the relationship, or a retaliatory rule violation that in some way is aversive to the original rule violator.

The family systems literature seems generally to treat rules as though they are implicit. Satir (1972, pp. 98–111), for example, wrote about unwritten rules and those that are difficult or impossible to articulate. Wertheim (1975) wrote about rules as largely unconscious. Thus, the rule metaphor highlights what appear to be unverbalized but effective understandings among family members.

Among the reasons for the difficultly or impossibility of articulating family rules is the fact that there may be rules blocking certain family communications. For example, a family member may not be allowed to disclose certain impressions, feelings, experiences, perceptions, disagreements, or confusions, either in general or to certain people. From Satir's perspective, rules blocking communication make trouble for families because they limit problem solving, honesty, and intimacy. From the perspective of an observer trying to understand a family system, blocks to family communications (and perhaps attendant blocks to paying attention to certain things or to thinking about them) may make family members poor informants about their rules, even if they are much more likely than the observer to know the family rules. Thus, it may be difficult or impossible for a family therapist or researcher to learn about certain family rules on the basis of direct reports from family members. Because family members are seen as unable or unwilling to articulate family rules, the metaphor of family rules highlights the special status of the family therapist or researcher as a person who can say (and perhaps "know") more about a family than family members do, and it also highlights the extent to which therapist or researcher assertions about regularities in family life are matters of inference from various clues.

The metaphor of family rules has been elaborated into a set of metaphors that includes the rules themselves, rules about how to apply the rules, rules about exceptions and qualifications to the rules, rules about what happens when the rules are broken, connections to related rules, and counterrules (Ford, 1983). The counterrule to a rule is something like the opposite of the rule. If the rule is "don't fight," the counter rule is "fight." According to Ford, there would be no need for a rule if the counterrule had no reality; for example, there would be no need for the rule "don't fight" if people were never disposed to fight. The rule that family members must be together as much as possible on weekends may seem like a powerful rule in a family where members are together almost all the time on weekends. But that rule, like any other, exists because some of the time at least some family members are disposed not to be with the rest of the family. Thus, if it is the case, as Minuchin asserted (1974, p. 52), that there are rules of intergenerational hierarchy and adult role complementarity in families, one would expect that those rules go against counterdispositions in some family members. Moreover, the apparent existence of a powerful and successfully compelling rule may lead us to miss people's private feelings of dissatisfaction with the rule and their disinclination to follow it. Nonetheless, there is within the set of metaphors dealing with rules a sense of inclinations to violate rules.

The metaphor of family rules has also been elaborated into a metaphoric system in which rules are thought of as ordered in hierarchies of abstraction and generality (Wertheim, 1975). According to that elaboration of the metaphor of rules, there may be a concrete rule dealing with a very specific matter, a more abstract rule that encompasses that concrete rule and still other concrete rules, still more abstract rules that encompass that specific abstract rule and other abstract rules, and so on. The higher-order rules may not only be general principles applying to many lower-order rules, but they may also qualify or limit the lower-order rules (Wertheim, 1975). Presumably, these higher-order, more inclusive, more abstract rules are slower to change, deal with issues that are played out over longer periods of time, are more difficult to describe and assess (Broderick & Smith, 1979, citing Mesarovic, Macko, & Takahara, 1970), and are more difficult to articulate (Wertheim, 1975).

The rules metaphor highlights complex systems of family constraint against individual actions, but the metaphor also leaves room for the apparent rules that pattern family interaction to be a resource to family members (Manning, 1991). Rules may be thought of as streamlining interaction and reducing the cost and complexity of repeated negotiation and conflict over various matters. By reducing the amount of time and energy that must be put into family interaction processes, rules can increase the time and energy available for other things. Family members can, moreover, use the rules to justify and rationalize their actions and as strategic tools enabling them to get what they need or want. Thus, a family's negotiations about rules or an individual family member's objection to a rule may be understood as dealing both with limits and resources.

The Relation of the Rule Metaphor to Other Systems Theory Metaphors

The rule metaphor is related to the metaphor of family structure. Families that have a relatively closed structure can be said to have relatively restrictive rules about information entering or leaving the family and about each member going along with family opinions, desires, and feelings no matter how much these may differ from the member's opinions or beliefs (Satir, 1983, p. 237). More generally, family structure—including role structure, gender structure, generational hierarchy, and coalitions—can be said to be created and maintained through family rules, and family rules can be said to have arisen from family structural arrangements. The theoretical relationship between family rules and family structure might simply be that they are two ways of characterizing the same thing. The relationship between rules and structure could also be said to be a complementary one: The rules reflect, reinforce, and create the structure; the structure provides a system to which rules must comply and in which rules are generated.

The rule metaphor is sometimes related in family systems theory writings to metaphors of the system's relationship with other systems. In this view family rules can be thought of as the family process (rules of transformation) that takes input from outside the family and produces output for the world outside of the family (Broderick & Smith, 1979). Thus, a description of the effect of the rules might not be a description of control but of the transformation of input into output.

The Origins of Family Rules

The metaphor of family rules may be used as a theoretical given; the question of origin may be taken as theoretically useless. However, in order to provide family professionals interested in intervention with conceptual tools for changing family rules, the metaphor of family rules can be elaborated to deal with the origins of rules.

Some theorists have seen rules as originating at least in part in the culture or even in the biology of the human species. Minuchin (1974), for example, wrote about "the universal rules governing family organization" (p. 52). His concept of universal rules includes the notions of hierarchy between parents and children and of complementarity of function between husband and wife. Family rules may stem from culture, not only directly but also indirectly through the restriction of options. That is, cultural pressure for rules may include not only the "thou shalt" statements in the culture but the ways the culture does or does not provide resources for meeting family needs. For example, the absence of good child care alternatives outside the home and the existence of wage differentials that give men higher earnings than women will push for family rules that say that child care is a mother's responsibility, even if the culture does not directly inculcate that rule.

Family rules may be understood as negotiated, however implicitly, most notably at the beginnings of an intimate adult relationship (Jackson, 1965b). Family rules may also be traced to families of origin, and combining rules from two families of origin may require implicit or possibly even explicit negotiation processes (Jackson, 1965b). From that perspective, family rules may be sustained by feelings of loyalty to previous generations or by a sense of what is right that is based on experiences in one's family of origin, and those family-of-origin forces may be supported and reinforced by older family members. Nonetheless, what emerges is shaped through ongoing family interaction and a blending of expectations, desires, abilities, preferences, and needs.

In considering the origins of family rules, it seems obvious that rules would have to be created or altered when new challenges arise, for example, when a first child is born or a family member becomes handicapped. From the perspective of the metaphor of family rules, part of the crisis of dealing with a new challenge would be that there are no rules prescribing or limiting action in the new situation or that there is a lack of individual confidence or family agreement about which rules apply or how to apply them. The metaphor of family rules includes the possibility that families have all-purpose crisis rules, but such rules may be inadequate to deal with a new situation or, at the very least, may require interpretation in order to apply to a new situation.

The metaphor of family rules also allows for the creation or alteration of a rule at a time when a rule seems to have been violated. Each instance of rule violation can be taken as a challenge to the validity of the rule or to how the rule is interpreted and applied and as a statement about the need for a qualification or exception to the rule. Thus, even if rules can be inferred from regularities, the absence of regularities may not mean that rules are absent. It may mean that the rules are changing or that what one perceives as irregularity is glossed by family members with interpretations, exceptions and qualifications that make things seem regular to them.

What Rules Metaphors Obscure

The metaphor of rules obscures the extent to which there is no need for a rule in some areas because people will always do what they do. Thus, there may seem to be a rule that says, "Talk to everyone in the family within an hour after waking up," but in a family where everyone always does that we may not be able to know whether the action conforms to a family rule (or to a societal rule) or is simply what people do. Perhaps morning sociability is so common in the species that it is only in cases where people are not at all sociable in the morning that it makes sense to entertain the possibility of a family rule operating.

The metaphor of family rules may obscure the extent to which rules are invented only after the fact—as family members try to explain to themselves why they do what they do or as they try to answer an outsider's question about family patterns and about why the patterns exist. The rules can also be understood as an outside observer's effort to make sense out of what is going on in the family (Jackson, 1965b). There may in fact be nothing like shared, implicit family rules a good deal of the time. The fact that a therapist or other outsider claims to identify rules that seem to apply to the observable patterns of a family may say nothing about the family and may only demonstrate the capacity of observers to select and organize information or to draw inferences. Apparent regularities in family actions may be maintained by many dynamics other than rules, for example, the selective perception of observers or the interplay of family member preferences.

Tomm (1987), basing his analysis on Pearce and Cronen's (1980) work on the "Coordinated Management of Meaning," differentiated regulative rules from constitutive rules. In that metaphoric dichotomy, regulative rules have to do with what should or should not be done in specific situations, and constitutive rules have to do with the meanings to be attached to particular events and actions. The conceptual system called the "Coordinated Management of Meaning" proposes that a network of rules guides communication in relationships. The notion of a constitutive rule adds another dimension to the metaphor of family rules. Without it, a rule may be only an outsider's construction. With the added dimension of a constitutive rule, the focus is at least partly on family members' understanding of things. From this perspective, a family conflict would be regulated and dealt with both by family rules about the forms and shapes of conflict (e.g., "Fairness issues are appropriate to bring up"; "Hitting is not allowed"; "Don't raise your voice when the children are present") and by family rules about interpretations (e.g., "Conflict is healthy"; "We argue so we can be intimate").

The constitutive rule metaphor seems to be a genuine addition to the definition of family rules that emphasizes their limit-setting aspect. Of course, that metaphor too may obscure. It may, for example, obscure the possibility that the family gives no meaning or no family-coordinated meaning to events. Asking family members for meanings may instigate them to create meanings—and they may even have common-meaning-creating rules, so that the meanings they come up with are coordinated—but they may actually have no meanings in mind for a good deal of what they do.

NEGATIVE AND POSITIVE FEEDBACK

The Feedback Metaphor

The second common control metaphor in family systems theory writings is the metaphor of negative and positive feedback. The metaphor of feedback, drawn from control systems concepts in engineering, refers to the flow of information through some sort of device (in humans the device might be a set of cognitive rules) that evaluates that information against some standard. Negative feedback (what Kantor & Lehr, 1975, p. 14, called "constancy feedback") reduces variation from the standard; for example, it draws a family member violating the standard "Be nice" back into niceness or sets into play family processes that dampen family boisterousness that exceeds the family comfort level for emotional expression. Positive feedback (what Kantor & Lehr, 1975, p. 14, called "variety feedback" or what Hoffman, 1971, following Maruyama, 1968, called "deviation-amplifying processes") increases variation from the standard; for example, family members might decide that their customary way of spending Sunday together is boring and might turn to new and potentially more rewarding activities. Although positive feedback produces change, it is not unlimited change (Constantine, 1986, p. 62); thus, even when positive feedback processes are producing marked change in system functioning, there are still processes within the system, within subsystems, or within the exosystem that limit the change. Feedback processes provide information to system components that enable the components to relate properly (by higher-level system standards) to one another and to the external environment (Kantor & Lehr, 1975, p. 12).

Family systems theorists claim that a family maintains and changes what goes on within it through a dialectic of stability and change, of negative and positive feedback (e.g., Constantine, 1986, pp. 64–65; Maddock, 1989, 1992b; Speer, 1970; Wertheim, 1975). They write of morphogensis, second order change, or meta-change as the process or outcome of a family's moving to a significantly new system, with new rules, structures, and the like. They write of morphostasis as the processes by which the family's system is maintained as it has been and as the steady-state outcome of those processes. Constantine (1986, p. 65), contrasting the operation of morphogenesis and morphostasis on structure with the operation of homeostasis on process, saw the feedback operations that affect structure as morphostatic or morphogenic and the feedback operations that affect process or ongoing behavior as homeostatic. The distinction between processes and structure is one of levels of the system (cf. Burr, 1991); however, Constantine (1986, pp. 52–53) also argued that the distinction between process and structure is a distinction of time scale. Summed across enough time, process blurs into structure and structures can be seen to have processes.

The feedback metaphor highlights how families must adapt and change in response to external events and to internal change in individuals and relationships; hence the need for morphogenesis. The feedback metaphor also highlights how families must maintain some stability in family relationships in order to maintain adaptations and in order to have at least modestly predictable relationships with one another and with others in their world.

The issue of stability is complicated (Richardson, 1991, pp. 321–322). A focus on stability can lead us to lose track of the complexity of systems and to ignore the dynamic interaction of system components with one another and the dynamic interaction of the system with its external environment. Keeping one piece of the system stable is not morphostatic if keeping that piece stable means other pieces of the system change. For example, morphostatic processes that keep a family watching its customary 6 hours a day of television would not be morphostatic at another level if the television watching means that the family is not continuing to make decisions and solve problems as it has been up to now. Thus, the dialectic in system functioning not only involves stability and change processes but also relations among various systemic levels (Maddock, 1989). Trying to understand what is going on systemically by examining only one systemic level is a mistake (cf. Maddock, 1989). For example, seeing estrangement in a family only in its own terms, we may miss how much the estrangement has to do with the links of that family to other families and other social groups (Gluckman, 1956) or to racist or classist dynamics in the larger society. And evaluating the health of a family purely in its own terms, without regard to what is happening in its ecosystem, may overlook unhealthy aspects of the family's functioning (Maddock, 1989). In fact, one of the feminist criticisms of family systems theory (Avis, 1986) is that as a therapy theory it has focused too much on the family and too little on the ecosystem of the family. As Avis pointed out, the feminist challenge in this regard may push family systems analyses to be more truly systemic.

What the Feedback Metaphor Obscures

The stability or change in a family may actually be the stability or change of interpretation, description, and understanding of outsiders evaluating the family (see Gubrium & Lynott, 1985). What seems like system stability or change is a matter of judgment by a family therapist, the therapist's supervisor, the therapist's colleagues on the other side of the one-way vision screen, the family researcher, or some other observer. Thus, the metaphor of system stability or change through negative or positive feedback obscures how much what is labeled stability or change and negative or positive feedback comes from the standards and cognitive/perceptual/interpretive processes of observers outside of the family. Recognizing how the metaphor obscures these standards and processes helps us focus our attention on how family therapists and researchers interpret, describe, and understand the words and actions of families in coming to their judgments of family stability and change. It also alerts us to the need to understand how the community of those who characterize families has developed its notions of how to make those judgments.

The feedback metaphor also obscures how iffy family realities are. There is a concreteness to how the feedback metaphor is often used that belies how much family members may disagree with each other and with outside observers about what is going on (Constantine, 1986, pp. 52–53) and belies how complex and unclear what goes on in family life often is to observers. For example, one observer may see parental criticism directed at a teenager who is going off to spend Sunday afternoon with friends as negative feedback in that the parent is trying to reduce deviation from the family standard of Sunday togetherness. Another observer may see the parental criticism as granting the teenager the right to deviate from the standard, as feedback concerning choice of friends rather than family togetherness, as feedback concerning a rule of timely warning of planned outings, or as an expression of parental hostility toward adolescent independence, a hostility that may be irrelevant to family rules about Sundays and friends. Still another observer may see what the parent says as pro forma and actually rather meaningless, that is, as more like the parent's customary form of good-bye than anything else.

Even when observers are in agreement, what they see may be so complicated that it seems to be positive feedback at one level and negative at another. Consider, for example, the behavior of a family that holds its members to a norm of emotional constraint following a fire that destroys the family home. The family may be limiting emotional expression according to established family rules (negative feedback) while producing change (positive feedback) at the level of rules about caring about material goods. More generally, it may be that most system change process, most morphogenesis, is an expression of morphostasis at a higher level. Also, most processes of system stability, most morphostasis, may be an expression of morphogenesis at a higher level. Thus, an apt characterization of feedback processes when change occurs would include descriptions of negative feedback processes at some levels coordinated with positive feedback processes at others. Similarly, an apt characterization of feedback processes when stability occurs would include descriptions of positive feedback processes at some levels coordinated with negative feedback processes at others.

When a family seems stuck at the task of dealing with an emergent problem, for example, unable to express feelings about a family member being diagnosed with cancer, it might be a matter of morphostatic struggle to keep the system as it was or a matter of lack of information about what the diagnosis means. Or it might be that there are no standards in this family to use in providing feedback about responses to the crisis. Until standards can be created, family members cannot judge crying as being more appropriate than calmness, optimism as being more appropriate than pessimism, discussing the cancer as being more appropriate than being silent about the issue. Creating such standards may be a daunting task, especially during a crisis. Thus, what seems like morphostasis or negative feedback may be something else—not control but a lack of a control standard.

Family "stuckness" may also represent competing systemic "shoulds," perhaps negative feedback that pulls in opposite directions. For example, a family that cannot decide what to do about a cancer diagnosis may be simultaneously wrestling with negative feedback about, on the one hand, trying not to alarm the person who is ill, on the other hand, trying to keep the system the same by keeping the person who is sick alive. Interpersonal conflict about such matters may represent competing systemic "shoulds," with different family members advocating for different "shoulds" but all maintaining loyalty to the same system. Although there may be controls at various levels of a family system for dealing with crises and novel situations, part of the struggle in accommodating to these situations may commonly involve developing new standards, interpreting old standards, or legislating among apparently competing standards.

WHAT BOTH CONTROL METAPHORS OBSCURE

Obscuring Noncontrol

Both the rules and the feedback metaphors of system control assert that families are internally controlled and that there is in the system some sense of what to do and what not to do. Both vocabularies for control can account for change, either through changes in lower-order rules that are consistent with higher-order rules or through positive feedback. Both the rules and the feedback metaphor obscure the ways in which families are not controlled. There are five aspects of this absence of control.

Absence of Regularity

Control metaphors obscure the absence of regularity in family functioning. Each interaction in the family may be unique. No two conflicts, no two mealtimes, no two sexual encounters between adult partners may be the same, so asserting that system control creates regularities in these and other family situations obscures that there are no true regularities. What appear to be regularities or what is labeled a regularity may be a matter of observer perception and generalization. But if these perceptions and generalizations are faulty, if there is no regularity, it is not clear what is being explained.

Constant Monitoring and Regulation Are Impossible

Another thing that may be obscured by the control metaphor is that a great deal may go on in families without any monitoring or regulating. People may not be able to attend to most of what is going on. They may not be interested in monitoring everything; they can only focus on so much and may have higher priorities most of the time than monitoring others. Thus, if control makes any sense in a family system, it may be a matter of haphazard sampling and occasional intense interest rather than constant monitoring.

Autonomy

Despite controls, family members function with a great deal of autonomy (see Katz, 1968). The family control system may set limits, prescribe actions, and taboo other actions, but a broad latitude of autonomy may still be allowed by the controls. The family rules may, for example, require family members generally to be together on Sundays, holidays, and birthdays, and the rules for these occasions may require certain kinds of actions (e.g., small talk) and prohibit others (e.g., spending most of one's family time talking on the phone with friends). Nonetheless, there is probably room for family members to engage in an enormous range of activities while in the company of other members. They may, for example, be permitted to watch television or read a newspaper some of the time, sit in bored silence, or be relatively inattentive; they may be permitted to choose the day's attire from a substantial range of clothing, eat a wide range of snack foods, or take a nap. Similarly, family rules may require one to keep clean but not prescribe precisely how one bathes. Or there may be rules about when and how to express disagreement with other family members but no rules about whether one should be sitting or standing at the time.

Understanding the place of these areas of autonomy in the functioning of the family system is important. Minuchin (1974, p. 52) offered one way of understanding areas of autonomy by suggesting that a family must have a sufficient range of alternative patterns and flexibility about mobilizing them in order to continue to exist. A family that is too rigid lacks the repertoire to adapt to the wide variety of demands placed on it externally and internally.

Another way to understand the issue of autonomy is to note that rules only apply to what counts to somebody. Although conceivably anything may matter to some member of some family, there may be in most families a great many things that are a matter of indifference to everyone.

The areas of autonomy may also represent a systemic allowance for meeting individual needs. If there are no areas of autonomy, it is likely that many individual needs will go unmet, which means that at least some individuals—and, presumably, then the whole family—are in a great deal of trouble.

Finally, there are probably spheres of individual and family life in which there is essentially no family control. One of those areas may be private thoughts, perhaps including what family members think about other family members, what they dream, what they think while watching television, and how much they think about other family members while apart from them. There may be no family rules in these areas because family members have no direct experience of another family member's mental activity and perhaps because people may assume such mental activity is uncontrollable. This suggests that there may be no control in any area of family life that is perceived as out of the direct experience of other family members or as incapable of being controlled. Those areas perceived to be out of the direct experience of others or incapable of control may be thought of as a matter of human nature, but they may in reality reflect beliefs that vary from culture to culture and family to family. It is easy, for example, to imagine a family system in which it is considered legitimate for members to question each other about what they think, feel, remember, or dream; to feel that they must report honestly; to develop sensitivity at reading indirect indicators of other members' private thoughts; and to learn how to control their private thoughts.

The Influence of Society and Culture

The metaphor of family system control obscures how much of the system control of a family is a product of society and culture (Hare-Mustin, 1987). Although family systems theories seem invariably to be based on a conception of the family system as linked to the larger systems of society, the focus of so much of family therapy on the individual family as a system makes it easy to obscure the extent to which the rules and standards, the sanctions, and the counterrules of the control system come from the larger society. For example, one may take a family's efforts to produce independent children and its tolerance of male physical threats as products of family rules without recognizing the extent to which the larger society supports, encourages, tolerates, and even pushes for these rules.

Critics of the way women are treated in the family field (e.g., Hare-Mustin, 1987) point out that family theory and therapy often operate with assumptions that disadvantage women—for example, that it is normal for a wife/mother to be responsible for most or all of the household chores and child care. Feminist critics suggest that family therapy, by obscuring the forces of society and culture, is a conservative force. They argue that family therapy helps to maintain societal and cultural rules and systems of enforcing rules even though, with other lenses, it is obvious how these rules and enforcement systems are injurious to women and children (and are not even in the best interests of men). One can also argue that the concept of control is part of a masculine view of science (Bleier, 1986, pp. 15–16) and that a theory like family systems theory, in which control is such a key concept, is suspect as one that provides, supports, and reinforces a male view of family life and misses and subordinates a female's view (one in which cooperation, connection, and democracy, for example, might be salient concepts). One can reply to feminist critics that control can be understood as a gender-neutral systems concept and that control takes many forms besides domination, oppression, victimization, and the covert assertion of privilege and power. However, feminists, for their part, would no doubt still alert us to how using a term that is purportedly gender-neutral to deal with families in a society in which much is structured in ways that are not gender neutral may mask societal biases.

The metaphor of system control may obscure how the players in a family's control system are to a very great extent not the members of the immediate family. Teachers, clergy, friends, colleagues at work, classmates, nonresident kin, and other people with whom family members have contact are potentially influential. However, the most influential people in regulating the life of a family may be unknown, nameless, and faceless. Laws are made and enforced by people the family members may never see. The norms that govern each person's sense of how to be a family member have arisen through the actions of people who, for the most part, have never been seen by any member of the family. The mass media provide standards, rules, and models of family control system functioning, and these are dictated by writers, editors, directors, advertisers, producers, and media executives who are not known to family members.

Thus, the focus on control systems in individual families obscures societal and cultural control forces and obscures the mass of people who are influential players in the family's control system. Obscuring these extrafamilial control forces leads, among other things, to missing how much the place for intervention for family control system problems might reasonably be the larger society.

Continual Change in Control Systems

The metaphor of system control in family systems theory obscures the extent to which there is no static control structure like a thermostat or a published legal code, that the system is constantly reengineered by family members. The metaphor of rules implies that there are fixed rules. The feedback metaphor, drawing its meaning from such fixed entities as thermostats, also implies a fixed system. Yet family rules are constantly being challenged, interpreted, and invented to deal with new situations and as family members and situations change. Similarly, the family system to which negative and positive feedback is applied is one that must be constantly challenged, interpreted, extended, and altered. There are quite possibly aspects of control systems that are constant in family life—rules that do not change, conceptions of rules that do not change, principles of enforcement, and so on—but it seems unlikely that a family control system could remain unchanging, even over a few days or weeks.

(Parenthetically, one of the challenges in dealing with theories of family systems is to find a place for the concept of individual dispositions. The reengineering of family rules seems to be one of those places—a conjunction between the system that regulates the whole family and the action of the individual as it affects the system. Consider, for example, some of the ways children are characterized— the terrible twos, teenage rebellion. These characterizations can be understood as describing family members who work at challenging and redesigning family controls. Although 2-year-olds and teenagers may be more conspicuous challengers of family system rules because they are defined in the culture as dependents and junior to adult family members, other family members may be equally active in revamping the rules as they offer their individual interpretations, come up with their individual reasons for challenging rules, and face dilemmas or go through personal changes that call for new rules.)

If one grants that control systems are continually changing (or that any other aspect of a system is continually changing), it becomes obvious that an apt systems analysis must characterize both the system at the moment and the processes involved in the system's continual change. Thus, to take one of many conceivable examples, an analysis of the rule system of a family therapy case should characterize both the rules that are relevant to the family's involvement in therapy and the processes by which the family's rules change.

Dialogic Relationship between Control and Power

Maddock (1992b) has argued that control is not freestanding in systems but is dialogically and reciprocally related to power. As he sees it, "power is the capacity of a system to influence other systems in its environment" (p. 13) and control is "the capacity of a system to limit the influence of other systems" (p. 13). From Maddock's perspective, "the power/control dialectic reflects the functional process of 'bounding' systems." Working within Maddock's view, family systems theory thinking that highlights control mechanisms obscures the dialectical relationship of control and power. If we focus on control, we will miss how control is associated with the exertion of power in the family's ecosystem and subsystems and how much the power–control dialectic has to do with defining boundaries and what the system seems to be at any given time. We would also miss the ongoing process of power–control dynamics, and we would miss the extent to which relations with ecosystem and subsystems have to do with the control reactions of these entities to the system's exertion of power.

Social Construction

Another approach to identifying what the control system metaphor obscures is from a social constructionist view, a perspective that denies the essentialness of givens, even of seemingly natural categories in social life (Gergen, 1985). From this perspective all realities are seen as arrived at through a process of implicit or explicit social collaboration or negotiation. According to some social constructionist views, the social construction of reality goes on constantly, with many bits of the reality simultaneously being dealt with in any ongoing interaction. In the social constructionist view, realities are not fixed but are perspectival; in different social contexts we will see different things, see what we see differently, understand differently, categorize differently, and believe profoundly in very different realities.

The social constructionist perspective is not inconsistent with a family systems theory conception of control systems. The rules, standards, and so on of a control system may be understood as socially constructed. People can be seen as collaborating in developing and maintaining rules, in defining rule violations and sanctions, and so on. Among family systems writers there are many who have written about what seem to be social construction processes. Minuchin (1974, p. 52), for example, wrote about mutual expectations of family members as a system of constraints idiosyncratic to each family. He saw the expectations as the result of years of explicit and implicit negotiations, often around small daily events, negotiations that may be lost to memory but are still in force. For Minuchin, the social construction of a rule system was part of what went on in families. Jackson (1959), to take another family systems writer, described the implicit and explicit efforts of all people constantly to define the nature of their relationships and saw these efforts as a facet of all relationship control activities (the "command" activities discussed in the next chapter).

Despite the social constructionist elements of paradigmatic systems theory thinking, a social construction perspective suggests two things that may be obscured in family systems conceptions of control systems. The first is that the therapist's or researcher's view of a family's control system is a social construction and is selective, perspectival, situation-bound, and influenced by social processes external to the phenomena being constructed (Gubrium, 1992). Obscuring the therapist's or researcher's construction of the family's system obscures how not taking the family's realities as given privileges the therapist's or researcher's view (cf. Erickson, 1988; Gubrium, 1992, pp. 48–51). By saying there is more there than the family can identify, therapists and researchers disqualify the family and present themselves as qualified to characterize the family.

Moreover, the therapist or researcher construction of a family's control system (or of anything else in the family) can be counted on to fit the theories that make sense to the therapist or researcher. To the extent that those theories are family systems theories, what will be selectively perceived, judged, shaped, and interpreted can be expected to fit systems theory (cf. Gubrium, 1992, p. 89). It may be in part an awareness of the potential selectivity, bias, and invalidity of a view of a family that is consistent with family systems theory that has made some therapists and researchers wary of using family systems theory. However, there may be no escaping one's own ideas about reality, even if they are inarticulate or very different from what is standard in one's field.

Another thing that may be obscured in family systems theory conceptions of control systems is that a family constructs the meanings its members give to the operation of the control system. Even if the system is in many ways implicit and undiscussed, family members will have evidence that something is going on and they may well construct a reality concerning that evidence. Meanings may be given to rules, to encounters that pull or push family members toward family standards, and to family discussions of what should be done about something. By giving meaning, by constructing a reality for some pieces of the control system, family members give a character to the control system and to its operation. Whether the family characterizes application of a rule or a standard as a matter of observing a divine commandment, staying healthy, getting along in the community, being respectable, being happy together, not crossing Dad, or being safe may make a difference, for example, in terms of how and when the system changes, in the consequences of deviating from the system, and of the therapeutic interventions that might change the system.

THE FAMILY IS A GOVERNMENT

As a means of developing alternative perspectives on family control mechanisms, consider the metaphor "the family is a government." A government controls itself, but it also controls all sorts of things besides itself. Thus, the government metaphor suggests, in contrast to the standard family control metaphors, how a family control system is designed not only to control the family but to control things outside the family. The rules and feedback processes of the family may be designed not only for internal family control but to control such social entities outside of itself as neighbors, related families, passing strangers, and school authorities. In fact, a case can be made that in a family's systemic linkage with any social entity there is a two-way operation of control mechanisms. If, for example, the school has some control on the family, the family has some control on the school.

The government metaphor highlights the internal limits in the family on regulating both itself and whatever is outside itself. Like a government, the family cannot always reach agreement on proposed regulations and rules. Internal conflict, lack of interest, the opposition of a strong lobbyist, the daunting complexity of some issues, or insufficient resources—all may block the addition or modification of some law or regulation.

When we consider the processes by which government operates, a social construction model seems both applicable and limited. It certainly fits that a great deal of the control that regulates a government and that a government imposes on outside entities is a matter of perception and of direct or indirect negotiation, but it is also the case that important things happen without negotiation. In governments sometimes a specific person or agency can stop something from happening, for example, by vetoing, delaying, or neutralizing through misinterpretation or indifference. Perhaps the same is true in families.

In American family life, in depictions of that life in the media, and surprisingly often in the texts of the family field, there is a sense that family life can and should be perfectly harmonious. Yet the government metaphor of family control suggests that in families, as in governments, system control is neither the product of perfect harmony nor the cause of it. In families, as in governments, there may always be opposition parties and an active system of checks and balances made necessary by the operation of competing interests, human greed, and much else that is less than noble. There may be areas of harmony: All those in government may support continuing to meet payroll obligations to government employees, and all family members may support continuing efforts to feed family members. But, the metaphor suggests, there will certainly be areas in which there will be disagreements about control, for example, about the intensity of control or whether controls that are in place are appropriate. For example, in government, as of this writing, there are disagreements about the extent to which politicians must be accountable for their income and the extent to which motorcycle helmet laws are desired, supported, and enforced. In families, examples might be disagreement about the extent to which each family member must account to the family for all income and disagreement about the extent to which family members desire and should support and enforce a ban on insulting other family members. In fact, just as government may be a device for channeling and dampening potentially dangerous and destructive conflict, so family control systems may be a way not of eliminating hatred and conflict but of keeping it safely channeled.

In governments there is corruption. Officials may be bribed or may find ways to divert resources to their own use or the use of their relatives and cronies. Seemingly general and fair laws may be promulgated that actually benefit a chosen few. Perhaps in some families too there may be control system corruption. A family member may divert collective resources (e.g., family savings) for personal use. Controls may be circumvented or created so as to benefit someone inside or outside the family. This entailment of the government metaphor suggests that in families, as in governments, there may be those who are in some ways unprincipled and that others must be alert to the selfish or covert deviations from what is considered appropriate and might well build in mechanisms for preventing, detecting, and stopping such deviations. The entailment also suggests that a fully comprehensive set of metaphors dealing with family rules or feedback systems in families must deal with the place of trust and responsibility in such systems.

SUMMARY

In this chapter the metaphor of systems control and the related metaphors of family rules and of negative and positive feedback have been analyzed. Control metaphors highlight regularity and regulation in family interaction. The rules metaphor highlights regularity in family functioning, the possibility of unverbalized but effective understandings in families, the status of the therapist/researcher as someone who can see what family members cannot, the possibility of systems of family constraints on actions, and the possible origins of family understandings about what should and should not be done. The metaphor of family rules obscures the possibilities that there is no need for family rules and the possibility that the so-called rules are after-the-fact inventions.

The feedback metaphor highlights the need for family stability and change and the mechanisms of achieving stability and change. It highlights the possibility of multiple levels of systemic guidance, with change on one level maintaining stability on another. The feedback metaphor obscures how family stability and change are matters of observer interpretation, the inherent ambiguity of family realities, and the complexity of interpreting negative and positive feedback when both may be going on. It also obscures the possibility that what appears to be morphostasis may be something else, for example, a lack of system guidance about how to change or a "stuckness" arising from competing systemic "shoulds."

All family control metaphors obscure that there may be no regularities and that it is unlikely that family monitoring and regulating of family process is continual. All family control metaphors also obscure the existence and importance of areas of autonomy in family life; the extent to which what appear to be family controls may more properly be understood as societal or cultural controls; the likelihood that if there is anything like a family control system, major aspects of it are constantly changing (so that there is, in a sense, no control system); the dialogic relationship between control and power; and the social construction processes that make it likely that what the family system observer and the family members themselves make of what appears to be a control system is cooked up and could be constructed in other ways.

Aspects of the metaphor, "the family is a government," have been developed in this chapter in order to provide alternative perspectives for thinking about family control systems. The government metaphor leads to a consideration of how family control mechanisms function to control externalities and to a sensitivity to the external constituencies, opponents, lobbyists, and so on, to which the family is in some sense responsive. The government metaphor alerts us to the limits on the development of controls that stem from a lack of internal consensus in support of certain controls, a lack of interest, or a lack of resources necessary to effect certain controls. The government metaphor highlights processes other than social construction that may shape control systems in families, for example, the exercise of vetoes or passive opposition. It highlights the extent to which conflict and disharmony may be normal in family life and the function of family controls as a way of channeling, not eliminating, conflict and disharmony. Finally, the government metaphor suggests that in families, as in governments, there may be corruption of various sorts, so that the operation of a family control system may itself be corrupt or may include various means of preventing, detecting, and stopping selfish or covert diversion of resources.

CHAPTER SEVEN

Metaphors of Communication in Family Systems

A family system cannot be regulated or bounded, cannot be internally differentiated or patterned, cannot relate to an outside entity, cannot change, and cannot exist without communication. A family system consists of patterned communicative relationships (Watzlawick et al., 1967, chap. 1). Fundamentally, family systems theory is a theory of communication. Consequently, an analysis of the metaphors of communication is central to understanding the power and possible limitations of the metaphors of family systems theory. This chapter explores the metaphors of communication, open and closed communication, metacommunication, paradox, and communication pathology, analyzing what each metaphor highlights and obscures.

THE METAPHOR OF COMMUNICATION

In everyday usage the word "communication" refers to concrete interaction between people, an interaction that is immediately available to the senses, talking, gesturing, signaling, writing, and moving closer to or farther away from someone. In everyday usage, communication is understood as the transmission by a sender of things the sender knows and knowingly sends—ideas, thoughts, opinions, feelings, impressions, facts. The Palo Alto group (Bateson, Beavin, Haley, Jackson, Satir, Watzlawick, Weakland, etc.), who developed the initial theoretical framework for family systems theory, grounded their understanding of communication and family systems in concrete verbal and nonverbal communications that an observer could hear and see (Weakland, 1967). These theorists were and are behaviorists. Thus, matters of communicator knowledge and intent were subordinated to what could actually be heard and seen by an observer.

Despite a grounding in what was available for an observer to hear and see, as the members of the Palo Alto group theorized about communication and interpreted the communications they used as data and illustrations, they extended the meaning of communication metaphorically. Their analysis of communication went far beyond what is immediately available to the senses, into such matters as the development and enforcment of family rules, system-maintaining and system-altering feedback, the use and monitoring of multiple communication channels, boundary maintenance, and symptoms as communication. That these elaborations of the meaning of communication are metaphoric extensions of the concept of communication may be difficult to appreciate because in the social sciences the word *communication* has been used for so long in so many metaphoric ways that the metaphoric extensions of the word can seem like concrete, ordinary usage. Nonetheless, when a systems theorist writes about communication rules in the family or about morphostatic and morphogenic communicative process, such use of the term "communication" is metaphoric because it goes far beyond standard meanings of communication into areas where the systems observer's capacity to perceive, classify, and generalize is informed and enhanced through metaphoric application of concepts such as rules, feedback, or openness in communicating. The Palo Alto group and others who have learned from them wrote not only about communication in the mundane sense but also about the concept of communication as it is greatly enriched and informed by insights gleaned from concepts brought metaphorically into the analysis of communication from other areas of thought.

What the Communication Metaphor Highlights

The concept of communication as it is used metaphorically in family systems theory highlights the potential of mundane communication to accomplish far more than the people communicating may realize or intend. It highlights how crucial communication is to a relationship and how much the dynamics of relationship, the processes of mutually getting along and remaining connected, are matters of communication, as opposed to individual attitudes and feelings, mere coresidence, or resource sharing. In using the word "communication" metaphorically, family systems theorists focus attention on the links among family members rather than on the individuals, on the interaction rather than on the coexistence, on the interplay of members of the system and not on the consequences of that interplay. The focus on communication makes family systems theory analysis necessarily work at attending to, studying, and modifying communication, rather than work at understanding individuals or the noncommunicative products of family relationship.

The metaphoric extensions of the concept of communication highlight that the metaphoric forms, the abstractions labeled by theorists as communication (e.g., boundary maintenance, feedback, rule enforcement, symptoms as communication), are as basic to family system functioning as are the communication processes that are part of the everyday conception of communication (e.g., talking and listening). Family systems theorists claim that the metaphoric communications processes on which they have focused are ubiquitous, basic, and fundamental. Related to this, family systems theories highlight how the processes that are metaphoric extensions of everyday experiences are like everyday experiences in that they require messages to be sent and received through such basic message-sending and message-receiving physical functions as speech, gesture, facial expression, hearing, and seeing. Thus, the metaphoric extensions of the concept of communication seem to highlight how virtually all humans have the capacity to function in the intricacies of patterning, pattern maintenance, and pattern change that family systems theorists claim are part of all family systems.

What the Communication Metaphor Obscures

The metaphoric extensions of the concept of communication were developed in conjunction with a behaviorism that seemed so objective that it was and is easy to miss the enormous inferential leaps and the awesome theoretical achievements of the systems theorists who were able to extend the meaning of the term "communication" metaphorically. Thus, one very important thing that is obscured by the systems theory metaphor of communication is that the concept has been extended metaphorically.

With family systems writings offering many penetrating analyses of the complexity and subtlety of communication, also obscured is the degree to which communication is challenging to capture, understand, and interpret. This is perhaps particularly so for the types of communication added by the metaphoric extensions of the meaning of "communication." Communication of any sort is a matter of guesswork. The event of A giving B a message that B "gets" is a matter of perception for A, for B, and for the observer. All have to make inferences about the message that A sent, the message that B perceived, and the validity of their bases for deciding these matters. Messages are often complicated, ambiguous, subtle, hard to articulate, inadequately expressed, internally contradictory, incomplete, qualified, content bound, contextualized, and open to alternative interpretations. Consequently, there may be no sure way to affirm that all parties have the same idea of what has been communicated. Even when A, B, and the observer all seem to agree, there is no sure way to know if they actually get the same thing or if what they get is what was there at the time the communication occurred.

The metaphoric extensions of "communication" seem often to be so grounded in what is concrete, so persuasive, and so brilliantly accurate that they obscure how much what is going on is the privileging of the family systems expert's focus and understandings. Even when practitioners and researchers make their account of communication seem simple and straightforward, it is still their account that is given most significance. Privileging their account does not change the complexity and ambiguity of the communications they analyze; nor does it do away with the possibility that the people whose communications they analyze might see things very differently.

The metaphor of communication also obscures how well or how often people get along in families with imperfect communication and vague or erroneous understandings. A family member may not understand a lot of what the other members say, gesture, signal, mean, or intend but may still get by without experiencing what he or she would consider serious problems. Many times a communicator may not be clear about what the intended message is; thoughts may be unclear or confused and may only be formed as the person tries to communicate or even after the communication recipient responds. A and B may commit a lifetime to each other because A says to B something that means to B "I love you," even though A, by A's own standards and honest self-awareness, may have felt and meant nothing in particular. Quite possibly, most of the fundamental concepts communicated in families—for example, "I feel healthy"; "I feel good about being with you"; "I am committed to you"; "Don't blame me"—may be imperfectly understood by any family member. And yet the members of the family may get along without serious difficulty. There may be enormous room for imperfect understanding in relationships in which all parties are satisfied and in which the necessary tasks of the relationship are carried out adequately. Or, to take an example closer to common family systems theory analyses, a family may seem to have patterned control of intimacy based on the repeated ways in which they are and are not intimate and based on their communications when family members deviate from the pattern. There may, however, be no communication about intimacy that a family member sends clearly or apprehends with certainty. There may be many messages sent that do not reach their target and many that are understood in very different ways by sender and intended receiver. What the systems analyst thinks are the active messages, the messages that make a difference in intimacy, may not be at all the messages that are making a difference. Indeed, it may not even be communication between family members that is responsible for a great deal of what is going on; it may be individual dispositions. How can we be confident that we understand a family's rules or that family members operate with the same rules when these are people who on a daily basis have confusions and misunderstandings over such simple communication matters as when a family member will come home from work or who will buy a carton of milk before arriving home?

The metaphor of communication at times has been used as though what was being characterized were a firm reality. To the extent that this has been so, it has obscured how the communication situation may often be one in which the people involved are co-constructing a reality (Berger & Kellner, 1964). There may be no firm rules, structures, boundaries, commitments, roles, and so forth. It is not, perhaps, that a system is built up into a solid structure that operates across time and situation but that in any interaction family members are building their perceptions and interpretations from their current and past communications and relationships.

The communication metaphor obscures the many situations in which the content is irrelevant and in which, as a consequence, our metaphoric extensions of the term "communication" are largely mistaken. Even when the communication is about matters that a family systems practitioner or researcher would take as centrally relevant to processes the theory deems important (e.g., core rules), what is going on may be something very different, perhaps only signalling that the channel of communication is open or that two people are in contact. Indeed, what may be going on in family communication may be something more like the development of communication processes rather than the expression and reinforcement of a system (Raush et al., 1979).

Finally, the communication metaphor obscures the reflexivity of communication (cf. Fisher, 1981). In order to understand something about communication, one must communicate about it. To the extent that a systems analysis of family communication focuses on a time-limited slice of ongoing communication processes, it stops the reflexivity process and thus obscures the importance of that process in correction and construction. How can we understand communication if our way of characterizing it limits the processes of the communicators and limits our own exposure to the communication process we hope to understand? From another angle, if reflexivity is so important in communication, how can we take an outside observer perspective on family communication and hope to understand it? To understand a family's communication, is it not necessary that we have ongoing interaction with family members as we work to understand their communication in their own terms?

OPEN AND CLOSED COMMUNICATION

One of the basic communication metaphors in family systems writings is that of open versus closed family communication (e.g., Bowen, 1978, chap. 15). Family communication can be characterized on a dimension of openness to closedness. Relatively open communication involves a great deal of freedom to communicate thoughts, feelings, opinions, fantasies, and so on among family members. Openness also involves the freedom to communicate congruently, completely, and honestly. Relatively closed communication involves blocking, walling off, distorting, or denying thoughts, feelings, opinions, fantasies, and truths. The closing may involve choices about what to communicate and what not to communicate, as well as "silencing strategies" (Zuk, 1965) to force compliance or conformity or to block or distort specific communications, communications in a specific area, or virtually all communications by a specific person. What makes openness–closedness a systems phenomenon, as opposed to a matter of personalities, is that it can be understood as a matter of interaction pattern (not individual disposition) and of family rules or mutual influence, with more than one family member supporting the pattern of relative openness or closedness and engaging in or complying with silencing strategies or strategies that promote openness.

Systems patterns of relative openness or closedness of communication are not necessarily simple. Bowen (1978, p. 322) argued that people are always closed about topics that at the moment are too threatening for them to deal with and that people also limit their communication to other family members in areas that make the others anxious. A family pattern of general openness or closedness may also be contingent on situational factors, such as who is present at the moment or what has happened in the family recently.

Closed communication is said to be associated with closed family systems (see Chapters 4 and 6) and hence with resistance to change and inflexibility. The closedness of a family system may be reinforced by closed communication so that family members do not interact about perceptions and feelings in ways that can open or change the system; it may also be reinforced by family rules that make it inappropriate to bring in new ideas or resources or to attempt to change family patterns. The association between closed communication and closed family systems can be seen in systems therapy writings about perverse family triangles (Haley, 1967) and about double binds (Bateson et al., 1956).

The metaphor of open versus closed communication draws on the elemental sense of things that open and close—doors, mouths, eyes, windows. When something is open, appropriate (and inappropriate) things can enter or exit; when something is closed, little or nothing passes through. The metaphor implies a mechanism of opening and closing as well as a palpability to openness and closedness (we can see what is open and closed directly or through the consequences of openness and closedness). The metaphor focuses on the sense of something real that is either held behind a barrier or allowed to pass through. It highlights how families seem to differ in how much family members disclose to one another, how much they tolerate disclosure, and how much of members' inner lives is a fit topic for conversation. The metaphor also suggests degrees of openness and the capacity for transformation to greater openness or closedness.

The metaphor obscures the transformability of communication. Very nearly the same message may be communicated in many different ways. People who seem closed to sending or receiving a message in one form may be much more open to another form. For example, family members may be closed to father saying, "The doctors say I have a metastasized cancer and am not likely to live more than six months." But they may be quite open to the message that father has a terminal illness if he says, "You all will have to do the taxes next year; be sure to check the tax file in my desk before you begin." Thus, the issue of open versus closed communication may often be a matter of whether family members have the flexibility, awareness, and skill to find a way to communicate that allows the message to get across. For family systems analysts, the parallel issue is whether they have the capacity to decode indirect communications the way the members of a given family decode them.

The open versus closed metaphor also seems to obscure how topics and situations, as opposed to families, may be crucial to consider when addressing matters of openness or closedness. Perhaps any family expresses quite a range from openness to closedness, so in some situations and on some topics family members will seem open while in other situations and on other topics they will seem closed. The question is then not so much one of characterizing a particular family but one of characterizing the topics or situations on which a particular family is open or closed.

As with many other systems metaphors that characterize a family, the metaphor of openness–closedness may obscure the ways in which the degree of openness may be a matter of personalities or dyads. In systems terms, the rules of openness and closedness may be quite different for different family members or different family pairs. Also, in some dyads or some families, there may be a great deal more openness coming from one family member than another, or family rules may allow some people more openness than others. For example, the rules may push children to be more open to saying certain things and more closed to being told or hearing certain things, or the rules may push parents or men or women to be relatively closed about certain feelings and thoughts and relatively open about others.

The implication in the open–closed metaphor of something real that is held back or sent ahead obscures the construction of social realities. When things seem closed, there may be no or very few actual messages held back; there may only be the avoidance of a process that through social interaction would cocreate feelings, thoughts, shared memories, facts, and so on. When things seem open, there may not be any or very few actual messages that are simply passed through the gates; instead, there may be an openness to an interaction process that cocreates realities. The metaphor of openness–closedness from this perspective obscures how inchoate and unformed private feelings and thoughts often are and how families that appear more open may simply be more active at working together to make something out of communications. Thus, the metaphor of openness–closedness may obscure how much openness and closedness is a matter of a family's interpretative process. In a closed communication setting the initial communications may typically be as available as in an open one, but in the closed one communications may be left uninterpreted or may be interpreted in ways that deny, trivialize, or obscure the realities that would be reached in an open communication situation.

Because it is in a sense a two-way metaphor, one of messages sent and messages received, the open–closed metaphor may obscure how in a family relationship there may be heterogeneity in openness–closedness. Family members may differ in how open they are to sending or to receiving certain messages. What appears to be family closedness on a given topic may, for example, be a matter of person X being closed to sending messages on that topic or of person Y being closed to receiving messages on that topic. For example, closed communication about a miscarriage in a heterosexual couple (Rosenblatt & Burns, 1986) may be an indication that the man does not want to burden the woman with his feelings, that the man does not want the responsibility of hearing about the woman's feelings, that the woman does not want to hear about her husband's feelings if they are different from hers, or that the woman does not want to tell her husband her feelings because it hurts too much to get in touch with the feelings. Questions about dispositional differences among family members that could lead to a pattern of openness or closedness on some topic are not trivial if a metaphor other than system openness–closedness would help to differentiate the various types and sources of openness and closedness.

Discussions of open versus closed communication almost always indicate that open communication is better. Bowen (1978, p. 323), for example, indicated that talking about death is always desirable for a person who is terminally ill. Perhaps there is truth to that, but one can wonder whether the metaphor of open versus closed communication obscures what can generally be lost from openness and gained from closedness. I do not want to persuade readers that closedness is desirable, since I myself value openness, but I want to make a case that family therapists, who are the principal creators and users of family systems theory ideas, may be biased in favor of open communication. Therapists must hear from clients in order to understand what is going on. They must talk to clients and be heard by them in order to do their work. Thus, therapists may, because of the requirements of their work, be biased in favor of open communication.

Nonetheless, in the values systems of many Americans, closed communication, by other names, is valued. It is often valued when, for example, it is called "tact," "circumspection," "keeping one's own counsel," or "not burdening others." Thus, the metaphor of open versus closed communication, to the extent that it is used to advocate open communication, may obscure the extent to which there is cultural valuing of closedness and the extent to which closed communication may be desirable in families.

Related to the point just made, the metaphor of open versus closed communication seems to imply that there is more freedom in families with relatively open communication, more freedom for members to express what is inside themselves and to know what is inside other members. However, there may be as much coercion in an open communication system as in a closed one. People may be as coerced to talk about their feelings, dreams, and so on in an open system as they are coerced in a closed system to keep things to themselves and to allow others to keep things to themselves. Moreover, if communication that is open involves active co-construction of reality, an open communication situation gives family members the opportunity to collaborate in reducing their freedom to perceive, think, and feel in uniquely individual ways.

METACOMMUNICATION

Metacommunication is another important theoretical metaphor dealing with communication in family systems (Watzlawick et al., 1967, chap. 2). It refers to communication about communication. Metacommunication is a metaphor because of the use of the prefix "meta-," which can modify a word in any of several different ways. In the compound word "metacommunication," "meta-" means "beyond," as in "Metacommunication is communication beyond the ordinary." The most common word in everyday English that uses the prefix "meta-" in the same way is "metaphysics," referring to the branch of philosophy that goes beyond the physical world to ultimate questions about existence, the universe, and the spiritual world. Metacommunication is beyond ordinary communication in that it is communication about communication.

As the term is used in family systems theory writings, metacommunication usually means communication by the family members being observed, though it may also be a therapist's communication to clients about their communication. Metacommunication may be explicit or implicit, verbal or nonverbal, rich and complex, or subtle and only hinted at. The verbalized form is defined in family systems writings as the communication level at which people make statements such as the following: "I am speaking to you this way because. . ."; "I don't want to answer your question because . . ."; "I want you to take what I am saying very seriously"; "When we try to problem solve together we need to stay more focused on the problem"; or "I think I misunderstood you; would you please say more?" With verbal metacommunication people comment about a communication or a general category of communication; make agreements about their communication; and discuss misunderstandings or in some other way evaluate, clarify, explain, comment on, or regulate their communication. Metacommunication implies a self-consciousness or self-awareness or a superordinate consciousness about communication, though conceivably metacommunication could go on without much self-consciousness, self-awareness, or superordinate perspective on communication. For example, a delay in answering a family member's question may be, even without awareness by the person who is delaying, a metacommunicative comment.

In family systems theory writings about communication it is the lack of metacommunication, or of truthful metacommunication, or of consistent metacommunication that is part of what is harmful and pathological about double-bind communications (Bateson et al., 1956) and perverse family triangles (Haley, 1967). Some family systems interventions are based on an analysis of metacommunication, and some teach skills at analyzing metacommunication and at metacommunicating in order to resolve family problems. From this perspective, metacommunication seems necessary for effective communication as family members recurrently come to terms with the fact that they understand or perceive things differently, that their assumptions about what is true or what has happened differ, and that their communication process does not always work well.

What Metacommunication
Highlights and Obscures

The metacommunication metaphor highlights the distinction be-tween communications that are not about communication and communications that are, the many different forms of communication about communication, and the potential metacommunications have to facilitate communication or to create problems.

Watzlawick et al. (1967, p. 95) speculated that the conviction that there is only one reality underlies a great deal of communication difficulty. To the extent that metacommunication is seen as a way of acknowledging and coming to terms with the multiplicity of realities, the metacommunication metaphor stresses a view of realities as multiple and also a sense that people can actually come to terms with their reality differences.

The metaphor of metacommunication may obscure the extent to which people function with no metacommunicational reality, that is, the extent to which there is "no comment" or no interpretable comment by family members at the level of communication about communication. Since it obscures how often realities may be fluid, metacommunication may have little value beyond the moment. A related point is that since family systems therapy realities are those dealing with ongoing relationship difficulty, there has been little or no interest or attention in metacommunication that is useful only momentarily (e.g., a metacommunication about the ambiguity of something specific a family member has just said), yet a great deal of metacommunication may be what Wilmot (1980) has called "epi-sodic," commenting on communication specifics more than on the relationship of the communicants.

The metaphor of metacommunication rests on distinctions among (1) content, (2) comments on the content, and (3) comments on the relationship of the communicators. Drawing those distinctions implies that some communications are not metacommunicative because they do not comment on content or on the relationship of the communicators. This way of understanding metacommunication obscures the ways in which all communications are metacommunica-tive because all content comments on all other content and on the relationship between the communicators (cf. Wilmot, 1980). That X communicates one content rather than another to Y is a comment on all subsequent communications from X to Y and also a comment on X's perception of the X–Y relationship.

To the extent that metacommunication is taken as a higher-order, relationship-protecting process, the metaphor of meta-communication may obscure how metacommunication can create or perpetuate difficulty, for example, by focusing attention on process to the detriment of important content, by framing simplistically what is best left as something not understood, or by disrupting and blocking information flow at the content level when that flow has a highly useful and cumulative information-giving effect. Finally, to the extent that the metacommunication metaphor highlights a sense that communication difficulties can be dealt with effectively it obscures the extent to which communication difficulties are irresolvable and the extent to which people with different realities cannot cross the gap of their differences.

Content and Command in Communication

In family system theory analysis of communication each message has a content or "report" level of facts, opinions, feelings, and experiences that can be evaluated as true or false. Each communication also has a "command" level, which comments on the relationship between the person sending the message and the person who is the intended recipient (Jackson, 1959, 1965a; Watzlawick et al., 1967, chap. 2). The command level, as a higher-order communication, that is, a communication about communication, can be understood to be a metacommunication (Watzlawick et al., 1967, pp. 53–54). It classifies the content of the communication. Watzlawick et al. (1967, p. 51) credited Bateson with originating the report and command metaphor (Ruesch & Bateson, 1951, pp. 179–181). His metaphor was based on a model of a linear chain of neurons—A, B, and C. The firing of B communicates (reports) the content that A has fired and, at the same time, commands C to fire. The command metaphor thus originated in metaphoric roots having to do with one entity's control over another. However, as Watzlawick et al. (1967, pp. 51–54) developed the metaphor, command seems more a matter of another level of communication that comments—and this usage seems to be the one that has been adopted in family systems thinking about metacommunication.

The command aspect of the communication "refers to what sort of a message it is to be taken as, and therefore, ultimately to the relationship between the communicants. All such relationship statements are about one or several of the following assertions: "This is how I see myself . . . this is how I see you . . . this is how I see you seeing me . . .' and so forth" (Watzlawick et al., 1967, p. 52). Thus, the command level of a communication defines the sender, the recipient, and the relationship between them.

In family systems analyses the command level of a family's communication can be expected to be patterned. The pattern may involve disagreements as well as agreements, and there may be as much patterning to disagreement at the command level as to agreement (Jackson, 1965a). Family members may, of course, be in conflict with each other about communication rules, or they may be in conflict because conflict is part of the communication rules. However, it seems reasonable to expect that as the typical relationship continues, the range of definitions in dispute tends to become narrower (Watzlawick et al., 1967, p. 133). This stabilization of definitions, and hence of the command level of communication, can be understood as an important aspect of family functioning. Definitional activities create realities. They make concrete what is unclear and open to multiple interpretations, focus people on whatever is consistent in their mutually communicated realities, and lead to interpretations of events, messages, and so on, in a way that supports the defined reality. There are also processes of self-fulfilling prophecy operating in family systems (Watzlawick et al., 1967, pp. 98–99) that lead a person to influence events so as to support her or his definition of reality.

The highlighting of the command level of communication alerts family systems analysts to the ways in which all family communications, no matter how trivial, are about family relationships. This awareness is valuable in therapeutic work and gives therapists powerful tools for family intervention, since therapists who are aware of the command level of communication can devise interventions that modify that level of communication in families and can themselves communicate at the command level in ways that affect the family.

The metaphor of command, by highlighting how much all messages can be understood to comment on self, other, and relationship, focuses on a crucial idea in family systems theory, namely, that a given communication contains many messages. With this comes the realization that in recognizing, replying to, or acknowledging only one of the messages contained in a communication one may miss or neglect what is central to what is going on.

As the metaphor of metacommunication is used in more recent family systems theory writings, it obscures what is clearer in the command metaphor—how any level of communication may comment on any other. Although Watzlawick et al. (1967, p. 54, n. 3) pointed out that the relationship aspect of a communication can be understood to classify or comment on the content level, so what communication is "meta" to another communication is a matter of analytic focus, the way they and others have written about command and content levels of communication seems to place the command level "meta" to the content level. By doing so the metaphor of command and content obscures how content can always be a comment on the relationship. For example, a content of assertions about the mistakes and immoral actions of a family member can comment very clearly on what the communicator thinks of that family member, and any communication is an indication of the communicator's perceptions of what the other is interested in and can understand. The command aspect of content is part of why family members can argue so much about "the facts." The identification by family members of the facts in any content that is a subject of communication may say too much about the relationship for feelings about the facts to stem solely from a cool analysis of truth and falsehood. For example, arguing over the facts concerning who in the family does the most housework can be understood as a matter for conflict because whatever the facts are says a great deal about relationships in the family.

The differentiation of content and command also obscures how much the command aspect of a communication may be all that is intended, with the content being arbitrary and of no real importance. In such cases, the word "content" is misleading; the command aspect of the communication *is* what counts. For example, in a couple in which one partner feels slighted and oppressed by the other, any and every content that is a matter of communication may be a vehicle for expressing those feelings. Neither partner may remember the content 5 minutes after they interact, but both may know clearly what feelings were expressed.

The metaphoric differentiation of content and command seems to imply that there is an essential reality to the differentiation that affects senders and receivers of a communication whether they can articulate anything more than the content level of the communication or not. The metaphor may, as a consequence, obscure the possibility that some people in some situations are unaware of the command level. Watzlawick et al. (1967, p. 52) claimed that the command level recedes to the background in spontaneous or "healthy" relationships, but it may be in the background in any relationship involving people who tune out or are unable to hear that level or whose communications are garbled or muffled at the command level.

The metaphoric differentiation of content and command also obscures how for some communicators the command level may be invariant across relationships and communication contents. In these latter cases, what is going on is not so much a family systems phenomenon as a personal disposition. For example, if a member of a family always communicates in all relationships a liking and respect for the communication recipient, characterizing the family communication command level in terms of liking and respect is misleading. There is something else or something more going on.

The metaphor of command also obscures, paradoxically, the systemic view of interaction that recognizes that all players in the system are playing (cf. Fisher, 1981), that interaction is *between* X and Y, not *from* X to Y. The command level of a communication is as much a matter of what the recipient of the communication perceives as it is what the sender sends. And the command level of a specific communication reflects both the current context and the entire history of communication of sender and recipient and their history of relationships with others in the family system and outside. Thus, the task of analyzing the command level of a specific message is complicated and enriched by an awareness of the role of all players in communicating and by the current and historical context of the specific message.

PARADOX

Borrowing from logic and mathematics, Watzlawick et al. (1967, p. 188) defined a paradox as a contradiction that follows correct deduction from consistent premises. Among the paradoxes found in family communication are paradoxical injunctions involving a demand for spontaneous behavior; spontaneity cannot exist if it is produced because of a demand. Another type of paradox in family communication is the self-description that seems internally illogical, for example: "I am a liar, so you must not believe me"; "I feel terrified that I have no feelings"; "I love you so much I could eat you up." If the recipient of a paradoxical communication cannot step outside the frame of the paradox, cannot find ways to make the logical contradictions no longer contradictory, or cannot escape the paradox, receiving a paradoxical communication will evoke a paradoxical response, one of internal contradiction, in the recipient. The paradoxical response of the recipient in turn produces renewed paradoxical response in the initial message-sender. Thus, paradoxical communication has a capacity to recur in a family (Watzlawick et al., 1967, pp. 214–215).

The metaphor of paradoxical communication in families highlights the ways in which family members may communicate to one another things that cannot simultaneously be true. It underscores the problems that can occur in relationships as a result of contradictory communication, especially if the contradiction cannot be cleared up through additional interaction or through individual processes of reframing. It highlights also how paradox in the family can drive a continuing pattern of paradoxical communication in the family.

Although Watzlawick et al. (1967, p. 188) recognized the

fuzziness of the metaphor of paradoxical communication (because of the extent to which additional knowledge or alternative perspectives can eliminate what seems to be paradoxical), the literature on paradoxical communication in families and in family therapy seems to lose that sense of fuzziness. Thus, as it is commonly used, the metaphor of paradoxical communication obscures the fact that a specific observer or family member may not be aware that a paradox has been stated. What seems contradictory to one person may not to another, who understands a way for the pieces to fit together and make sense, who understands unvoiced assertions that neutralize the paradox, or who understands the words differently from someone who hears them as paradox. Similarly, what seems like no paradox at all to one person may seem quite paradoxical to another.

The metaphor of paradoxical communication also obscures how much communication in families is not necessarily subject to the logic adhered to by the systems observer or to the need for rigorous clarity that is present in mathematics and logic. Although the metaphor of paradoxical communication has made many a family clinician or researcher into something of a logician, many people may function in the family context without any concern about what may appear to an observer to be illogical. Even those family members who have concerns about logic may adhere to a logic that is different from that of the family clinician or researcher. (There is more than one logic taught in university philosophy departments, and there is a diversity of logics across cultures.) In everyday life people may comfortably live with paradox and contradiction. Indeed, a case can be made that paradox is common, central, and necessary in the lives of many people. For example, Brice (1991) has written about the many paradoxes that seem understandable, normal, and psychologically appropriate in the life of a bereaved mother who may simultaneously desire talk and shun talk about a deceased child and may believe both that the death is final and that the death has not ended her relationship with the deceased. The metaphor of paradoxical communication may alert us to problems that can arise in family communication, but we may need a more precise notion of which paradoxes are paradoxes for family members and which paradoxes create serious problems.

THE METAPHOR OF COMMUNICATION PATHOLOGY

There is a rich literature on communication pathology in families, with numerous clinical examples and conceptual approaches. The metaphor of pathology in family communication is borrowed from concepts of physical disease. When extended metaphorically to communication, the pathology metaphor implies communication patterns that are harmful to family relationships and to individual family members (see Watzlawick et al., 1967, chap. 3). One example of such a pattern involves recurrently saying something critical of another family member while appearing to be talking about trivia, doing so in a way that makes it impossible to challenge or to speak to the criticism. Another example involves a pattern of recurrently saying nothing while apparently saying something. If family members must act as though something has been said when they have no idea what might have been said, it can make great difficulty for them.

The metaphor of communication pathology enables creative use of all the concepts associated with ideas of disease. It stimulates questions about etiology, epidemiology, contagion, cure, and so on. It highlights how family communication patterns can cause difficulty in the family, and it sets a negative value on those patterns. The pathology metaphor highlights the possibilities for diagnosis, research on treatment and prevention, and cure.

The communication pathology metaphor obscures the ways in which a disease concept of communication may not be appropriate. It obscures how what goes on in family communication rarely has anything to do with biological mechanisms of illness and health but has everything to do with language and social relationships; how what one person considers a pathology may not be considered a pathology by another or how what is harmful in some sense in one family may not be harmful in that sense (or, perhaps, in any other) in another family; how other metaphors may be more appropriate when dealing with family communication (e.g., metaphors about the negotiation of reality, selective attention, or the coding and decoding of language). The communication pathology metaphor, like all the communication metaphors discussed in this chapter, has been enormously rich and productive in family systems thinking, but entirely different metaphors might also be enriching and productive and might get at what the communication pathology metaphor obscures.

SUMMARY

This chapter has explored the metaphors of communication, open and closed communication, metacommunication, paradox, and communication pathology. "Communication," as it is used in family systems theory, is metaphoric in that it imports concepts that go far beyond the everyday meaning of communication. The metaphor of communication highlights the potential of communication to accomplish far more than the people communicating may realize, the extent to which family relationships are matters of communication, and the ways the aspects of communication incorporated in the metaphoric extensions (e.g., boundary maintenance, feedback) are as basic to family system functioning as the aspects of communication that are part of the everyday conception of communication. The metaphor of communication obscures that the metaphoric extensions of the concept of communication are metaphoric extensions and the degree to which all communication is challenging to capture, understand, and interpret. It also obscures how much systems analysis of communication privileges the observer's views, how much people get by with imperfect communication, how the communication situation may be one in which people are co-constructing a reality, the many situations in which communication content is irrelevant, and the place of reflexivity in family members' understanding one another.

The metaphor of open and closed communication highlights the sense of something real that is either held behind a barrier or allowed into the open and the apparent differences among families in how much family members disclose to one another. The metaphor obscures how a family that is closed to one version of a communication may be open to another; how topics and situations, as opposed to families, may be crucial to consider when addressing matters of openness or closedness; the extent to which openness–closedness may be a matter of individual dispositions; and how when things seem closed, there may be no or very few actual messages held back but an avoidance of certain kinds of processing of messages.

Metacommunication refers to communication about communication. The metaphor highlights the distinction between communications that are not about communication and communications that are, the many different forms of communication about communication, and the potential metacommunications have to facilitate communication or to create problems. The metaphor of metacommunication may obscure the extent to which people function with no metacommunicational reality, how often realities may be so fluid that metacommunication may have little value, and the extent to which all content comments on all other content and on the relationship between the communicators. To the extent that metacommunication is taken as a relationship-protecting process, the metaphor of metacommunication may obscure how metacommunication can create or perpetuate difficulty and cannot clear up some kinds of problems.

In family systems theory analysis of communication, each message has a content or "report" level that can be evaluated as true or false and a "command" level, which comments on the relationship between the person sending the message and the person who is the intended recipient. The command level can be understood to be a metacommunication. The metaphor of command level alerts us to the ways in which all family communications are about family relationships and the ways that any communication contains several messages. The differentiation of content and command obscures how much the command aspect of a communication may be all that is intended and seems to imply that there is an essential reality to the differentiation that affects communication senders and receivers whether or not they can speak about it. The metaphor of command also obscures the systemic view of interaction, namely, that interaction is *between* X and Y, not *from* X to Y.

The metaphor of paradox in family communication, borrowed from logic and mathematics, highlights the ways in which family members may communicate to one another things that cannot simultaneously be true and the problems that can occur in relationships as a result of such communication. The metaphor of paradoxical communication obscures the iffiness of any specific observer's sense that there is a paradox and the way in which families are not necessarily subject to the logic of the observer.

The metaphor of pathology in family communication, borrowed from concepts of physical disease, highlights how communication patterns can be harmful in families and the possibilities for diagnosis, research on treatment and prevention, and cure. The pathology metaphor obscures the ways in which a disease concept of communication may not be appropriate, obscuring, for example, how what one person considers a pathology may not be a pathology for another or how what is harmful communication in one family may not be harmful in another.

CHAPTER EIGHT

Metaphors of Family
Systems Therapy

F amily systems therapy is often metaphor-
sensitive—with careful attention to client metaphors and with
therapeutic use of metaphors. This chapter looks at metaphor in family
systems therapy in a different way. Instead of looking at client
metaphors or the metaphors used to facilitate client change, this
chapter explores the metaphors used to characterize family systems
therapy and its outcomes. Exploring these metaphors is important
because the metaphors that are used create certain realities at the
expense of other conceivable realities. Understanding what the
metaphors of family systems therapy highlight and obscure will help us
to understand what family systems therapy highlights and obscures.
From a Lakoff and Johnson perspective, one could say that the choice
of theoretical metaphors constrains the way family systems therapists
think about therapy.

Family therapy is itself a metaphor. It is drawn from medical
concepts of healing. The family therapy metaphor highlights how
clients need something like healing, that there is a problem that needs
fixing or pain that needs to be relieved. It also highlights a need for
healer expertise. Just as physicians require specialized training and
knowledge to heal, so too do family therapists require training to
become experts with technical competence and advanced knowledge.
However, with a key organizing metaphor borrowed from medicine,
the family therapy metaphor obscures much that is important in family
therapy and leads to limitations in therapeutic practice and in

understanding of the therapeutic process. In order to understand what the metaphors of family systems therapy highlight and obscure, it seems crucial to first analyze the metaphors of therapeutic goals, the metaphors of the therapist in the system, and the metaphors of family response to therapeutic intervention.

THERAPEUTIC GOALS IN FAMILY SYSTEMS THERAPY

Metaphors That Fit Intervention Goals

Family systems therapists are interested in intervening with families to change them or to help them change. Many family systems therapists are interested in theoretical approaches that enable them to help families become "unstuck," that is, to help families recognize, circumvent, or minimize whatever might be destructive, causing pain, or blocking them from healthy relationships and healthy individual functioning. Consequently, most of the creative work, most of the work of editorial gatekeepers for the family therapy literature, and most of what there is to learn about family systems therapy is directed toward ways therapists can help troubled families change. Understanding therapeutic work as involving a therapist as a facilitator of change highlights the value of therapist actions, understanding of family systems, concern about therapeutic goals, and therapist responsibility for the process and outcomes of therapy. However, understanding therapeutic work as involving the therapist as facilitator of change limits the kinds of metaphors that can be used to characterize family therapy. Very different theoretical metaphors could be applied if the therapist were defined not as an intervenor but as, say, a witness to family interactions, a describer of the family, a resource for the family, a referee, or as one who acknowledges what family members say and do. Similarly, very different theoretical metaphors could be applied if family members were understood to be in therapy to work on things themselves rather than to experience intervention or if they were understood to have goals other than change, for example, achieving understanding, putting words to their experience, or learning how much they are like other families.

The constraints of intervention lead to metaphors that characterize families as not being able to find the requisite transformative processes in themselves or in their environment. With such metaphors, family systems therapy may minimize or ignore transformative processes in families and in the environment of families. With intervention metaphors, family systems therapy theories may minimize or ignore how what seems to be family pathology may be reduced or disappear without intervention. They may miss how much a family seeking intervention may find what it needs without the help of a therapy professional.

The constraints of intervention lead to metaphors that indicate the possibilities for intervention in depicting client families. Consequently, the standard metaphors of family systems theory may miss what is not useful in intervention. There must be something that the practitioner can do that will make something different. Perhaps that is why control mechanisms receive so much attention in the family systems literature. It is not simply that system control keeps the system doing whatever it has been doing; control mechanisms are also a place for intervention. The concern with family boundaries may also represent the intervention focus; it is partly because the therapist is on the outside and needs to find entrances to the system so as to intervene that boundaries are so interesting.

The metaphor of client resistance also can be understood to arise from an intervention approach to therapy. Intervention implies what de Shazer (1982) called "The contest model of therapy." He described how the contest model arose, prior to the advent of family therapy, in individual therapy, with the therapist pushing for change through client insight into anxiety-evoking experiences and the client resisting. With the move toward interactional therapy, de Shazer said, the resistance was still seen as located in the client, though therapists like Milton Erickson (Haley, 1973) and Watzlawick, Weakland, and Fisch (1974) moved to forms of therapeutic contest that tolerated or made use of the resistance rather than combatting it. Consequently, de Shazer pointed out, even in more interactional therapies the resistance metaphor obscured the ways that resistance is interactional rather than located in the client or clients. That is, resistance can be understood to be the joint product of therapist and client. Other ways to conceptualize client resistance in family therapy certainly have been useful and influential (e.g., Anderson & Stewart, 1983). However, thinking of client resistance as a metaphor can empower a therapist to see the part she or he may have in the apparent client resistance. Seeing resistance as interactional, the therapist may be freer to explore alternative approaches to dealing with the resistance.

With metaphors that fit intervention goals, the family systems theories that family therapists work with are a fraction of all the family systems theories that can be conceived. There are many alternative family systems theory metaphors that do not serve the goals of intervention but meet numerous conceivable alternative goals that might be helpful to families, for example, understanding a family, appreciating a family, organizing and integrating information about a family, developing a complete history of a family, witnessing family interactions, contextualizing family experiences, or disclosing to members of a family what they do not know about one another. The metaphors that would be useful in gathering the history of a family that has come for help or in working to provide the maximum amount of self-disclosure among family members have not been developed. Nor are they likely to be developed in the family therapy field unless they seem to be useful for intervention or unless there is less investment in intervention as the model of therapy.

Metaphors of Presenting Problems and Therapeutic Goals

Therapy is carried out and evaluated in terms of therapeutic goals. Early in therapy there must be goal setting in order to provide coherence and direction to the therapeutic process. The metaphor of therapeutic goal setting is drawn from other areas of life in which people establish goals. However, the goals of therapy may often be much less concrete and much more difficult to articulate than goals in many other areas of life. Compared to other goals of family members—for example, buying a house, getting off to school or work on time, taking a vacation—the goals of therapy seem indefinite and subjective. Moreover, it seems much harder to evaluate whether a family has achieved therapeutic goals than to evaluate whether a family has bought a house or taken a vacation.

Therapeutic goal setting begins with the metaphor of the presenting problem, the concern that family members are said to offer as their reason for coming to therapy. The idea of presentation is drawn from such areas of life as presenting someone with a gift or an award. The metaphor of the presenting problem highlights the ways in which clients can and do explain why they have come to therapy. It underlines the value of therapist respect for the goals clients verbalize and the relevance of what goes on in a first therapeutic session to what happens over the entire course of therapy.

The metaphor of the presenting problem obscures how there may be no problem presented or no problem that all family members agree upon, how people may not be able to articulate their problems or articulate them clearly, and how a family may only present individual problems (so that any translation into a family presenting problem is a distortion of family reality).

The metaphor of presentation obscures how much the presenting problem is a device created by the therapist. This is a matter that will be discussed further in the next section of this chapter, but it is important to say here that the word "presenting" makes the clients the players and defines the therapist as an outsider with no apparent responsibility for the presenting problem or perhaps even for defining the initial therapeutic goals. Yet therapists often actively elicit the presenting problem from clients, discuss it with them in order to clarify it, and make it a focus that obscures other matters that are harder to articulate or to discern. Thus, the metaphor of the presenting problem obscures how much therapists are players in defining the problem (see Sluzki, 1992) and denies their responsibility in setting up a situation in which they try to heal the very problem they have defined or have co-constructed.

The metaphor of initial goal setting in therapy obscures how often therapists fish for goals as the therapy goes on, how they may come to many different goals through the course of therapy, and how it is often only after the therapy that they come to articulate what the goals of the therapy were. Thus, the metaphor of therapeutic goals obscures both the trial-and-error nature of therapy and the ways social construction goes on from the beginning to some time after the end of therapy in order to make sense of the therapy.

THE METAPHORS OF THE THERAPIST IN THE SYSTEM

There is a substantial therapy literature using the metaphor of the family system that is misleading in that it leaves out the therapist (Berger & Jurkovic, 1987; de Shazer, 1992; Keeney, 1982, 1983, pp. 134–135). One of the ways the therapist is in the system has to do with the therapist's role in defining the family. Although many metaphors for families in therapy seem to characterize the family as an objectively describable entity, they are misleading in not acknowledging how the therapist's subjectivity and selectivity are involved in the characteriza-tion. In part because of this subjectivity and selectivity, the therapist is part of the system (Erickson, 1988; Hoffman, 1990). It is misleading to speak in objective terms of a family system that existed prior to therapy and that exists outside of the therapy office.

A metaphor for characterizing the system that includes the therapist as depicter and definer of the family might be the artist who paints a portrait of a family. With the metaphor of the artist painting the family, it would also be important to show how the family is posed by the artist, who also establishes an emotional tone for the family through the interactions she or he has with them. Despite discussions in the therapy field about when to choose to practice therapy inside or outside the system, once the therapist interacts with family members in any way, it is a system that includes the therapist, not an entity that exists independently of the therapist. While performing therapy, the therapist is part of the system. Sometimes the shared nature of the system is represented directly, as in written, audio, or video records of dialogue that include the therapist as *a*—if not *the*—key player. Sometimes the shared nature of the system is represented more indi-rectly, with the therapist taking the role of director or playwright for the family cast of players. In these cases the system that includes the therapist is represented through the therapist's report of having worked with the family to set a therapeutic contract or of having given the family challenging questions or a task to carry out in the therapy office or at home.

As was said earlier in this chapter, the metaphor of the presenting problem provides another way in which the therapist is a system player. This metaphor indicates that it is clients who bring something into therapy that must be worked on and that what they bring in is a problem (as opposed, say, to a curiosity about themselves or a desire to be known). This problem is open to reinterpretation by the therapist, who may see it as only part of the family difficulty, as masking other problems, or as defining the family's situation in a way that blocks desirable family change. In fact, it is common in published family therapy reports to show how incorrect or incomplete the presenting problem as initially defined by the family was by showing that it was later found to distort or overlook crucial family difficulties. For example, the child genius in the family turns out to be retarded or the family member alleged to have agoraphobia turns out not to be the one who really has this disorder or not to be the only spouse with agoraphobia. By eliciting the presenting problem, negotiating agreement from key members of the family that it is the problem, defining the presenting problem as a symptom of system problems, and then interacting with the family in a way that makes the therapist a player in dealing with the problem, the family system therapist invalidates a family systems model that omits the therapist. If presenting problems could be taken on face (Lowe, 1990), without therapeutic irony, the significance of the therapist in the family's process would be reduced though not eliminated. This is partly because the therapist would not have such an active role in defining what is to be dealt with. It is also because defining what families bring into therapy as problems may create a situation in which the therapist continues to be more active than is necessary. Some of what families bring to the therapist may actually require much less therapist activity if understood as something other than a problem. For example, a dilemma, confusion, concern, or misunderstanding may require much less therapeutic action than a "problem" would to be dealt with effectively by a family.

Another metaphor that reflects the place of the therapist in the system is the metaphor of the therapy session. It is a metaphor that is presumably based on the concept of medical treatment sessions. Typically, in medicine the problems that are treated in an office session are identical to the problems outside the office; a broken leg or a tumor in the office is not different from what it is outside of the office. However, the metaphoric transfer of meaning to family therapy obscures the ways in which what the therapist sees may be different from what goes on outside the therapy office. The processes of the therapy session that involve the therapist as participant and that occur in a location that is not the family's own turf may be taken in some family therapy writings as having a strong relationship to what goes on in the client family outside of the therapy office. Thus, if the therapy seems to work, it is assumed to do so by getting things to happen in the therapy office that are presumed to be strongly connected to the rest of the client family's life. However, the links between therapy sessions and the rest of what goes on in a family's life are not necessarily straightforward.

METAPHORS OF FAMILY RESPONSE TO THERAPEUTIC INTERVENTION

There is nothing more important in the literature on family systems therapy than the metaphors of family response to intervention. It is through these metaphors that therapists decide on therapeutic goals or on how to transform presenting problems into therapeutic goals. It is through these metaphors that therapists come to understand what they are doing and the relative importance of client action versus therapist action (Wahlström, 1990) and to decide what to do with families, what is good for families, and when therapy is complete. The potential for good rests on these metaphors—and also the potential for mischief. What follows is a discussion of what seem to me to be the core metaphors of family change in therapy.

Metaphoric Criteria of Family Well-Being

The Metaphor of Becoming a Healthy Family

The health metaphor is commonly explicit in family systems therapy writings and is almost always implicit if it is not explicit. A healthy family is understood to have certain characteristics, to have characteristics within a certain range, and to lack certain other characteristics. Health is so much a positive value in the United States and in the other countries in which family therapy most often is carried out that it is scarcely a value to be questioned. Yet it is surely a metaphoric leap to move from a medicine that deals with viruses, cancers, and broken limbs to the social science and psychology of relationships.

One thing that is obscured in metaphorically defining certain family system characteristics as healthy or unhealthy is how much the criteria of family system health are bound to culture and class. Family therapists come up against the culture- and class-bound nature of their conceptions of family system health when dealing with families that have members who are from a different culture or class than that of the therapist. Consider, for example, treating people from a culture or class that values what is commonly disapproved of in family therapy—for example, denial rather than the expression of anger or sorrow, corporal punishment of children defined as misbehaving, or communication cutoffs in the family as a legitimate reaction to perceived insults or unfairness. Even when dealing with people who are ostensibly from the same culture or class, therapist interest in helping a family move to what the therapist sees as a healthier relationship—something less chaotic, more respectful, or with less conflict—may be based on an obscuring of the diversity and relativity of values within what could appear to be a homogeneous culture or class. In fact, a case can be made that any family structure can be healthy or unhealthy (Constantine, 1986, pp. 26, 40–41), depending not only on the values one applies in evaluating families but also on how the structure meets or does not meet the goals and needs of the individual family members and of the family as a whole.

In defining certain family system characteristics as healthy or unhealthy, not only is a medical concept extended metaphorically to apply to family systems, but the concept of individual health is extended metaphorically to the family. In that metaphoric extension what is understood by most therapists as healthy in the individual is often seen as healthy in family systems. The healthy family is seen as a good communicator, trusting, a respecter of others, responsible, a good citizen, avoidant of great danger, reasonably careful about diet, and so on. Extending individual concepts of health highlights how what is good for individuals often seems to be good for a collection of individuals. However, the metaphoric extension obscures how good communication, trust, and so on, at the family level are qualitatively different phenomena from those at the individual level. For example, good communication at the individual level may involve generic skills at listening, saying things clearly, and knowing how to be aware of one's feelings and thoughts in ways that allow them to be communicated. Good communication at the family level, by contrast, may involve social dynamics that include not only saying things clearly but checking out the meanings of what is said, not only knowing feelings and thoughts but helping to make an environment in which it is safe for others to know feelings and thoughts. It is all too easy when extending an individual metaphor to the level of the family to lose track of how a social entity like a family has important emergent properties that do not exist in the individual.

The extension of the medical model also brings with it the concept of cure. The concept of cure makes sense when applied to a broken leg, a cancer, or a bacterial infection. The concept of cure, when extended metaphorically to family difficulties, can make mischief. Who is to say what a cure is in relationships? Family members can say they are getting along fine, but by somebody's standards there may be serious problems. Family members may be extremely distressed and committed partners may be thinking of leaving each other in response to something in each other that a therapist or other outsider fails to see as a problem or even considers healthy. Experts may disagree about what is a cure in relationships, and a cure in the sense of dealing with a presenting problem or providing a family with skills or orientations to deal with one specific problem may leave other problems still festering or may be dynamically linked to the development of new problems.

What therapists who reject the medical model may work for is not cure but something else: for example, greater skills at communicating or coping, new perceptions of self or other family members, the uncovering of family secrets, increased willingness to work on the relationship, or more realistic expectations for the relationship. Nothing is healed; no illness disappears. But something may happen that makes a family more livable or survivable, that increases members' comfort in the family, or that gives someone a clearer sense that his or her family is not the best place to stay.

The concept of cure implies the healing of a single entity. But the family is a collection of people, and what is optimal for one person may not be for another. What is welcomed as a change by one person may be anathema to another. How do we define "cure" when family members differ?

Finally, the concept of "cure" implies a great deal that does not apply to families: the absence of recurrence of problems, the implication that something is abnormal about the problems families bring to therapy (though they often come with the normal distress concomitant to normal family living—e.g., grief over a death, struggles to work out gender roles, concerns about teenagers). "Cure" also implies that the problems are in the family even when the problems may be in the community or society. It is the society, for example, that creates the environment for chemical dependency or for gender relationships in the family. The discussion could be extended, but the basic point is clear. Cure is a metaphor that comes with the medical model and makes trouble in family therapy.

The Metaphor of Being Stuck

Another central metaphor in family systems therapy writing is the metaphor of being stuck (i.e., being in a place of pathological homeostasis or morphostasis, being rigidly unresponsive to family or environmental factors that make change desirable, lacking adaptability, being inflexible, being unable to get past problems that other families get past). Presumably, if a family were not in some way stuck, it would not need help. The metaphors of "stuckness" are drawn from many sources. People experience stuckness in many concrete ways, for example, vehicles mired in mud or broken down mechanically, dresser drawers that won't pull out, bus riders stranded when the bus doesn't show up, doors that are jammed shut, household appliances requiring repairs that stump them.

The extension of the concept of stuckness to family systems highlights the ways that family systems resist change and are disabled in the face of certain problems. The metaphor is used to explain why a family cannot seem to solve its own problems and why clinical intervention is necessary. The metaphor is thus key in legitimating family therapy. It is also useful in explaining apparent failures of therapeutic intervention. We can talk about stuckness when a clinical intervention intended to make a desired change leads to family actions that either cancel the effects of the change or seem to make the change a disaster (Watzlawick et al., 1967, pp. 134–135). For example, progress at helping a child who is the family scapegoat to cope better at home and in school may lead the family to attack the child in new ways or may lead to another member of the family being scapegoated.

The metaphor of family stuckness in the face of attempts at therapeutic change may seem to imply that the mechanisms for the stuckness are in the family (as opposed to being in the therapy or in the larger society). The implication that the stuckness is in the family has its uses in stimulating the family system therapist to search for something in the family that blocks change. The therapist may find, for example, that the previously scapegoated child may miss the attention or the feelings of power that came with being the scapegoat, or another child in the family who is newly acting out may resent the loss of the favored child role. Other possibilities include that the pre-intervention roles are maintained because they are comfortable for family members or that the child who had been identified as the scapegoat enacted a symptom that is widespread in the family (e.g., all children in the family have school phobias or are antisocial). Related to this is the idea that the symptom bearer is in some sense covering for other family members, as, for example, when one adult partner's anxiety obscures the extent to which the other adult partner has similar anxieties (Fry, 1962). All these possibilities are interesting and may lead to effective intervention, but they also may miss what is obscured by the metaphor of the stuck family.

One thing the metaphor of stuckness obscures is that it is often the observer's view of what goes on in the family (cf. Erickson, 1988). Family members may see things very differently. For example, they may think that they have changed enormously, or they may perceive the change the therapist has been trying to facilitate as unhealthy, immoral, or of too little benefit to be worth their effort.

The metaphor of overcoming stuckness in the face of attempts at therapeutic intervention (and in fact every metaphor of family systems therapy) also obscures how much what goes on in therapy can be understood as talk (Lowe, 1990). The therapy literature emphasizes how much what is dealt with in therapy is behavior and feelings. However, since a considerable amount of what a therapist learns about client behaviors and feelings is communicated through client words, it is fair to say that much of what therapy is about is talk. Thus, it is possible that what seems like an overcoming of stuckness may be more a matter of words than of behavior, and a family that is understood to be stuck may be stuck primarily at the level of words. Moreover, a family that seems to have changed may not have changed at the level of behavior or feelings as much as at the level of words.

The Metaphor of Family Coping

Coping (e.g., with separation and divorce, the birth of a handicapped child, terminal illness, a death, economic difficulties) is an important concept in the family systems therapy literature. The concept of coping refers to a degree of success in struggling with some sort of adversity. The application of the concept of coping to families can be considered a metaphoric extension of a concept from individual psychology. There were extensive writings on the "psychology of adjustment" and on individual coping with stress prior to the development of an extensive literature on family coping. Extended to family systems, the metaphor of individual coping stresses how a family faces adversity as a unit, how standards of doing better or worse at dealing with the adversity can be applied to entire families, how adversities dealt with poorly at the level of the family may disrupt or even shatter family relationships, and how many difficulties are not matters of individual coping but of family members coping together.

Extended to families, the metaphor of coping obscures the diversity of family experience. What seems like coping at the family level may be beneficial, helpful, and comfortable for some family members and harmful, unhelpful, and painful for others. For example, some family members may flourish when the family copes with a death by talking about feelings whereas other family members may find it agonizing and very disruptive to engage in such talk.

Coping is a matter of standards. To say that coping has occurred requires that somebody's standards be applied. But whose? The observer's? That of each individual family member? The metaphor of family coping implies an objectivity that obscures the question of whose standard is to be applied. Often it is the therapist or other family specialist who evaluates coping, with the coping metaphor and the language of objectivity obscuring the extent of observer subjectivity in the choice of means of assessment and in the choice of the standards themselves. The metaphor of coping also obscures how much it may be the observer's judgment about what is or is not a source of stress. Were family members to be asked about sources of stress, it might be discovered that some of the things that family researchers and clinicians consider sources of stress (e.g., a child's handicaps, a family member's alcohol addiction) are taken for granted by some family members and not experienced by them as stressful. By contrast, other things that are not counted as stressful by family researchers and clinicians (e.g, shopping for groceries, answering the phone) are experienced as stressors by some individuals and families.

Metaphors of Reconnecting

In various ways family systems therapy can be a therapy of reconnecting. Estranged spouses or siblings may be reconnected, as may parents and offspring who have been distant from each other. The metaphors of reconnecting are of course rooted in the many other concepts of connection in American English: connecting electronic equipment to power sources, connecting railroad cars, connecting telephone circuitry.

The metaphors of connecting suggest the ways in which family members may be more or less in contact, both in terms of behavior and in terms of feelings. However, the metaphors of connecting obscure how much family members may be connected or have the potential to be connected even when appearing estranged. They obscure the connection that comes with conflict and hostility and the ways that estrangement may sustain a relationship (Simmel, 1955). Nor do they indicate how limited the connections may be that seem to have been engineered in therapy, limited in terms of durability and the number of changes that have actually been made. They obscure what systems theory might lead us to suspect, namely, that a strengthened connection in one place in a person's life may result in weakened connections (at least in terms of time and energy available for interaction) elsewhere. Thus, reducing the estrangement between parent and adult offspring may well reduce the connections of one or both of them with a spouse or friends. Finally, the metaphors of connection obscure the fact that what links people is very different from what links railroad cars or electronic equipment. What links people are such intangible things as feelings, acknowledgment, acceptance, shared experience, and similarity, things far more insulated from observation than are most connections in the physical world.

Metaphors of Insight

Historically, in the family systems therapy field there has been a great deal of hostility to therapies with insight goals. Nonetheless, there have always been family system therapies designed to produce insights that lead to behavior change (e.g., Benson, Schindler-Zimmerman, & Martin, 1991). Techniques such as role playing or circular questioning can give family members insights into how they are perceived by other family members or how the family deals with difficulties. Having achieved the insights, family members may then be motivated or enabled to change.

Like insight metaphors in individual therapy, the insight metaphors in family systems therapy are drawn from the realm of perception and discovery. Family members are helped to see, to realize, to perceive, and so on. Such metaphors highlight the clarity of realization and discovery that can come when a person is faced with evidence, including the words of the therapist and the words and actions of other family members. Insight metaphors also highlight how powerful an impetus for change new perceptions and discoveries occurring in therapy can be.

One thing insight metaphors applied to families obscure is the differentiation of experience. It is unlikely that all family members will see things in the same way or make the same sense of some input. Thus, it may be that a specific insight is gained by some family members and not others. Consequently, changes may not be spread evenly through the family; even if all family members seem to be changing, some may be changing through dynamics that have nothing directly to do with insight.

Another thing that may be obscured by insight metaphors is that it may not be the insight but the significance given to the insight that is crucial in the insight process. It is not merely that on circular questioning family member X said such and such or that in a role play the children did Y after a parent did Z. The point is that someone, quite possibly the therapist, has pushed all to accept a seemingly new view of things. It may even be that a transforming insight is not new to anyone in the family (e.g., that Dad is an alcoholic), but it has been given a different significance through the therapeutic process. For example, even though the story of Dad's alcoholism is new to no one in the family, the story may become useful in new ways, now accounting for assorted difficulties experienced by individual family members and the family as a whole.

Family System Test Scores as Metaphors

Paper-and-pencil tests of family system functioning may be used to index family change. These measures are usually linked to family systems therapy concepts through the labels attached to the family scores. In fact, all family system test scores can be understood as metaphors (see the discussion of the FACES measure in Chapter 5). The names of the scales are borrowed from other areas of discourse, and the response of family members to the scales is not an enactment of the family patterns that the scales are intended to assess.

Test scores may be reified and families may be labeled because of their scores, but the family's performance on the test is usually not part of the domain of family systems at all (the family did not enact its systemic qualities). Thus, any paper-and-pencil test measuring family functioning is linked to family functioning, at best, indirectly. Nor does a test escape being metaphoric when validated against criteria (e.g., other tests, therapist ratings) that are themselves metaphoric and metaphorically connected to everyday family system functioning. The validation process does not make the test score any less a metaphor. Thus, to say that on a test a family is coping, healthy, adjusted, or communicating well is to borrow concepts from other arenas and apply them to the test scores.

That paper-and-pencil test scores are considered useful may come in part from the metaphoric power of the labels they apply to families. However, it is not merely the labels that are useful but also the metaphoric connections of the labels to more elaborate scripts, stories, concepts, and theories about families. Consider a family that receives a low score on a paper-and-pencil test on communication. The test score is considered useful at least in part because the concept of poor communication on the test is linked to so much else that is known about poor communication. If the metaphoric representation of the family is reified, we may lose track of how scores on the test have no real relationship to all those other things we know about poor communication.

Feminist Views on Metaphors of Therapeutic Change

Feminist critics of family systems therapy (e.g., Goldner, 1985, 1988; McGoldrick et al., 1989; Hare-Mustin, 1987) have pointed out how much theories of family system therapy focus on the microdynamics of the family and not on the societal context of the family that disadvantages women and privileges men. These critics help us to see that theoretical metaphors that ignore these contextual factors perpetuate the status quo. To the extent that family systems therapy metaphors seem to argue for a kind of democracy of equal treatment, they support the privileged at the expense of the disadvantaged; this is because the equal treatment fails to correct for the inherent inequities created by the larger context. To the extent that family systems metaphors can be applied in a therapy that takes for granted a society that pushes women to be heterosexual and married, to bear children, to have primary responsibility for children, to accept disadvantaged work roles and wages, and so on, those metaphors reduce the range of choices, resources, and rewards available to women.

Can any process that focuses solely on helping families to function better in a society biased to disadvantage some family members and privilege others avoid reflecting the biases of that society? Is a professional stance that is passive toward such societal factors benign? Without active opposition to societal sexism, can family systems therapy be anything other than an agent of that sexism? One could argue that treating all family members with equal respect is a revolutionary therapeutic intervention. But one can also argue that therapeutic neutrality on the gender biases in the family and in society supports the pattern of privilege and disadvantage. If family problems can be traced to societal institutions, why are family therapists not working to change societal institutions? Why, for example, are interventions designed to end a particular husband's violence against his wife not expanded and aimed also at male violence depicted on television and in movies, at the tolerance (if not encouragement) of male violence on playgrounds, or at the ways domestic violence is tolerated by the police and the courts? Why are the goals of a family therapy intervention peace and mutual respect only for the members of the client family rather than for the members of all families throughout the client's social environment?

The feminist perspective is also useful in highlighting hierarchy in the metaphors of family systems therapy. When members of a family are in relationship to someone who is labeled the therapist, the implication is that they are dealing with a person who, as healer, ranks above them. A striking expression of this hierarchy in therapy is the use by many therapists of techniques designed to work toward goals that go beyond what family members have asked for or expect. Hierarchy in therapy reinforces patriarchal models of helping relationships elsewhere in the society and of rank in the family. Hierarchy in helping relationships and in the family often effectively obscures the reality that a high-ranking helper or family member may be not only ignorant of much that is going on in the family but also inexpert and even capable of causing harm. Models of helping relationships that involve no hierarchy, such as models of the helper as an interaction partner (Lowe, 1990), might allow more honest and beneficial helping relationships and might model more honest and beneficial family relationships.

OBSCURING THE SHADOW REALITIES OF FAMILY THERAPY

When a reality is constructed, all the information, arguments, beliefs, feelings, organized counterrealities, and fragments of counterrealities that did not fit the constructed reality enter a kind of shadow reality (Rosenblatt & Wright, 1984). What remains in the shadows may be out of awareness, but some or all of it may be brought to awareness and into a challenging relationship with the constructed reality by any of a number of processes.

Much that has been in the shadows in family systems therapy has been discussed in this book: for example, the ways that women may have been disadvantaged and the way a therapist's assumption of objective reality may disadvantage clients. The adoption of a constructionist perspective or of any other perspective on therapy that seems to eliminate the problems of the past may be a boon. However, there may well be shadow realities in constructivist therapy, realities in which what is suppressed is information about the continued existence of hierarchy, therapist manipulation, and much else that is inconsistent with a constructivist view of collaboration in the construction of reality (Golann, 1988; Held, 1990; Weingarten, 1992). One thing that is obscured by the metaphor of social construction in therapy is the possible continued operation of therapeutic power, with clients and therapists no closer to being coequals than when therapists use highly manipulative, power-laden models of therapy (Golann, 1988). Power obscured may be quite corrosive, both to clients and therapists. Another thing that is obscured is the inherent contradiction in constructivists claiming, without co-constructing a reality with the reader and without the sense of iffiness they apply to the realities they talk about co-constructing with clients, that constructivist realities are valid (Held, 1990).

The metaphors of therapy based on family systems theory also obscure the ways in which family therapists may be self-serving and insincere. The metaphors of systems-based therapy give a picture of a therapist or an agency providing therapy without conflicts of interest, with the best interests of the clients as paramount. Yet the conflict of interest is obvious in that clinicians earn their living from clients and keep their jobs by not offending many people, by retaining clients, and by drawing new clients. Many years ago a Mexican spiritualist healer (who took no fees for her services) asked me a question that translates into English as the following: "How can you trust a doctor who charges to heal you?" From her perspective, a healer who was so little interested in one's welfare as to only heal if paid to do so could not be trusted. Beyond the economic motives that create conflict of interest, there are other motives that can be sources of conflict of interest. Therapists may satisfy an enormous array of personal needs through engaging in therapy, for example, the need to feel useful, to be in the middle of dramatic encounters, to be acknowledged as someone important, and to see others who seem less healthy than themselves.

As therapy theorists explore what family systems theory has obscured and as social constructionist, feminist, narrative analysis, and other sorts of theoretical work point toward new ways of thinking about family dynamics, family systems theory will undoubtedly be altered to accommodate these changes that penetrate into the shadows created by standard systems theory analyses. Lowe (1990), who has pioneered in juxtaposing the thinking of Lakoff and Johnson with family systems theory, describes the therapeutic metaphors of the future as follows:

> I have a sense that therapists are looking to metaphors which might entail a greater emphasis on respect for the views, desires and abilities of our clients, both as individuals and as family members, an associated sense of therapist humility, a reorientation to the basic condition of therapy—that it is fundamentally a form of talk or dialogue conducted over time—and an emphasis on the responsibility therapists face in choosing their maps and exercising their privileges. (p. 3)

In Lowe's view, the movement toward family therapy theories emphasizing talk, dialogue, and narrative is an acknowledgment that family systems theory has obscured the importance of talk in therapy. Although communication has always been a central concept in family systems therapy, family systems therapy frameworks seem to have inappropriately emphasized the importance of therapeutic strategies and to have privileged the therapist's view at the expense of client views. Along with therapist privilege has come the imposition of therapist views on clients (Erickson, 1988; Fine & Turner, 1991) and on professionals who are the audience for therapeutic accounts. There are, of course, situations in which therapists are required legally and morally to impose their ideas on clients, for example, when a client intends to harm another person. But there are many situations in which there is no such requirement but in which therapists, overtly or covertly, impose their will. Such imposition may come in many forms—for example, in how the therapist thinks about the client, the client's family, and the client's experience; by the therapist's ideas of what a professional should and should not do; and by the therapist's ideas of normality, health, and coping (Fine & Turner, 1991).

The need for therapists to make their interventions through a limited range of words and actions (within ethical, practical, and customary constraints) limits the metaphors that therapists use in thinking about and relating to client families. For example, the need for therapists to carry on therapy with a family in brief sessions once or a few times a week over relatively few weeks (as opposed to, say, being in continuous contact for days, weeks, or months) leads therapists toward certain metaphors for family systems. The preferred therapeutic metaphors are those that allow, enable, and highlight abrupt and substantial, rather than gradual, change and change that can be facilitated in an office setting. Consequently, in the shadow realities of family systems therapy are all the metaphors and models that could be of benefit to clients if the practicalities were other than what they seem to be now. For example, a systems theory that focuses on gradual developmental processes or on habituation processes requiring many months would not be of interest in the context of the present ideal of short-term, office-based therapy. Yet there may be, in the conceivable slow-process systems theories, much that could be useful and practical with some client families or with family members who try to make change without the benefit of therapeutic intervention.

WHAT IF WE CALLED IT LISTENING?

As was mentioned at the beginning of this chapter, therapy is a metaphor rooted in medical concepts of healing. The therapy metaphor highlights what medical metaphors highlights—cure, disease, healer knowledge and expertise—and obscures a great deal of what goes on in family therapy. Although the name given to what goes on in therapy offices does not control what goes on, it still implies and encourages certain arrangements and discourages others. What if some metaphor other than therapy were the central metaphor to use in what has been understood as family therapy? O'Hanlon and Wilk (1987, pp. 177–179) suggested such alternative metaphors as consultant, coach, and pit stop. Or what if the central metaphor were educating, witnessing, conversing, exploring, or carrying out an archeological dig? Each metaphor suggests a different process, with different goals. It might be extremely useful to explore these and other metaphors for therapy and the therapist's role. Here I will explore only one alternative to the therapy metaphor: the metaphor of listening.

Listening is a foundation for the co-construction of reality. One cannot engage in reality co-construction involving spoken words if one is not hearing or being heard. Listening is also a foundation for work with narratives (Anderson & Goolishian, 1988; Hoffman, 1990; Parry, 1991; Sluzki, 1992). If therapists were called listeners, a greater premium might be placed on good, patient listening, on effective acknowledgment and validation of what people said, on active checking out with them, and on using people's own words and meanings rather than transforming them or dealing with them selectively.

Good listening can facilitate a person's own processes. When a person talks to a good listener, he or she can move with freedom and creativity into new personal discoveries, new connections among ideas, and new reconstructions (Rosenblatt, 1981). Individuals, couples, and families who are seemingly stuck may find that with a good listener they move past or around the places in which they are stuck.

If listening were the metaphoric alternative to therapy, good listening would be modeled for clients, and clients would be held accountable for listening well to one another and to the therapist. One implication of an emphasis on listening would be that client family members might come to terms with their problems with one another through better listening and through efforts at genuine understanding and acknowledgment of one another's meanings. With an emphasis on listening, there would be a premium on each family member respecting the others enough to hear them well and to remember what they have to say however much each member may wish not to hear the others, may disagree, or may feel threatened by something. Family pathologies, then, would include not listening, talking so much that others cannot be heard, not spending enough time together talking and listening, and using television and other devices to block listening. Perhaps there would be "hearing aid" therapies, both to help clients become better listeners and to ensure that they are better listened to. Value would be placed on relationships in which one was listened to well and in which one enjoyed hearing what the other had to say. A highly valued parenting skill would be to listen to a child, and child neglect would include putting children in situations where no one listened to them. In asking that clients listen well to the therapist, the therapist would be defined not as an expert but as someone who deserves, like anyone else, to be heard and understood.

A therapy based on client narratives challenges the therapy metaphor, with its implication that a member of a healing elite can somehow cure the afflicted. Through narrative, the client is given a voice with which to choose, discover, and invent personal identity, experience, and realities. With a focus on client narrative, the therapist can give up the presumption of the therapy metaphor that therapist insight and knowledge can explain the experience of clients at a plane that is superior to client knowledge and experience (Parry, 1991).

"Narrative" is a metaphor, too. Drawn from realms of story telling and applied to what goes on between the therapist listener and the client narrator, the metaphor highlights the stories client narrators tell and the power of those stories to define realities. The narrative metaphor also highlights how much client change may be created or expressed by changes in narratives. It may obscure the extent to which the old therapy model may continue to operate under cover of narrative; the extent to which clients simultaneously entertain several narratives, are aware that their narratives are not the whole story or even an accurate story, and that some things cannot be put into words; and the extent to which people are captured by cultural conventions for narrative in ways that may block, shape, or camouflage experiences and awarenesses.

The listening metaphor is only one of many conceivable alternative metaphors for therapy. Because the narrative metaphor, like any metaphor, is limiting, therapists and clients would do well to explore alternative metaphors for what goes on in their mutual interactions. Doing so might make clear what each wants and does not want, what each will and will not do, and what each is able to do. Consider such metaphors as family guidance, family exploration (with therapist as coexplorer or expedition leader), family detective work, family truthtelling, family archeology, family repair, and family re-creation. Each implies different goals, different client roles, different therapist roles, and different processes. This approach is consistent with a modest view of therapy (Ryder, 1987), one that recognizes that there are no unequivocal right answers to some questions and that there is no "real" reality.

ECOSYSTEMIC PERSPECTIVE ON THERAPEUTIC METAPHORS

The ecosystemic approach to therapeutic epistemology (Keeney, 1983; Keeney & Sprenkle, 1982) challenges us to examine our assumptions about what is real and true in families and in family therapy. The ecosystemic challenge rests in part on the distinction between two types of family therapy, characterized by the metaphors of "aesthetic" and "pragmatic." The two approaches to therapy, Keeney and Sprenkle (1982) argued, are on "different logical levels such that questions of the aesthetic cannot be answered from the pragmatic and vice versa" (p. 3). Because of this, they argued, neither approach provides an appropriate base for critiquing work using the other approach. Extending that perspective to the multiple realities for thinking about therapy suggested in this chapter and this book, one must be cautious about judging work within a specific metaphoric frame from the perspective of another metaphoric frame.

It would be unfortunate, however, to restrict the criticism of work within a given therapeutic metaphor to comments consistent with that metaphor. We must be able to recognize when work within a given metaphoric frame or work on a given logical level has limitations. One approach to transcending differences in frames or logical levels that has been suggested by ecosystemic/epistemological critics (Keeney, 1983; Keeney & Sprenkle, 1982) is to take a systemic view of systemic approaches. Such a systemic view can show how all levels of therapy are part of a whole and are connected and how good therapy requires a bonding of levels. For example, aesthetic work without pragmatics and pragmatic work without aesthetics are both inadequate (Keeney & Sprenkle, 1982).

Another approach to working across frames or logical levels is to focus on the frames and logical levels themselves, as opposed to what goes on within those frames and logical levels. With a Lakoff and Johnson perspective on the metaphors used in thinking about families in therapy, we can analyze what those metaphors highlight and obscure. This gives us one way to work across frames and logical levels. Any approach to examining ways of thinking that are in some way at different logical levels or within different realities has its limits; it is a frame or a logical level itself. As such, it may miss much and may be more appropriate in some sense for analyzing some frames or logical levels than others. Nonetheless, metaphoric analysis of frames or levels seems a valuable tool in comparing and evaluating frames for thinking about family therapy.

SUMMARY

Most of the growth in family systems thought has been devoted to family therapy. This chapter has begun with an exploration of three key metaphors in family systems therapy, the metaphor of therapeutic goals, the metaphor of the therapist in the system, and the metaphors of family response to therapeutic intervention. Because of the focus on therapeutic intervention, many of the metaphors of family systems theory and family systems therapy are metaphors that accommodate intervention. With goals other than intervention (e.g., promoting full self-disclosure in families, entertaining families, or witnessing what goes on in families) other metaphors would be used. The focus on intervention may also lead to metaphors that obscure the transformative processes in families and in the environment of families outside of the therapy office. The active nature of intervention is masked by the metaphor of the presenting problem, which downplays the role of the therapist in defining therapeutic goals and belies the complexity and fluidity of what may be labeled therapeutic goals.

The metaphors applied to families in therapy often characterize families as freestanding and objectively real, yet the therapist is very much in the system, both as someone whose subjectivity is crucial in characterizing the family and as someone who is a player in the system. In this chapter the metaphoric nature of the following five key concepts in characterizing family responses to therapy have also been explored: family health, stuckness, coping, reconnecting, and insight. Each metaphor can be useful and can also create a great deal of mischief because of what it obscures. In further analysis of the metaphor of family response to family therapy, the metaphoric nature of test scores has been explicated and several aspects of the feminist critique of family therapy have been explored, including concern that family therapy fails to deal with male privilege, female role overload, and the disadvantaging of women in the family and fails to challenge societal forces that create and sustain such problems.

The chapter has also explored how the metaphors of family therapy obscure the shadow realities of family therapy, including the ways therapy might be in the therapist's interests and the ways various practical and customary constraints on therapist action limit therapeutic metaphors and alternative approaches to healing.

The chapter has explored some of the implications of using one of many conceivable alternative metaphors for what therapists do, namely, the metaphor of listening. Alternative metaphors for what goes on with clients may suggest radically different but nonetheless useful models of relating to clients, of conceptualizing client needs and problems, and of defining quality work with clients. The chapter has concluded with a framing of the metaphoric approach toward therapy within the ecosystemic framework, indicating that the metaphoric approach is one, but only one, of the conceivable ways of bridging different levels of systemic therapy.

CHAPTER NINE

Multiple Theoretical Metaphors and Multiple Realities

But the greatest thing, by far, is to be a master of metaphor. It is the one thing that cannot be learnt from others; and it is also a sign of genius since a good metaphor implies an intuitive perception of similarity of dissimilars. Through resemblance, metaphor makes things clearer.

— ARISTOTLE, *Poetics*

NEW METAPHORS FOR FAMILY SYSTEMS

This book offers analyses of the standard metaphors of family systems theory, showing how those metaphors structure, highlight, and obscure family phenomena. The book also suggests a few of the many possible alternatives to the standard metaphors. I do not advocate abandoning family systems theory. I believe the theory is still of enormous value. In this chapter I outline some approaches to developing new systemic metaphors and consider what to make of new systemic metaphors.

Abstract versus Grounded Metaphors

Most versions of family systems theory are written in abstract terms. I think there are two reasons for that. One is an interest in broad applicability. Social science theorists seem generally to believe that more general theories are more broadly applicable. The belief creates an aesthetic for theory as well as a criterion.

I believe the second reason why family systems theories have been written in such abstract terms is that they are partially rooted in general systems theory, a theory intended to deal with all natural systems. Loyalty to the goals and character of general systems theory seems to many people to require abstract theoretical language. However, Bertalanffy (1968), who has been the most influential general systems theorist, argued strongly for the importance of cultural, linguistic, and perspectival differences in human thought (chap. 10). This view led him to conclude that "ultimate reality is a unity of opposites; any statement holds from a certain viewpoint only, has only relative validity, and must be supplemented by antithetic statements from opposite points of view" (p. 248). Thus, abstraction without grounding in a diversity of experiences and perspectives is disloyal to the Bertalanffian view of general systems. Not only do abstract theories obscure variations in experienced realities, but they may well privilege the theorist's reality at the expense of alternative realities. That is, it may be only the theorist's reality (not the reality of most or all other people) that is expressed in abstract language that seems so broadly applicable.

Although it might seem that metaphors grounded in experience or in what is well known are too specific and narrow to be as useful as more abstract metaphors, I believe that they can be. The usefulness comes out of their familiarity, which makes them easy to use, and out of the rich entailments of what is most familiar. The processes by which we generate new metaphors may at times be very abstract, but the best novel metaphors we generate might involve familiar referents with well-known entailments.

No Single Set of Metaphors May Suffice

It may be that the universe of ideas encompassed by family systems theory is bigger and more complex than what can be understood from a single set of metaphors designed to lay out the theory. One aspect of that complexity is that family life is full of contradictions. Quinn (1991) addressed the contradiction in what she believed to be the cultural model of marriage, between marriage as an enduring relationship and marriage as a mutually beneficial relationship. The many other contradictions in family life include that family life is both intense and dull, both loving and full of hate, both a haven and a place of violence, both a place where one finds emotional support and a place where one's self-esteem and sanity are undermined, both a place to heal and a place where one catches most of one's contagious diseases and where one's ego may be most at risk.

If no single set of metaphors speaks to all that goes on in family systems, being able to move among alternative system metaphors can help us to conceptualize more of what seems to be there to conceptualize. The sense of alternative metaphors helping us to conceptualize more of what seems there to be conceptualized lends a peculiar quality to the new insights we achieve with novel system metaphors. New metaphors for family systems may typically give us insights that we feel are in some way familiar, even if we were not able to articulate those insights prior to thinking in terms of the new metaphors (cf. Manning, 1991, p. 83).

Cultural Barriers to Thinking Systemically

American culture makes it difficult to think about family systems. Perhaps the greatest difficulty in finding useful theoretical metaphors for family systems is that thinking in terms of families is much less significant in most American cultural groups and in the social sciences than thinking in terms of individuals. When thinking about families, many Americans and many social scientists actually think in terms of the individual in relationship to the family or of family dyads. Thus, most social science and psychological literature dealing with families is about the individual in the family (e.g., the teenager struggling to individuate, the overburdened homemaker, the abuse victim) or about specific dyadic family relationships (e.g., mothers and daughters, wives and husbands). Even a considerable amount of research that is ostensibly focused on family systems is actually based on the perceptions of individual family members. It is a challenge to carry out research at the level of the family system. Family systems theory thinking was revolutionary when it was first developed—and it still is.

Despite the barriers in the dominant American culture to thinking about whole families, we should not be deterred from analyzing familiar family systems metaphors or developing new ones. If anything, the barriers to thinking about whole families should give us additional incentives for developing metaphors that seem particularly valid to ourselves and our audiences and provide insights that make it obvious how important a family level of analysis is.

For professionals who want to understand, help, or study families there are additional cultural barriers to working at a systems level. The family clinician must contend with a medical model of the sick individual, with respect not only to the presenting problem but also to the diagnostic categories that must be used so that an insurer, health maintenance organization, or other umbrella organization will pay for clinical services. The family educator must deal with the individual model of education, where most often only one member of a family is present and where educational resources and approaches to conceptualizing outcomes are typically geared for the individual.

Family research is most often carried out within a "science" framework in which cause-and-effect relationships or the relationships among "variables" are key metaphors for data gathering and data analysis. As these scientific metaphors are applied, they are almost invariably inconsistent with family systems metaphors. The metaphors of scientific research used in studying families lead to research based on the perspectives of individual respondents and produce linear accounts of what goes on in families. If a family is a river, how can research describe and evaluate the "river-ness" of the families studied? If a family is a tapestry, how can research pick up the "tapestry-ness" of the families studied? An individual level of measurement may identify interesting things about families, but to be sensitive to the interactive events that fit systemic metaphors like "the family is a tapestry," information must be gathered at the interactive level. For the family researcher, then, the challenge of metaphoric analysis may be to stay with systemic metaphors to move research beyond metaphors of cause and effect, linear causality, and relationships among variables.

FINDING NEW METAPHORS

Fresh insights and perspectives on families require escape from the standard, trite accounts of human lives, even perhaps from the metaphors of the high theories of the family field. Family clinicians, researchers, educators, and policymakers who find themselves stuck may have to escape the standard theoretical metaphors to do good work (see Pratt, 1986, for analogous considerations about ethnographic representation). To escape, one must first be *willing* to escape, to be willing, as Brown (1977) has said, "to say 'No' to the organization of experience as it is given to us in preordained categories" (p. 84). The escape cannot be outside of human thought process or familiar languages; it cannot even be an escape from metaphor; it can only be an escape to fresh metaphors. Even if one does not escape systemic metaphors, finding new systemic metaphors will give one an augmented set of lenses for perceiving families.

Crucial consideration is the necessity of working with metaphors that connect with other metaphors or that can be elaborated into submetaphors (Brown, 1977, p. 96). That is, the best new metaphors can be linked to other metaphors and allow a certain grain of detail in our theorizing. For example, a tennis match might be a good metaphoric base for family systems therapy because it links to other metaphors (games, competition) and because it breaks down into submetaphors (rules, turn taking, the value of endurance, the value of practice).

Theoretical metaphors that are illuminating and give rise to many interesting entailments have to come out of the experience and verbal fluency of the persons who develop and use them. This makes it necessary to turn to known and shared language, culture, and experience in developing theoretical metaphors. The more richly we know the areas of experience to which to apply a metaphor and from which to draw a metaphor, the more disciplined can be the implicit or explicit analogy making that is involved in drawing metaphoric connections. In the average U.S. household a television set operates 6 hours a day and an automobile is enormously important. By contrast, most Americans probably know little about paramecia and the politics of Sri Lanka. One might expect that television watching, television programs, and automobiles would provide Americans with detailed and more richly elaborated theoretical metaphors for a wide range of topics, including the family, than would paramecia or the politics of Sri Lanka.

Central to widely shared experience is the experience of our bodies and their interaction with the environment (Johnson, 1987;

Lakoff, 1987). When talking about the metaphor of the family as a river, it helps to think of the sight, sound, and feeling of the river. In thinking of the family as a group of people traveling together in a vehicle, it helps to think of the feeling of movement and confinement, the sight of scenery going by, the sound of an engine.

Beyond being grounded in the culture, language, and experience of the people who will use it and being compatible with the phenomena to which it will be applied, a useful and powerful metaphor will be concise, will fit into a larger structure, and will be sufficiently different from what it is being applied to (see Lakoff & Johnson, 1980; Nilsen, 1986). A concise metaphor can be expressed in a few words, even though it may yield pages and years of interesting development and implications. A metaphor that fits into a larger structure draws on connections with the larger structure, even if it does so only implicitly. A metaphor that is sufficiently different takes us into a new reality, perhaps with a momentary bump or hesitation as we move into a new way of thinking.

Although alternative metaphors might be most useful if they come from areas of rich experience, this does not mean that they have to come out of concrete experiences. Any culture is rich in experiences with what may never have been directly touched, tasted, seen, or smelled—for example, mythology, religious stories and symbols, children's stories, plays, and other sources of thought that are not grounded in concrete physical activity or sensory experience.

Despite my advocacy of familiar metaphors, it is at times useful to develop a metaphor based on what few people know about or have experienced (see, e.g., Doherty's [1986] stimulating paper that makes use of concepts from particle physics). One can even turn to cultures outside of the majority culture of the United States for preexisting metaphors of family systems. There are, for example, fascinating, mind-stretching metaphoric applications to families based on concepts from Hopi language and culture (Dell, 1980) and from Hawaiian language and culture (Ito, 1985). These metaphors provide strikingly new perspectives on families, both new ways of seeing and new things to see. For example, the Hopi way of thought described by Dell includes an emphasis on verbs, not nouns, on becoming, not being, and on intensity, preparing, and repetition. Hawaiian culture, as described by Ito, includes a ritual of "mental cleansing," *ho'oponopono*, which is intended to clear away all possible grievances or *hihia* (hostile entanglements) prior to conflict resolution or medical treatment. Ito focused on the adoption of ho'oponopono for therapy with native Hawaiian families. But her descriptions of Hawaiian ways of framing family difficulty and of the ritual (which includes an exchange in which offender and offended both apologize and forgive) provide novel and useful lenses for looking at difficulties in families from any culture.

Core Metaphors for Family Systems

One way of thinking about family systems theory is that underlying a great deal of it is a set of core metaphors; that beneath, the standard metaphors of family systems theory is an implicit model of family systems. Many of the theoretical metaphors discussed in this book can be traced back to core metaphors. If one asks how we arrived at such family systems metaphors as subsystem, boundary, and cohesion, one kind of answer can be found by examining the properties of these core metaphors.

The core metaphors might themselves be used in family systems thought, but they may not be sufficiently evocative to get us to the many insights that are possible with the standard family systems theory metaphors. Still, believing that there are core metaphors and that we know what they are may help to guide development of new metaphors.

The idea that there may be core metaphors for family systems rests on a view that even though there may be many metaphors that can illuminate any important concept, the number of core metaphors underlying those metaphors is small (Lakoff & Turner, 1989; Quinn, 1991). Quite possibly, all fluent speakers who are well grounded in their culture intuitively know and understand the core metaphors for the concepts important in their language and culture. Nonetheless, explicitly identifying the core metaphors for a domain reveals what may be the basic dimensions of thinking about the domain and provides a coherent, organized view of the many linguistic expressions of those core metaphors. Lakoff and Turner (1989) provide a fascinating analysis of the core metaphors in English for the concepts of life, death, and time (e.g., they see time as a changer, as something that moves, and as a pursuer).

To explicate the core metaphors for family systems I have gone back to some of the cultural and linguistic roots in English for the idea of family. I have looked at biblical and Shakespearean references to family and at "family" and related entries in the *Oxford English Dictionary* (1989). I have reviewed how families are talked about in family textbooks and in collections of stories about families and listened to people talking about families. Judging by what I have read and heard, I believe there are five core metaphors for family systems: the family is a thing, the family is a living entity, the family is a primary relationship, the family is a container, and the family is a machine. These five metaphors overlap the core metaphors that Quinn (1991) identified for marriages: entity, trajectory, relation, and container. Quinn's work provides inspiration and a model for my analysis of the core metaphors for family systems.

The Family Is a Thing

Biblical references to the family are most often to the family of a specific patriarch. Such references seem to imply that the patriarch in some sense owned the family, that the family is a thing that can be owned. The Bible also refers to the family of someone as the "house" of that person, again implying a thing.

A thing is a bounded entity, separate from other entities. It has a location in space and time. As a material object it functions in a world of physical principles. It may belong to someone, or someone may be a part of it. A thing is a generic entity, but among things there is enormous diversity. Families seem that way too. Furthermore, things consist of basic constituents that are bonded together. With families too there is a sense of basic constituents and of relationships among them. The constituents, at the most obvious level, are people, but they may also be kinds of relationships (e.g., mother–infant versus wife–husband) or roles, beliefs about identity, etc.

Gubrium (1988) wrote about the family as a socially constructed thing, separate from its members and used to understand the relationships of its members. In some cultures, thinking that way would be natural. In the United States, however, people may often think so much in terms of individuals that they fail to consider how family members can be perceived as a collectivity or as collectively responsible, for example, for care of a family member who has Alzheimer's disease (Gubrium, 1988). Considering the family as a thing enables one to recognize emergent and collective attributes, at the risk, of course, of obscuring individual actions and the ways in which the family is not or is only partially an entity with emergent attributes.

The Family Is a Container

The second core metaphor for family systems, related to the first, is the family as a special kind of thing, a container, something that separates inside from outside. The family is often thought of as a vessel, a box, or a structure within which people who could be called a family live. According to Lakoff and Johnson (1980), the container metaphor is a primary one in English and perhaps in all human languages. We talk about being *in* a family, about social service agencies and the community putting resources *into* the family, and about people being inside and outside the family.

The Family Is a Living Entity

A common metaphor used in social theories is to liken a social system to an organism (Brown, 1977, chap. 4). Use of this metaphor in Western culture was common long before the rise of modern social theory. For example, some biblical references to family mention blood; people who are related are seen as of one blood. Blood can be seen as a life force of the family. In using an organismic metaphor for the family, one can talk about the family's life and death and can refer to it as healthy or ill and as living somewhere or having the vitality to move somewhere else. The living entity that is a family can be described in terms that are used for plants—growing, being nurtured, blossoming, withering, dying—or in terms that characterize people—feelings, needs, conflicts, fears, health, strength, intelligence, education, and so on.

The Family Is a Primary Group

The fourth core metaphor is commonly used in American social science textbooks. It is that the family is a person's primary (literally, "first" but also "most important") group. Thus, the family has priority and great importance for its members and is more basic, emotionally involving, and irreplaceable than other groups to which a person might belong. This is analogous to a finding in Quinn's (1981) study of marriage metaphors, namely, that a primary relationship is one of the basic metaphors for marriage. Thinking of the family as a primary group can help us to understand *Oxford English Dictionary* (1989) definitions of the family that differ from contemporary understandings of the family. For example, defining the family as the whole household, including the servants, makes sense if one thinks of the servants as part of the household primary group, including people with whom children first have contact and people who are of utmost importance to household members.

The Family as a Machine

The machine is a core metaphor in modern society (Brown, 1977, p. 90) and, at least through the influence of family systems thinking, a core metaphor for the family. Thus the family, like a machine, has parts, does things, has controls, can break down, requires energy input, operates with some friction, produces an output, has a physical existence in space and time, and so on.

Relations among the Core Metaphors

As with core metaphors for the individual (Jung, 1987), the core metaphors for family systems can be seen as contradictory. The thing, container, living entity, and machine metaphors are about single entities; the group metaphors are about collectivities. The thing, container, and machine metaphors deal with what seems inanimate, whereas the other two deal with what is living. The primary group metaphor emphasizes importance and early connection, while the other metaphors seem neutral about both importance and early connection. These differences (and others) make it seem difficult to use all five core metaphors together, but it may not be necessary to do so, since any core metaphor could be developed to give a relatively comprehensive view of family systems.

Despite their obvious differences, the core metaphors are related. A container may be seen as a thing, although it is a very special kind of thing. Living beings, groups, and even things may be seen as containers. A machine is also a special kind of thing. Thus, although core metaphors may arise from different focuses and conceptual bases, they can be complementary because there are relationships among them.

Core Metaphors as a Basis of New Systems Metaphors

In organizing thought about metaphoric alternatives to family systems theory, it may be useful to use the five core metaphors to stimulate the search for alternative metaphors. The five core metaphors could be seen as foundational for thinking about families. They bring with them connections to significant entailments. Once we think about the family as a living entity, for example, we can think about the family as coming into existence, having biological antecedents, and being capable of dying. To get to richer entailments while using the core metaphor of the family system as a living entity, one may try out metaphors based on any of a wide range of living entities—for example, a tree, a cell of a living organism, a flower, a human being.

Theoretical metaphors that stray too far from a theory are, by definition, not relevant to the theory. Conceivably, one could take any conceptualization and stretch it to fit family systems. However, it seems more appropriate for any new theoretical metaphor for family systems to hold some aspects of the phenomenon of interest constant and to try to find new metaphors in which to embed those aspects. For example, one might move from a standard family systems discussion of boundaries and rules in blended families by holding constant the idea of putting things together from different places (the blending) and setting them in a new metaphor (e.g., the mixing of chemicals, the creation of a union between previously independent countries). Obviously, a key issue in developing new metaphors, then, is the choice of what to keep constant. A decision to make a certain piece of family systems theory or a certain phenomenon that makes sense in terms of that theory a given in developing a new metaphor is a decision about what is central to one's family systems analysis.

As was argued in the discussion in Chapter 3 of the metaphor "the family is a rock," once one thinks systemically, it is impossible not to see systems in any metaphor. A system is not a thing but a way of thinking. Quinn (1991) has argued that people choose metaphors that fit their underlying cultural model, and in the case of family systems it seems difficult to find a metaphor that does not fit systems thinking. The challenge in developing family systems metaphors is not in finding a starting place that can be thought of as a system but in finding metaphors that can highlight what the metaphors we have been working with obscure. Searching for new metaphors pushes us to consider standards for evaluating theoretical metaphors (Simons, 1981). How can we know that a metaphor is a good one?

EVALUATING NEW THEORETICAL METAPHORS

Lack of Firm Ground for Evaluation

There is no firm ground for evaluating theoretical metaphors. A metaphor that is exhilarating and delicious to one person is meaningless or grossly inappropriate to another. What one person counts as an insight another counts as an absurdity. It is possible to bully people into accepting one's reality. It is possible, as a scholarly gatekeeper, to keep others from learning about the metaphors one rejects. But there is no escaping diversity and subjectivity of evaluation. This book is a vote for fresh metaphors, but it offers no objective grounds for sorting out metaphors for family systems.

I do not think of metaphors as true in the sense that they can be compared with some objective standard and judged to be consistent with all facts. Metaphors have to fit what seem to be facts, but there are more facts—as well as greater diversity in what people count as the facts and greater diversity of interpretation of those facts—than anyone can take into account. So the fit to facts always leaves a metaphor open to challenge by additional or alternative facts and by alternative interpretations of the so-called facts. The facts are not objective constants but are open to analysis and negotiation of meaning. The truth of a metaphor cannot be ascertained against something that has permanent solidity. Indeed, the unfolding nature of experience guarantees an unfolding, impermanent nature for what might be called facts. Even things that could be called immutable facts are subject to reinterpretation and are changed by new discoveries and new selectivities of perception. Nor can any single observer or participant in events know all that all other observers and participants know. Thus, a number of metaphors may be equally true or consecutively true. Whatever it is, the family is a construction, an entity that has been created, defined, construed, or invented to account for relationships among individuals (see Shotter, 1987, on the third party, the relationship, that connects lovers). That additional entity may become the basis for understanding what goes on among those individuals, but it remains a hypothetical entity.

That I think it is valuable to write about a theory of family systems does not mean that I think there is a single uncontroversial all-purpose definition of family. However, focusing on the metaphoric representation of family systems makes the question of definition less important and moves us to issues of representation. Even if the question of definition cannot be resolved, it is useful, as Gubrium and Lynott (1985) pointed out in discussing the controversy over defining the family, to consider how the family represents itself and how to represent families. Then the question is not "What is a family?" but "What are useful ways to represent families?" This book does not offer a resolution to the question of how to define the family, but it does speak extensively to the question of how to represent families and family processes.

Family systems theory was made by metaphor makers (de Shazer, 1982). There is nothing sacred or unalterably real about the family systems theory metaphors that have been codified in books, articles, and teaching. The theoretical metaphors that are current in the field have their uses, but so will many new theoretical metaphors.

When Is a Theoretical Metaphor Good?

One starting place in deciding whether a theoretical metaphor is good is to ask whether the distinctions drawn by the new metaphor are different from those drawn by other metaphors (Keeney 1983, chap. 2, citing Spencer-Brown, 1973, on distinction as the starting place for epistemological analysis and theory). However, distinctions are not separable from how they are used. If I seem to be drawing different distinctions when thinking about families using metaphor A than when thinking about them using metaphor B and if I then bend the metaphors so that both cover the same territory, the distinctions are not meaningfully different. This is not a small matter because metaphors are inherently flexible (Manning, 1991). We use them because they stretch to fit a variety of situations, but we may find them giving us nothing new because of that flexibility. Put another way, the power of a good new metaphor is that it is strange in useful ways.

Another starting place in evaluating a new theoretical metaphor is to explore the coherence of different parts of the metaphor. Does it hang together as a metaphor or seem to consist of disconnected pieces? For example, thinking of a family system as a piece of candy being eaten by a loaf of bread driving an automobile would be a challenge in part because the three elements of the metaphor do not cohere.

Another starting place in evaluating a new theoretical metaphor, though based on what is inevitably subjective and idiosyncratic, is its truthfulness to experience. Given our own experiences and perceptions, does the metaphor seem to fit the phenomenon of interest? The metaphor "the family is a forest" will seem appropriate to some people and not to others, depending on how the metaphor is developed and how it coincides with what people have experienced and perceived.

Ultimately, a family systems metaphor might best be evaluated by asking the questions "Does it give new perceptions and associations?" and "Does it structure the phenomena in useful ways?" Metaphors that are good will lead us and others to what we may not have known (or not have known so fully) or to what we have been overlooking. Metaphors that are good will help us to organize what we see, hear, believe, and know. And that organization may lead us to comprehend more fully, to see gaps in our knowledge, and to see connections with other phenomena. Good metaphors can lead to new questions about families, and our attempts to answer those questions may lead us to more knowledge and to still other metaphors. Good metaphors are about what is not in front of us and perhaps what could never be in front of us without their metaphoric assistance.

Evaluation of a metaphor assumes some sort of stable frame of reference, but in using metaphors frames of reference may shift. For example, what was once taken to be a fact about a family or about families in general may, in the light of some newly considered metaphor, become transformed into a quite different fact. Gubrium and Lynott (1985), for example, wrote about a staff review of a client family in which the fact of the family's being close-knit (a tapestry metaphor) is transformed when a psychiatrist suggests that the family is close-knit without emotional intimacy but with a calculated closeness that enables individual family members to get what they want from one another (perhaps a game-playing metaphor).

Metaphors are not only cognitive. They also speak to feelings. The feelings associated with the metaphor of a family as a rule system are no doubt different from those associated with the metaphor of a family as a group of people battling for survival. This book is primarily about perspectives, and in fact the function of metaphors can be considered to be the provision of perspective (Kittay, 1987, pp. 13–15). But the discussion has touched repeatedly on the matter of feelings. Perhaps the discussion has missed crucial aspects of feelings or has made use of them in covert ways, but perhaps perspectives and feelings are difficult to separate. At any rate, a good metaphor would probably have the potential to connect with our feelings. Ultimately, however, the answer to the question "What is a good metaphor?" is one that recognizes that different metaphors are good for different purposes or in different situations or with people who have had different experiences.

METAPHORS TO DEAL WITH METAPHORIC COMPLEXITY

The theoretical metaphors presented in this book may simplify how much multiple metaphors are needed to characterize families in general or even a particular family. Although the metaphors developed in this book have overlapping properties and entailments, no metaphor captures the full range. It is not merely that a family is like a group of people traveling in a vehicle, but it is simultaneously like a group of people playing a game, a river, a tapestry, a government, a group of people in a mystery story, and much more.

Synthesizing a holistic view of a family that incorporates its full metaphoric complexity may require still other metaphors. How are we to think of the family in a way that pulls together the whole range of appropriate metaphors? How can we capture the metaphoric complementarities, contradictions, and paradoxes?

One metaphor that gives a view of the joining of complexities and differences is the metaphor of a crossroads. A crossroads is a coming together. The roads are separate most of their way, but where they join there is a combining. Perhaps the "riverness" of a family is in some sense separate from the "tapestryness" and so on, but at times they and other metaphoric qualities come together. For example, consider how families are timeless and exist independently of any specific members. Yet at any specific time families are formed and given an aesthetic by their constituents of the moment.

A more complicated and perhaps more apt metaphor for capturing the complexity of metaphors that can account for family systems is that of the city. The family is like a city, with its different neighborhoods, industries, social activities, simultaneous sorrow and happiness, safety and danger, wakefulness and sleep, creativity and banality. Like a city with all its complexity, a family may combine its nature as a river, as a tapestry, as people riding in a vehicle, and so on.

WHAT ALL FAMILY SYSTEMS THEORY METAPHORS OBSCURE

"In the face of the vague, indescribable, open, fluid, and ever changing nature of human life (its messy nature), language can work 'to make it appear as if' it is well ordered and structured" (Shotter, 1990, p. 158). One metaphor may highlight what another obscures, but all obscure how much our theoretical language is constructive and simplifying, and all obscure how little certainty and sure knowledge we have after we have carefully applied all conceivable metaphors. All obscure how much of what comes out in writing is limited and shaped by the necessary constraints of language (Gergen & Gergen, 1986; see Shotter, 1990, on deconstructionist applications to social psychology). All obscure the extent to which language processes that are even more fundamental than metaphors (e.g., grammar) influence thinking about families and family therapy (Wahlström, 1990).

Like family systems theory, all the alternative metaphors offered for family systems are an outsider's perspective. An insider would see different things, but, perhaps what is even more important, an insider would feel different things. Observers tend to be dry, "objective," and neutral, and so do their theoretical metaphors. There is not very much of the love, passion, rage, fear, grief, and pain of family life in metaphors of family systems. This book is a theorist's construction of reality, but to achieve appropriate connections with feelings it might be useful to dialogically develop realities anew in each specific situation, that is, in interaction with family members.

Perhaps the discussions of this book will help to revitalize family systems theory by moving us away from the rigidities that develop when theoretical metaphors become realities and block the exploration of alternatives. I have no need for family systems theory to survive or to become a theory everyone uses, but I also have no need to throw it out because some people see it as sterile, unhelpful, or irrelevant. I hope that the "re-imagining" (Lowe, 1990) of family systems theory offered in this book will lead to renewed enthusiasm for systems thought and to creative developments in systems theory.

SUMMARY

This chapter has begun by making a case for continuing to focus on family systems and for working toward new insights with a variety of experience-based metaphors. It has explored cultural barriers to thinking systemically and ways of developing new theoretical metaphors for family systems. One approach to developing new theoretical metaphors is to turn to what seem to be the core metaphors for family systems: the family is a thing, the family is a living entity, the family is a primary relationship, the family is a container, and the family is a machine. The core metaphors can help to guide our search for more specific and lively metaphors. However, a challenge in the search for new theoretical metaphors is to hold on to what seems basic in the phenomena we are trying to understand, to hold on to the kernel of "reality" that is captured by the metaphors we want to leave behind. In the end, the question to be asked of new metaphors is what they give us that standard metaphors do not. While rejecting any notion of ultimate truth, the chapter has offered a number of approaches to evaluating new theoretical metaphors. Because multiple and seemingly inconsistent metaphors are appropriate in analyzing families, we need metaphoric frames for combining metaphors that seem on face not to fit together. The chapter has suggested two such frames: the crossroads and the city. The chapter has concluded with a recognition of some of what all family systems theory metaphors obscure and with the hope that this book will lead to renewed enthusiasm and creative growth in systems thought.

References

Ackerman, N. J. (1984). *A theory of family systems.* New York: Gardner.

Allman, L. R. (1982). The aesthetic preference: Overcoming the pragmatic error. *Family Process, 21,* 43–56.

Anderson, C. M., & Stewart, S. (1983). *Mastering resistance: A practical guide to family therapy.* New York: Guilford Press.

Anderson, H., & Goolishian, H. A. (1988). Human systems as linguistic systems: Preliminary and evolving ideas about the implications for clinical theory. *Family Process, 27,* 371–393.

Anderson, S. A., & Sabatelli, R. M. (1990). Differentiating differentiation and individuation: Conceptual and operation challenges. *American Journal of Family Therapy, 18,* 32–50.

Andolfi, M., Angelo, C., Menghi, P., & Nicolo-Corigliano, A. M. (1983). *Behind the family mask: Therapeutic change in rigid family systems.* New York: Brunner/Mazel.

Atwood, J. D., & Levine, L. B. (1991). Ax murderers, dragons, spiders and webs: Therapeutic metaphors in couple therapy. *Contemporary Family Therapy, 13,* 201–217.

Avis, J. M. (1986). Feminist issues in family therapy. In F. P. Piercy & D. H. Sprenkle (Eds.), *Family therapy sourcebook* (pp. 213–242). New York: Guilford Press.

Bandler, R., & Grinder, J. (1975). *The structure of magic.* Palo Alto, CA: Science and Behavior Books.

Barker, P. (1985). *Using metaphors in psychotherapy.* New York: Brunner/ Mazel.

Bateson, G. (1972). *Steps to an ecology of mind.* New York: Ballantine.

Bateson, G. (1980). *Mind and nature: A necessary unity.* New York: Bantam.

Bateson, G., Jackson, D. D., Haley, J., & Weakland, J. (1956). Toward a theory of schizophrenia. *Behavioral Science, 1,* 251–264.

Beavin, J. B., Black, A., Chovil, N., & Mullett, J. (1990). *Equivocal communication.* Newbury Park, CA: Sage.

Belenky, M. F., Clinchy, B. M., Goldberger, N. R., & Tarule, J. M. (1986). *Women's way of knowing: The development of self, voice, and mind.* New York: Basic Books.

Benson, M. J., Schindler-Zimmerman, T., & Martin, D. (1991). Accessing children's perceptions of their family: Circular questioning revisited. *Journal of Marital and Family Therapy, 17,* 363–372.

Berger, M., & Jurkovic, G. J. (1987). Family therapy in context. *Journal of Family Psychology, 1,* 187–204.

Berger, P. & Kellner, H. (1964). Marriage and the construction of reality. *Diogenes, 46,* 1–24.

Bertalanffy, L. von (1968). *General systems theory: Foundations, development, applications.* New York: Braziller.

Black, M. (1962). *Models and metaphors: Studies in language and philosophy.* Ithaca, NY: Cornell University Press.

Bleier, R. (1986). *Feminist approaches to science.* New York: Pergamon Press.

Boss, P. G. (1977). A clarification of the concept of psychological father presence in families experiencing ambiguity of boundary. *Journal of Marriage and the Family, 39,* 141–151.

Boss, P. G. (1980). The relationship of psychological father presence, wife's personal qualities, and wife/family dysfunction in families of missing fathers. *Journal of Marriage and the Family, 42,* 541–549.

Boss, P. G. (1992). Primacy of perception in family stress theory and measurement. *Journal of Family Psychology, 6,* 113–119.

Boss, P. G., & Greenberg, J. (1984). Family boundary ambiguity: A new variable in family stress theory. *Family Process, 23,* 535–546.

Boszormenyi-Nagy, I., & Spark, G. M. (1973). *Invisible loyalties: Reciprocity in intergenerational family therapy.* Hagerstown, MD: Harper & Row.

Boulding, K. E. (1985). *The world as a total system.* Beverly Hills, CA: Sage.

Bowen, M. (1978). *Family therapy in clinical practice.* New York: Jason Aronson.

Brice, C. W. (1991). What forever means: An empirical existential–phenomenological investigation of maternal mourning. *Journal of Phenomenological Psychology, 22,* 16–38.

Broderick, C. B., & Pulliam-Krager, H. (1979). Family process and child outcomes. In W. R. Burr, R. Hill, F. I. Nye, & I. L. Reiss (Eds.), *Contemporary theories about the family: Vol. 1. Research-based theories* (pp. 604–614). New York: Free Press.

Broderick, C. & Smith, J. (1979). The general systems approach to the family. In W. R. Burr, R. Hill, F. I. Nye, & I. L. Reiss (Eds.), *Contemporary* theories about the family: Vol. 2. General theories/theoretical orientations (pp. 112–129). New York: Free Press.

Brown, R. H. (1977). A poetic for sociology. New York: Cambridge University Press.

Bruner, J. S., Goodnow, J. J., & Austin, G. A. (1956). A study of thinking. New York: Wiley.

Buckley, W. F. (1967). Sociology and modern systems theory. Englewood Cliffs, NJ: Prentice-Hall.

Burr, W. R. (1991). Rethinking levels of abstraction in family systems theories. Family Process, 30, 435–452.

Campbell, D. T. (1956). Perception as substitute trial and error. Psychological Review, 63, 330–342.

Campbell, D. T. (1958). Common fate, similarity, and other indices of the status of aggregates of persons as social entities. Behavioral Science, 3, 14–25.

Campbell, D. T. (1959a). Methodological suggestions from a comparative psychology of knowledge processes. Inquiry, 2, 152–182.

Campbell, D. T. (1959b). Systematic errors on the part of human links in communication systems. Information and Control, 1, 334–369.

Campbell, D. T. (1966). Pattern matching as an essential in distal knowing. In K. R. Hammond (Ed.), The psychology of Egon Brunswik (pp. 81–106). New York: Holt, Rinehart & Winston.

Campbell, D. T. (1974). Evolutionary epistemology. In P. A. Schilpp (Ed.), The philosophy of Karl Popper (pp. 413–463). La Salle, IL: Open Court.

Chodorow, N. (1978). The reproduction of mothering: Psychoanalysis and the sociology of gender. Berkeley: University of California Press.

Constantine, L. L. (1986). Family paradigms: The practice of theory in family therapy. New York: Guilford Press.

Cozby, P. C. (1973). Self disclosure: A literature review. Psychological Bulletin, 70, 73–91.

Dell, P. F. (1980). The Hopi family therapist and the Aristotelian parents. Journal of Marital and Family Therapy, 6, 123–130.

Dell, P. F. (1986). In defense of "lineal causality." Family Process, 25, 513–521.

de Shazer, S. (1982). Some conceptual distinctions are more useful than others. Family Process, 21, 71–84.

de Shazer, S. (1992). What question is being asked? AFTA Newsletter, 47, 31–32.

Doherty, W. J. (1986). Quanta, quarks, and families: Implications of quantum physics for family research. Family Process, 25, 249–263.

Dolan, Y. M. (1986). Metaphors for motivation and intervention. In S. de Shazer & R. Kral (Eds.), *Indirect approaches in therapy* (pp. 1–10). Rockville, MD: Aspen.

Edie, J. (1967). Comments on Dr. Natanson's paper. In E. W. Straus & R. M. Griffith (Eds.), *Phenomenology of will and action: The second Lexington conference on pure and applied phenomenology* (pp. 221–228). Pittsburgh: Duquesne University Press.

Erickson, G. D. (1988). Against the grain: Decentering family therapy. *Journal of Marital and Family Therapy, 14,* 225–236.

Erickson, M. H. (1967). *Advanced techniques of hypnosis and therapy.* New York: Grune & Stratton.

Ferreira, A. J. (1963). Family myth and homeostasis. *Archives of General Psychiatry, 9,* 457–463.

Fine, M., & Turner, J. (1991). Tyranny and freedom: Looking at ideas in the practice of family therapy. *Family Process, 30,* 307–320.

Fisher, B. A. (1981). Implications of the "interactional view" for communication theory. In C. Wilder & J. H. Weakland (Eds.), *Rigor and imagination: Essays from the legacy of Gregory Bateson* (pp. 195–209). New York: Praeger.

Fogelin, R. J. (1988). *Figuratively speaking.* New Haven, CT: Yale University Press.

Ford, F. (1983). Rules: The invisible family. *Family Process, 22,* 135–145.

Friedman, E. H. (1989). Systems and ceremonies: A family view of rites of passage. In B. Carter & M. McGoldrick (Eds.), *The changing American life cycle* (2nd ed., pp. 119–147). Boston: Allyn and Bacon.

Fry, W. F., Jr. (1962). The marital context of the anxiety syndrome. *Family Process, 1,* 245–252.

Geertz, H., & Geertz, C. (1975). *Kinship in Bali.* Chicago: University of Chicago Press.

Gergen, K. J. (1985). The social constructionist movement in modern psychology. *American Psychologist, 40,* 266–275.

Gergen, K. J., & Gergen, M. M. (1986). Narrative form and the construction of psychological science. In T. R. Sarbin (Ed.), *Narrative psychology: The storied nature of human conduct* (pp. 22–44). New York: Praeger.

Gluckman, M. (1956). Estrangement in the family. *Custom and conflict in Africa* (pp. 54–80). London: Basil Blackwell.

Goffman, E. (1959). *The presentation of self in everyday life.* New York: Doubleday Anchor.

Golann, S. (1988). On second-order family therapy. *Family Process, 27,* 51–65.

Goldner, V. (1985). Feminism and family therapy. *Family Process, 24,* 31–47.

Goldner, V. (1988). Normative and covert hierarchies. *Family Process, 27,* 17–31.

Goldner, V., Penn, P., Sheinberg, M., & Walker, G. (1990). Love and violence: Gender paradoxes in volatile attachments. *Family Process, 29,* 343–364.

Griffith, J. L., Griffith, M. E., & Slovik, L. S. (1990). Mind–body problems in family therapy: Contrasting first- and second-order cybernetics approaches. *Family Process, 29,* 13–28.

Gubrium, J. F. (1988). The family as project. *Sociological Review, 36,* 273–296.

Gubrium, J. F. (1992). *Out of control: Family therapy and domestic disorder.* Newbury Park, CA: Sage.

Gubrium, J. F., & Buckholdt, D. R. (1982). Fictive family: Everyday usage, analytic, and human service considerations. *American Anthropologist, 84,* 878–885.

Gubrium, J. F., & Holstein, J. A. (1990). *What is family?* Mountain View, CA: Mayfield.

Gubrium, J. F., & Lynott, R. J. (1985). Family rhetoric as social order. *Journal of Family Issues, 6,* 129–152.

Haley, J. (1967). Toward a theory of pathological systems. In G. Zuk & I. Boszormenyi-Nagy (Eds.), *Family therapy and disturbed families* (pp. 11–27). Palo Alto, CA: Science and Behavior Books.

Haley, J. (1973). *Uncommon therapy: The psychiatric techniques of Milton H. Erickson, M.D.* New York: Norton.

Handel, G. (1985). Central issues in the construction of sibling relationships. In G. Handel (Ed.), *The psychosocial interior of the family* (3rd ed., pp. 367–396). New York: Aldine.

Hare-Mustin, R. (1978). A feminist approach to family therapy. *Family Process, 17,* 181–194.

Hare-Mustin, R. (1987). The problem of gender in family therapy theory. *Family Process, 26,* 15–27.

Held, B. S. (1990). What's in a name? Some confusions and concerns about constructivism. *Journal of Marital and Family Therapy, 16,* 179–186.

van Heusden, A. & van den Eerenbeemt, E. M. (1987). *Balance in motion: Ivan Boszormenyi-Nagy and his vision of individual and family therapy.* New York: Brunner/Mazel.

Hill, R., & Klein, D. (1973). Toward a research agenda and theoretical synthesis. In E. B. Sheldon (Ed.), *Family economic behavior* (pp. 371–404). Philadelphia: Lippincott.

Hillman, J. (1975). *Re-visioning psychology.* New York: Harper.

Hoffman, L. (1971). Deviation-amplifying processes in natural groups. In J. Haley (Ed.), *Changing families: A family therapy reader* (pp. 285–311). New York: Grune & Stratton.

Hoffman, L. (1990). Constructing realities: An art of lenses. *Family Process, 29,* 1–12.

Imber-Black, E. (1986). Maybe "lineal causality" needs another defense lawyer: A feminist response to Dell. *Family Process, 25,* 523–525.

Ito, K. L. (1985). Ho'oponopono, "to make right": Hawaiian conflict resolution and metaphor in the construction of a family therapy. *Culture, Medicine, and Psychiatry, 9,* 201–217.

Jackson, D. D. (1959). Family interaction, family homeostasis and some implications for conjoint family psychotherapy. In J. H. Masserman (Ed.), *Individual and familial dynamics* (pp. 122–141). New York: Grune & Stratton.

Jackson, D. D. (1965a). The study of the family. *Family Process, 4,* 1–20.

Jackson, D. D. (1965b). Family rules: Marital quid pro quo. *Archives of General Psychiatry, 12,* 589–594.

Johnson, M. (1987). *The body in the mind: The bodily basis of meaning, imagination, and reason.* Chicago: University of Chicago Press.

Jordan, J. R. (1985). Paradox and polarity: The Tao of family therapy. *Family Process, 24,* 165–174.

Jung, R. (1987). A quaternion of metaphors for the hermeneutics of life. In J. A. Dillon, Jr. (Ed.), *General systems: Yearbook of the International Society for General Systems Research, 30,* 25–31.

Kantor, D., & Lehr, W. (1975). *Inside the family.* San Francisco: Jossey-Bass.

Katz, F. E. (1968). *Autonomy and organization.* New York: Random House.

Keeney, B. B. (1982). What is an epistemology of family therapy? *Family Process, 21,* 153–168.

Keeney, B. B. (1983). *Aesthetics of change.* New York: Guilford Press.

Keeney, B. B., & Sprenkle, D. H. (1982). Ecosystemic epistemology: Critical implications for the aesthetics and pragmatics of family therapy. *Family Process, 21,* 1–19.

Kirschner, S. R. (1990). The assenting echo: Anglo-American values in contemporary psychoanalytic developmental psychology. *Social Research, 57,* 821–857.

Kittay, E. F. (1987). *Metaphor: Its cognitive force and linguistic structure.* New York: Clarendon.

Kopp, S. B. (1972). *If you meet the Buddha on the road, kill him!* Ben Lomond, CA: Science and Behavior Books.

Laird, J. (1989). Women and stories: Restorying women's self-constructions.

In M. McGoldrick, C. M. Anderson, & F. Walsh (Eds.), *Women in families: A framework for family therapy* (pp. 427–450). New York: Norton.

Lakoff, G. (1987). *Women, fire, and dangerous things: What categories reveal about the mind.* Chicago: University of Chicago Press.

Lakoff, G., & Johnson, M. (1980). *Metaphors we live by.* Chicago: University of Chicago Press.

Lakoff, G., & Turner, M. (1989). *More than cool reason: A field guide to poetic metaphor.* Chicago: University of Chicago Press.

Lankton, C. H., & Lankton, S. R. (1989). *Tales of enchantment: Goal-oriented metaphors for adults and children in therapy.* New York: Brunner/Mazel.

Lasch, C. (1977). *Haven in a heartless world: The family besieged.* New York: Basic Books.

Livingstone, S. M. (1987). The representation of personal relationships in television drama: Realism, convention and morality. In R. Burnett, P. McGhee, & D. D. Clarke (Eds.), *Accounting for relationships* (pp. 248–268). New York: Methuen.

Lowe, R. (1990). Re-imagining family therapy: Choosing the metaphors we live by. *Australian and New Zealand Journal of Family Therapy, 11,* 1–9.

Maddock, J. W. (1989). Healthy family sexuality: Positive principles for educators and clinicians. *Family Relations, 38,* 130–136.

Maddock, J. W. (1992a). *Power, control, and victimization: Conceptual and clinical considerations.* Unpublished manuscript, Department of Family Social Science, University of Minnesota, St. Paul.

Maddock, J. W. (1992b). *Ecological dialectics: An approach to family theory construction.* Unpublished manuscript, University of Minnesota, Department of Family Social Science, St. Paul.

Manning, P. (1991). Drama as life: The significance of Goffman's changing use of the theatrical metaphor. *Sociological Theory, 9,* 70–86.

Maruyama, M. (1968). The second cybernetics: Deviation-amplifying mutual causal processes. In W. F. Buckley (Ed.), *Modern systems research for the behavioral scientist* (pp. 304–313). Chicago: Aldine.

McGoldrick, M., Anderson, C. M., & Walsh, F. (1989). Women in families and in family therapy. In M. McGoldrick, C. M. Anderson, & F. Walsh (Eds.), *Women in families: A framework for family therapy* (pp. 1–15). New York: Norton.

McNamee, S. (1992). Social construction and the process of inquiry. *AFTA Newsletter, 47,* 37–39.

Merkel, W. T. & Searight, H. R. (1992). Why families are not like swamps, solar systems, or thermostats: Some limits of systems theory as applied to family therapy. *Contemporary Family Therapy, 14*, 33–50.

Mesarovic, M. D., Macko, D., & Takahara, Y. (1970). *Theory of hierarchical, multi-level systems.* New York: Academic Press.

Meyer, C. J. (1988). *Social support and couple closeness among lesbians.* Unpublished doctoral dissertation, University of Minnesota.

Meyer, C. J., & Rosenblatt, P. C. (1987). Feminist analysis of family textbooks. *Journal of Family Issues, 8*, 247–252.

Mills, J., & Crowley, R. J. (1986). *Therapeutic metaphors for children and the child within.* New York: Brunner/Mazel.

Minuchin, S. (1974). *Families and family therapy.* Cambridge, MA: Harvard University Press.

Minuchin, S., Montalvo, B., Guerney, B. G., Jr., Rosman, B. L., & Schumer, F. (1967). *Families of the slums.* New York: Basic Books.

Montgomery, J., & Fewer, W. (1988). *Family systems and beyond.* New York: Human Sciences Press.

Morgan, G. (1986). *Images of organization.* Beverly Hills, CA: Sage.

Nilsen, D. L. F. (1986). The nature of ground in farfetched metaphors. *Metaphor and Symbolic Activity, 1*, 127–138.

O'Hanlon, W., & Wilk, J. (1987). *Shifting contexts: The generation of effective psychotherapy.* New York: Guilford Press.

Olson, D. H. (1990). The triple threat of bridging research, theory, and practice. In F. W. Kaslow (Ed.), *Voices in family psychology* (pp. 361–374). Newbury Park, CA: Sage.

Olson, D. H. (1992). Family continuity and change: A family life cycle perspective. In T. H. Brubaker (Ed.), *Family relations: Challenges for the future* (pp. 17–31). Newbury Park, CA: Sage.

Olson, D. H. (in press). Family systems: Understanding your roots. In R. Day, K. Gilbert, B. Settles, & W. Burr (Eds.), *Advanced family science.* Belmont, CA: Brooks/Cole.

Olson, D. H., & Lavee, Y. (1989). Family systems and family stress: A family life cycle perspective. In K. Kreppner & R. M. Lerner (Eds.), *Family systems and life-span development* (pp. 165–195). Hillsdale, NJ: Erlbaum.

Olson, D. H., Portner, J., & Lavee, Y. (1985). *FACES III.* St. Paul: Department of Family Social Science.

Olson, D. H., Russell, C. S., & Sprenkle, D. H. (1980). Circumplex model of marital and family systems: II. Empirical studies and clinical intervention. *Advances in Family Intervention, Assessment and Theory, 1*, 129–179.

Olson, D. H., Sprenkle, D. H., & Russell, C. S. (1979). Circumplex model of marital and family systems: I. Cohesion and adaptability dimensions, family types, and clinical applications. *Family Process, 18,* 3–28.

Oxford English dictionary (2nd ed.). (1989). Oxford: Clarendon.

Palazzoli, M. S., Boscolo, L., Cecchin, G. F., & Prata, G. (1977). Family rituals: A powerful tool in family therapy. *Family Process, 16,* 445–453.

Papp, P. (1982). Staging reciprocal metaphors in a couples group. *Family Process, 21,* 453–467.

Parry, A. (1991). A universe of stories. *Family Process, 30,* 37–54.

Pearce, W. B., & Cronen, V. E. (1980). *Communication, action, and meaning: The creation of social realities.* New York: Praeger.

Penn, P. (1983). Coalitions and binding interactions in families with chronic illness. *Family Systems Medicine, 1*(2), 16–25.

Pinderhughes, E. (1982). Afro-American families and the victim system. In M. McGoldrick, J. K. Pearce, & J. Giordano (Eds.), *Ethnicity and family therapy* (pp. 108–122). New York: Guilford Press.

Pittman, F. S., III, & Flomenhaft, K. (1970). Treating the doll's house marriage. *Family Process, 9,* 143–155.

Pratt, M. L. (1986). Fieldwork in common places. In J. Clifford & G. E. Marcus (Eds.), *Writing culture: The poetics and politics of ethnography* (pp. 17–50). Berkeley: University of California Press.

Quinn, N. (1981, August). Marriage is a do-it-yourself project: The organization of marital goals. In *Proceedings of the Third Annual Conference of the Cognitive Science Society* (pp. 31–40). Berkeley, CA.

Quinn, N. (1982). "Commitment" in American marriage: A cultural analysis. *American Ethnologist, 9,* 775–798.

Quinn, N. (1987). Convergent evidence for a cultural model of American marriage. In D. Holland & N. Quinn (Eds.), *Cultural models in thought and language* (pp. 173–192). New York: Cambridge University Press.

Quinn, N. (1991). The cultural basis of metaphor. In J. W. Fernandez (Ed.), *Beyond metaphor: The theory of tropes in anthropology* (pp. 56–93). Stanford, CA: Stanford University Press.

Rapp, R. (1978). Family and class in contemporary America: Notes toward an understanding of ideology. *Science and Society, 42,* 278–300.

Raush, H. L., Greif, A. C., & Nugent, J. (1979). Communication in couples and families. In W. R. Burr, R. Hill, F. I. Nye, & I. L. Reiss (Eds.), *Contemporary theories about the family: Research-based theories* (Vol. 1, pp. 468–489). New York: Free Press.

Reiss, D. (1981). *The family construction of reality.* Cambridge, MA: Harvard University Press.

Richards, I. A. (1936). *The philosophy of rhetoric*. London: Oxford University Press.

Richardson, G. P. (1991). *Feedback thought in social science and systems theory*. Philadelphia: University of Pennsylvania Press.

Romanyshyn, R. D. (1981). Science and reality: Metaphors of experience and experience as metaphorical. In R. S. Valle & R. von Eckartsberg (Eds.), *Metaphors of consciousness* (pp. 3–19). New York: Plenum.

Rosenblatt, P. C. (1964). Origins and effects of group ethnocentrism and nationalism. *Journal of Conflict Resolution, 8*, 131–146.

Rosenblatt, P. C. (1981). Ethnographic case studies. In M. B. Brewer & B. E. Collins (Eds.), *Scientific inquiry and the social sciences* (pp. 194–225). San Francisco: Jossey-Bass.

Rosenblatt, P. C., & Burns, L. H. (1986). Long-term effects of perinatal loss. *Journal of Family Issues, 7*, 237–253.

Rosenblatt, P. C., & Elde, C. (1990). Shared reminiscence about a deceased parent: Implications for grief education and grief counseling. *Family Relations, 39*(2), 206–210.

Rosenblatt, P. C., Johnson, P. A., & Anderson, R. M. (1981). When out-of-town relatives visit. *Family Relations, 30*, 403–409.

Rosenblatt, P. C., & Wright, S. E. (1984). Shadow realities in close relationships. *American Journal of Family Therapy, 12*(2), 45–54.

Roth, S. (1989). Psychotherapy with lesbian couples: Individual issues, female socialization, and the social context. In M. McGoldrick, C. M. Anderson, & F. Walsh (Eds.), *Women in families: A framework for family therapy* (pp. 286–307). New York: Norton.

Ruesch, J., & Bateson, G. (1951). *Communication: The social matrix of psychiatry*. New York: Norton.

Ryder, R. (1987). *The realistic therapist*. Newbury Park, CA: Sage.

Ryder, R., & Bartle, S. (1991). Boundaries as distance regulators in personal relationships. *Family Process, 30*, 393–406.

Salaff, J. W. (1981). *Working daughters of Hong Kong: Filial piety or power in the family?* New York: Cambridge University Press.

Satir, V. (1972). *Peoplemaking*. Palo Alto, CA: Science and Behavior Books.

Satir, V. (1983). *Conjoint family therapy* (3rd ed.). Palo Alto, CA: Science and Behavior Books.

Schneider, D. M. (1980). *American kinship: A cultural account* (2nd ed.). Chicago: University of Chicago Press.

Searight, H. R., & Merkel, W. T. (1991). Systems theory and its discontents: Clinical and ethical issues. *American Journal of Family Therapy, 19*, 19–31.

Seltzer, W. J., & Seltzer, M. R. (1983). Material, myth, and magic: A cultural approach to family therapy. *Family Process, 22,* 3–14.

Shotter, J. (1987). The social construction of an "us": Problems of accountability and narratology. In R. Burnett & P. McGhee (Eds.), *Accounting for relationships* (pp. 225–247). New York: Methuen.

Shotter, J. (1990). Social individuality versus possessive individualism: The sounds of silence. In I. Parker & J. Shotter (Eds.), *Deconstructing social psychology* (pp. 155–169). New York: Routledge.

Simmel, G. (1955). *Conflict and the web of group affiliations.* New York: Free Press.

Simons, H. W. (1981). The management of metaphor. In C. Wilder & J. H. Weakland (Eds.), *Rigor and imagination: Essays from the legacy of Gregory Bateson* (pp. 127–148). New York: Praeger.

Sluzki, C. E. (1992). Transformations: A blueprint for narrative changes in therapy. *Family Process, 31,* 217–230.

Sluzki, C. E., Beavin, J., Tarnopolsky, A., & Verón, E. (1967). Transactional disqualification: Research on the double bind. *Archives of General Psychiatry, 16,* 494–504.

Smith, D. (1987). *The everyday world as problematic: A feminist sociology.* Boston: Northeastern University Press.

Speer, D. C. (1970). Family systems: Morphostasis and morphogenesis, or "Is homeostasis enough?" *Family Process, 9,* 259–278.

Spencer-Brown, G. (1973). *Laws of form.* New York: Bantam.

Spender, D. (1983). Theorising about theorising. In G. Bowles & R. D. Klein (Eds.), *Theories of women's studies* (pp. 27–31). London: Routledge.

Spiegel, D. (1982). Mothering, fathering, and mental illness. In B. Thorne & M. Yalom (Eds.), *Rethinking the family: Some feminist questions* (pp. 95–110). New York: Longman.

Sprenkle, D. H., & Olson, D. H. (1978). Circumplex model of marital systems: An empirical study of clinic and nonclinic couples. *Journal of Marriage and Family Counseling, 4,* 59–74.

Stack, C. (1974). *All our kin: Strategies for survival in a black community.* New York: Harper & Row.

Taffel, R. & Masters, R. (1989). An evolutionary approach to revolutionary change: The impact of gender arrangements on family therapy. In M. McGoldrick, C. M. Anderson, & F. Walsh (Eds.), *Women in families: A framework for family therapy* (pp. 117–134). New York: Norton.

Thorne, B. (1982). Feminist rethinking of the family: An overview. In B. Thorne & M. Yalom (Eds.), *Rethinking the family: Some feminist questions* (pp. 1–24). New York: Longman.

References

Tomm, K. (1987). Interventive interviewing: Part II. Reflexive questioning as a means to enable self-healing. *Family Process, 26,* 167–183.

Tourangeau, R. (1982). Metaphor and cognitive structure. In D. S. Miall (Ed.), *Metaphor: Problems and perspectives* (pp. 14–35). Atlantic Highlands, NJ: Humanities.

Trinh, T. M. (1989). *Woman, nature, other: Writing postcoloniality and feminism.* Bloomington: Indiana University Press.

Turbayne, C. M. (1970). *The myth of metaphor* (rev. ed.). Columbia: University of South Carolina Press.

Turner, M. (1987). *Death is the mother of beauty: Mind, metaphor, criticism.* Chicago: University of Chicago Press.

Turner, R. H. (1962). Role-taking: Process versus conformity. In A. Rose (Ed.), *Human behavior and social processes* (pp. 20–40). Boston: Houghton Mifflin.

Vaillant, G. G. (1985). Loss as a metaphor for attachment. *American Journal of Psychoanalysis, 45,* 59–67.

Wahlström, J. (1990). Conversations on contexts and meanings: On understanding therapeutic change from a contextual viewpoint. *Contemporary Family Therapy, 12,* 455–466.

Walsh, F., & Olson, D. H. (1989). Utility of the circumplex model with severely dysfunctional family systems. In D. H. Olson, C. S. Russell, & D. H. Sprenkle (Eds.), *Circumplex model: Systemic assessment and treatment of families* (pp. 51–78). New York: Haworth.

Watzlawick, P. (1978). *The language of change.* New York: Basic Books.

Watzlawick, P., Beavin, J. H., & Jackson, D. D. (1967). *Pragmatics of human communication.* New York: Norton.

Watzlawick, P., Weakland, J. H., & Fisch, R. (1974). *Change: Principles of problem formation and problem resolution.* New York: Norton.

Way, E. C. (1991). *Knowledge representation and metaphor.* Dordrecht, The Netherlands: Kluwer.

Weakland, J. H. (1967). Communication and behavior: An introduction. *American Behavioral Scientist, 10*(8), 1–4.

Webster's new collegiate dictionary. (1956). Springfield, MA: Merriam.

Weingarten, K. (1991). The discourses of intimacy: Adding a social constructionist and feminist view. *Family Process, 30,* 285–305.

Weingarten, K. (1992). A consideration of intimate and non-intimate interactions in therapy. *Family Process, 31,* 45–59.

Weisner, T. S., & Gallimore, R. (1977). My brother's keeper: Child and sibling caretaking. *Current Anthropology, 18,* 169–190.

Wertheim, E. S. (1973). Family unit therapy and the science and typology of family systems. *Family Process, 12*, 361–376.

Wertheim, E. S. (1975). The science and typology of family systems II: Further theoretical and practical considerations. *Family Process, 14*, 285–309.

Wikan, U. (1990). *Managing turbulent hearts*. Chicago: University of Chicago Press.

Wilmot, W. W. (1980). Metacommunication: A re-examination and extension. In D. Nimmo (Ed.), *Communication Yearbook* (Vol. 4, pp. 61–69). New Brunswick, NJ: Transaction Books.

Wood, B. (1985). Proximity and hierarchy: Orthogonal dimensions of family interconnectedness. *Family Process, 24*, 487–507.

Wood, B., & Talmon, M. (1983). Family boundaries in transition: A search for alternatives. *Family Process, 22*, 347–357.

Wood, B., Watkins, J. B., Boyle, J. T., Nogueira, J., Zimand, E., & Carroll, L. (1989). The "psychosomatic family" model: An empirical and theoretical analysis. *Family Process, 28*, 399–417.

Wright, S. E. (1985). An existential perspective on differentiation/fusion: Theoretical issues and clinical applications. *Journal of Marital and Family Therapy, 11*, 35–46.

Zborowski, M., & Herzog, E. (1952). *Life is with people: The culture of the shtetl*. New York: International Universities Press.

Zuk, G. H. (1965). On the pathology of silencing strategies. *Family Process, 4*, 32–49.

Name Index

Subject Index

T

Tests and test scores as metaphors, 109–112, 190–191

Theoretical metaphors, value of examing, 27–31

Therapeutic epistemology, 198–199

Therapeutic goals, 176–179

Therapist in the system, 180–182

Therapy metaphors, 175–200

Triangles, 117–119, 159, 163